Philippians: An Exegetical Commentary

Philippians
An Exegetical Commentary

William Varner

Fontes

Philippians: An Exegetical Commentary

Copyright © 2021 by Fontes Press

ISBN-13: 978-1-948048-56-9 (paperback)

All rights reserved. No part of this publication may be reproduced, stored in a retrieval system, or transmitted in any form or by any means—electronic, mechanical, photocopy, recording, or any other—except for brief quotations in printed reviews, without the prior permission of the publisher.

All Scripture quotations except where designated otherwise are taken from the (LSB®) Legacy Standard Bible®, Copyright © 2021 by The Lockman Foundation. Used by permission. All rights reserved. Managed in partnership with Three Sixteen Publishing Inc. LSBible.org.

FONTES PRESS
DALLAS, TX
www.fontespress.com

Contents

FOREWORD ix

PREFACE xi

ABBREVIATIONS xiii

INTRODUCTION 1
    Author 1
    Provenance 1
    Linguistic Background of Philippi 2
    Literary Unity 3
    Purpose/Occasion 4
    The Language of Philippians 5
    Discourse Analysis 7
        Thinking Beyond the Clause and the Sentence 9
        Cohesion and Coherence 9
        Prominence 10
        Discourse Peak as Foreground Prominence 10
    Text-Critical Issues 11
    Verbal Aspect and Aktionsart 13
    Semantic Analysis 15
    Spiritual Value 15

ANALYSIS OF PHILIPPIANS ONE 17

ANALYSIS OF PHILIPPIANS TWO 67

ANALYSIS OF PHILIPPIANS THREE 107

ANALYSIS OF PHILIPPIANS FOUR 143

GLOSSARY 177

BIBLIOGRAPHY 185

Foreword

IN THE EARLIER DAYS OF SOCIAL MEDIA, my Facebook discussion group "New Testament Textual Criticism" (https://www.facebook.com/groups/11404207692) frequently received requests to post excellent queries pertaining to New Testament linguistics that were otherwise irrelevant to textual criticism. Such queries were consistently referred to William Varner's Facebook discussion group "Nerdy Language Majors" (now renamed as Nerdy Biblical Language Majors: https://www.facebook.com/groups/NerdyLanguageMajors). I began to view Nerdy Language Majors as a sister group to my textual criticism page, and I found Prof. Varner to be a congenial and authoritative conversation partner.

Varner's *Philippians: An Exegetical Commentary* is one of a score of Philippians commentaries I consistently used in writing my monograph on the text of the letter. Of these twenty commentaries, Varner's commentary had its own unique niche and was reliably helpful in various kinds of linguistic analysis. Those who read the Greek text carefully will invariably stumble on unfamiliar or less familiar elements, prompting them to ask, "What is this construction?" Varner's very focused commentary provides accessible answers. Elsewhere, such answers are often buried in voluminous data in the larger commentaries, or maybe overlooked entirely. The layout in Varner's commentary provides answers in quick fashion; the commentary is a tool that should be in reach while reading through the Greek text.

In any given passage, users of the commentary can confirm, for example, a particular word's function with the proper grammatical terminology, or its typical meaning when used with one case and not the other. Varner very typically supports his analysis by references to important grammars or other advanced commentaries where the user can learn more. An essential tool for the twenty-first century, the commentary thus provides an advance from the old analytical Greek lexicons that earlier generations of seminary students used for grammatical parsing. It provides help far beyond what many digital Greek applications and software programs can offer.

The formatting and scope of this work is ideal for a shorter commentary. Varner writes brief and cogent summaries by section, including key exegetical information that most users will appreciate. Varner provides introductory discussions of recent developments in reading Philippians (e.g., discourse analysis, text-critical method, verbal aspect, and semantic analysis). As a committed Christ-follower, Varner also does not ignore the spiritual dimension of this letter which so emphatically urges believers to conform their thinking to the mind of Christ.

One might hope that companion volumes will be forthcoming to cover all of the New Testament, book by book.

Rev. James M. Leonard, PhD
Educator, The Garden Christian Academy, Cleveland, OH

Preface

THIS BOOK IS A REVISED EDITION of an exegetical commentary on Philippians published privately. This edition has allowed me to benefit from several volumes that have appeared in recent years. The English third edition of Montonari's Greek-Italian dictionary now titled *The Brill Dictionary of Ancient Greek* (GE, 2015) has been particularly helpful in both affirming and revising my comments on many important lexemes. Mathewson and Emig's *Intermediate Greek Grammar* (ME, 2016) has also been useful in some important syntactical discussions. I have also benefited from the new Tyndale House edition of the Greek New Testament (2017) and have strengthened some of my earlier text critical observations and added a few others. I have updated the bibliography and added a "summary" of each pericope in Philippians before my analysis of its Greek clauses. A few "expository" comments have also been included at the end of the four chapters with additional semantic references. These additions have made the analysis of the Greek text more helpful also as a commentary. I am also pleased that this commentary is the first to include the English text of Philippians from the Legacy Standard Bible (2021). I was privileged to be part of that translation committee. The LSB translation follows my own at each passage for the reader to compare. It follows the practice of the NASB of capitalizing OT quotations. Through the courtesy of Bible Works and the Center for the Study of NT Manuscripts, I have also included images of Philippians from Codex Sinaiticus and Codex Vaticanus.

I first worked through the Greek text of Philippians to prepare for an expository sermon series at the Independent Bible Church of

Willow Grove, PA in 1978. I had no idea that more in-depth examinations of the Greek text of this book yet lay ahead. With my Biblical Language majors at The Master's University, I have labored again on the Greek text of Philippians from 1998 through 2021, endeavoring also to apply the tools of discourse analysis to its overall macro-text as well as to the details of its micro-text.

Among those Master's University students analyzing Philippians with me in 2000–2001 was my own daughter, Lynda. When I began again to work on the Greek text of Philippians for this volume, I was reminded that her middle name, Joy, is a prominent word in the Apostle's message to the Philippians. Therefore, it is with great *joy* that I dedicate this work to the memory of Lynda Joy Varner.

Abbreviations

1st	first person
2nd	second person
3rd	third person
acc	accusative
act	active
aor	aorist
ASV	American Standard Version
BDAG	Danker, *A Greek-English Lexicon of the New Testament*, 2000
BDF	Blass, Debrunner, Funk, *A Greek Grammar of the New Testament*
ca.	circa
CBGM	Coherence-Based Genealogical Method
CEV	Contemporary English Version
CGELNT	Danker, *The Concise Greek-English Lexicon of the New Testament*
ch(s).	chapter(s)
CSB	Christian Standard Bible
DA	Discourse analysis
dat	dative
ECM	*Editio Critica Maior*
EDNT	Balz and Schneider, *Exegetical Dictionary of the New Testament*, 3 vols.
ESV	English Standard Version
fem	feminine
fut	future
GAGNT	Zerwick and Grosvenor, *Grammatical Analysis of the GNT*
GE	Montonari, *Brill Dictionary of Ancient Greek*
gen	genitive
GNB	Good News Bible
ILNTG	Beale, Brendsel, Ross, *An Interpretive Lexicon of New Testament Greek*
impf	imperfect
impv	imperative
ind	indicative

inf	infinitive
KJV	King James Version
LN	Louw and Nida, *Greek-English Lexicon*
LSB	Legacy Standard Bible
LSJ	Liddell, Scott, Jones, *A Greek-English Lexicon*
LXX	Septuagint
masc	masculine
ME	Mathewson and Emig, *Intermediate Greek Grammar*
mg	marginal reading
MHT	Moulton, Howard, Turner, *A Grammar of New Testament Greek*, 4 vols.
mid	middle
MM	Moulton and Milligan, *The Vocabulary of the Greek Testament*
mrg	margin
mss	manuscripts
Muraoka	Muraoka, *A Greek-English Lexicon of the Septuagint*
NA28	Nestle-Aland, *Novum Testamentum Graece*, 28th ed.
NASB	New American Standard Bible, 1995
NET	New English Translation
neut	neuter
NIDNTTE	Silva, *New International Dictionary of NT Theology and Exegesis*, 5 vols.
NIV	New International Version, 2011
NJB	New Jerusalem Bible
NLT	New Living Translation, 2nd ed.
nom	nominative
NP	noun phrase
NRSV	New Revised Standard Version
NT	New Testament
opt	optative
OT	Old Testament
OV	Object/Complement–Verb
OVO	Object/Complement–Verb–Object/Complement
pass	passive
PGL	Lampe, *Patristic Greek Lexicon*
pl	plural

plprf	pluperfect
PP	prepositional phrase
pr.	prologue
pres	present
prf	perfect
ptc	participle
RSV	Revised Standard Version
sg	singular
subj	subjunctive
s.v.	under the word (*sub verbo*)
TDNT	Kittel, *Theological Dictionary of the New Testament*, 10 vols.
THGNT	Tyndale House *Greek New Testament*
TLNT	Spicq, *Theological Lexicon of the New Testament*, 3 vols.
TR	*Textus Receptus*
Tregelles	Greek New Testament, 1872
UBS5	Aland, Metzger, et.al. *The Greek New Testament*, 5th ed.
voc	vocative
WH	Westcott-Hort

Introduction

SINCE THERE ARE MANY excellent treatments of the standard NT "introduction" issues generally and of Philippians particularly, this introduction focuses on linguistic issues that affect the questions of the letter's provenance, destination, literary unity, purpose, and language. Crucial language-related matters are included, such as discourse analysis, text-critical issues, verbal aspect, and semantic analysis.

Author

The claim of Pauline authorship in 1:1 was affirmed by the overwhelming testimony of the early church fathers such as Clement of Rome, Polycarp, Clement of Alexandria, Irenaeus, Tertullian, Hippolytus, Origen, and Eusebius. Suffice it to say that Pauline authorship is also supported by "virtually the whole of NT critical scholarship" (Hagner, 557).

Provenance

That Paul was in prison is indisputable (1:7, 13, 17), but where he was in prison is still debated. The three hypotheses that have attracted attention are Caesarea, Ephesus, and Rome. Rome appears to be the most likely option by default. A surprisingly strong argument for an Ephesians provenance can be made from what we know of Paul's intentions in Romans, written during his third journey. In this letter Paul expresses his hope to visit Philippi a second time, but as Romans explicitly tells us, even before Paul reached Rome, his attention had already turned westward to Rome and beyond to Spain (15:22–29). In light of this, a visit to Philippi would have required him to backtrack from Rome to the east before the launch of the Spanish mission. The silence in Acts about an imprisonment in Ephesus is a factor, but 2 Corinthians states he had suffered great affliction in Asia (1:8) and was imprisoned many times (11:23). Clement of Rome (5:5–6) states that he "wore chains seven times" while the much later *Acts of Paul and Thecla* speaks of an Ephesian imprisonment. Also, in Rom 15:23 he states that "his work was done" in Asia and Greece. Would he go against all his plans and desire to go back to Philippi after the third journey? Such a return from Ephesus while he was still active in the area during the third journey would be much easier (see Roetzel, 128–29). While an Ephesian provenance is attractive, in the end there is simply no clear statement in Acts nor in any of the epistles that Paul was actually imprisoned in Ephesus. With that absence, the Roman imprisonment is still the best option for the location of Paul's writing (Witherington, 2017).

Linguistic Background of Philippi

The letter's destination—Philippi—is located some eight miles northwest of the ancient seaport Neapolis (modern Kavala). The name recalls Philip of Macedon (father of Alexander), under whose control the city came when the people sought his intervention against from Thracian invaders in 356 BC. In 42 BC Antony and Octavian battled with Brutus and Cassius in the plain before the acropolis, which led to the establishment of Philippi as a Roman colony named *Colonia Victrix Philippensium*. Octavian would eventually control the colony, so it was named *Colonia Iulia Augusta Philippensis* (27 BC). Roman control continued well into the Christian era including the time when Paul visited there (Acts 16) and when he wrote this letter to the church. The colony was not primarily comprised of Roman citizens but both Romans and Greeks lived there together. Roman influence was evident, however, as can be witnessed even today in the surviving Latin inscriptions. The city was diverse, perhaps with tensions between Romans and Greeks within the congregation (for the above see Oakes, especially pages 1–76). Many commentators have noted the special "citizenship language" Paul uses in 1:27 (πολιτεύεσθε) and 3:20 (πολίτευμα). Brewer and others argue that Paul uses this language to promote faithfulness to the Roman colony of Philippi within the bounds of obedience and allegiance to Christ (76–83). "Paul seems to have employed these words to say, 'Continue to discharge your obligations as citizens and residents of Philippi faithfully and as a Christian should; but do not yield to the patriotic pressure to give to Nero that which belongs to Christ alone. Remember that while you are members of a Roman colony you are also a colony of heaven from which you are awaiting the return of your divine Lord and Savior. So stand firm. Never waver in the conflict. You may have to suffer for Christ, but remember that he is your deliverer too'" (Brewer, 83). We do not know how many members of the congregation would have been actual Roman citizens, but all the original hearers of the letter being read to them would have recognized Paul's not-so-veiled references to the standing of Philippi in the Roman Empire and how allegiance to Christ and heavenly citizenship greatly surpassed even this special privilege (Roberts, 325–28; followed by Fee, 161–62).

Literary Unity

To illustrate one way in which an author's language use (the "register," to use a linguistic term) can impact matters of "introduction," we must address the debate about the unity of Philippians. The letter has undergone a good amount of critical analysis addressing whether it is one letter or a pastiche of two or more. Some early critical scholars held that Philippians was a compilation of three letters (4:10–20; 1:1–3:1, 4:4–9, 4:21–23; 3:2–4:1/3). One of the main reasons is because 3:1 appears to terminate a letter (note Τὸ λοιπόν), while 3:2–4:1 "is marked by a tone of polemic and personal *apologia* absent from the rest of the epistle" (Sellew, 17, elaborated in 17–19). David Garland's significant article (141–73) has encouraged a greater support for the integrity hypothesis (see also the comments of Watson, 57–88; O'Brien 1991, 10–18; Reed 1997, 63–90; Silva, 12–15). Currently this is the view that holds the scholarly consensus and has the most to commend it (for a recent dissenter, see Reumann, 9–13).

Furthermore, the following pattern of shared words and concepts from both halves of the letter (chs. 1–2 and 3–4), noted by Garland (141–73, et.al.), supports the integrity and unity of the letter.

φρονέω	1:7; 2:2, 5 / 3:5, 19; 4:2, 10
κερδ- cognates	1:21 / 3:7, 8
πολιτευ- cognates	1:27/3:20
συναθλέω	1:27 / 4:3
ἡγέομαι	2:3, 2, 25 / 3:7, 8
ταπεινο- cognates	2:3, 8 / 3:21; 4:12
μορφ- cognates	2:6, 7 / 3:10, 21
σχημ- cognates	2:7 / 3:21
ἐπίγειος	2:10 / 3:19
κυρίου Ἰησοῦ Χριστοῦ	1:2 / 4:23 (*inclusio*)

In the comments on the text, attention will be given to other shared words and phrases in the two "halves" such as the common language in the prayer of 1:9–11 and the personal thoughts in 4:10–20.

Purpose/Occasion

Although there is no explicit statement providing Paul's rationale for writing, we may discern from his language three main purposes for the letter, namely (1) to express his sincere gratitude to the congregation for their recent gift brought by Epaphroditus, (2) to fiercely warn the church in quite strong language about the danger of false teachers, and (3) to loving exhort the church to live out their visible unity. This third purpose—to admonish the brethren to lovingly express their oneness—constitutes, in my opinion, the warp and woof of the letter. Philippians 1:27–2:4 and 4:2–3 are particular passages that underscore this theme. Paul desires that the church, comprised of both Romans and Greeks, exist in harmony (for the above see O'Brien 1978, 9–18; as well as Black 1995b, 16–49). This stress on unity will impact the interpretation of other passages, such as the celebrated "Carmen Christi" passage in 2:5–11, and place them in their correct context.

The Language of Philippians

Although not the only way to analyze the language of writers, tabulating statistics of their vocabulary can sometimes be enlightening and provide at least a place to start the analysis. If we count the words that are unique to Philippians (these statistics are based on those in Köstenberger and Bouchoc), the total number is forty, a proportionately higher number than in most epistles. The longer Galatians and Ephesians, for example, contain respectively thirty-one and thirty-five of these *hapax legomena*. In the comments on the text, I call attention to when a word has been used only once in the NT and the few times that it is unknown in the rest of Greek literature.

A better understanding of the lexical uniqueness of Philippians can be gained from recognizing certain words and semantic fields that appear with a higher frequency than in other epistles by the same author. To mention only two: the noun δέσμιος (prisoner) occurs four times in Philippians, but elsewhere only once in Colossians and once in 2 Timothy while the verb ἡγέομαι (regard, consider) occurs 6 times, but only once in 2 Corinthians, 1 Thessalonians, 2 Thessalonians, and twice in 1 Timothy.

Many commentators have noted the abundance of "joy" terminology (the verb χαίρω and the noun χαρά). These cognate terms occur 14 times (3.5 times per chapter) in Philippians, while the total for the rest of the Pauline writings is 36 times (less than once per chapter). As a caution that the concept of joy is not unique to this letter, however, it should be observed that the verb χαίρω appears eight times in 2 Corinthians and five times in the few verses of 2 John. More significant than the "joy" language are the ten occurrences of φρονέω (think), elsewhere used only 13 times in Paul (nine times in Romans). When we combine this word (φρονέω) with others that stress oneness (αὐτός [7], ἕν [4], and the συν-compounds [15]), the resulting collocation conveys the commitment to unity that Paul commends in the letter. This language helps his readers to understand that even joy is a sort of by-product of the humility that exemplifies unity. Consider the collocation of thinking, oneness, and joy in 2:2: πληρώσατέ μου τὴν χαρὰν ἵνα τὸ αὐτὸ φρονῆτε, τὴν αὐτὴν ἀγάπην ἔχοντες, σύμψυχοι, τὸ ἓν φρονοῦντες (fulfill my joy by thinking the same way, having the same love, being united in spirit, thinking the one thing).

While the register of the Koine Greek in Philippians is not necessarily high, there are a surprising number of words that appear in the New Testament only in the book. Following is a chart that lists them with the reference where each word is found in Philippians.

Hapax Legomena in Philippians		
There are around thirty words that appear in the NT only in Philippians, not counting personal names. These words appear below with their basic lexical meaning (drawn from BDAG) and the reference where each occurs.		
Word	Meaning	Reference
ἀγνῶς	"purely" "sincerely"	1:17
αἴσθησις	"discernment"	1:9
ἀκαιρέομαι	"have no opportunity"	4:10
ἄλυπος	"free from anxiety"	2:28
ἀναθάλλω	"cause to bloom again"	4:10
ἀπουσία	"absence"	2:12
ἁρπαγμός	"robbery"	2:6
αὐτάρκης	"content"	4:11
γνησίως	"genuinely"	2:20
ἐξανάστασις	"resurrection"	3:11
ἐπεκτείνομαι	"stretch out"	3:13
ἐπιπόθητος	"longed for" "desired"	4:1
ἑτέρως	"otherwise"	3:15
λῆμψις	"receiving"	4:15
μεγάλως	"greatly"	4:10
μυέω	"learn the secret"	4:12
ὀκταήμερος	"eighth day"	3:5
παραβουλεύομαι	"be careless"	2:30
παραμύθιον	"consolation"	2:1
παραπλήσιος	"resembling"	2:27
πολίτευμα	"commonwealth"	3:20
προσφιλής	"pleasing" "agreeable"	4:8
πτύρω	"be frightened"	1:28

σκοπός	"goal" "mark"	3:14
σκύβαλον	"refuse" "garbage"	3:8
σύζυγος	"true comrade"	4:3
συμμιμητής	"fellow imitator"	3:17
συμμορφίζω	"have the same form as"	3:10
σύμψυχος	"harmonious"	2:2
ὑπερυψόω	"raise" "exalt"	2:9
The following proper names appear only in Philippians: Ἐπαφρόδιτος (Epaphroditus, 2:25, 4:18); Εὐοδία (Euodia, 4:3); Κλήμης (Clement, 4:3); Συντύχη (Syntyche, 4:2); and Φιλιππήσιος (Philippian, 4:15).		

These micro-features of the language in Philippians are also related to larger literary analyses that appeal to argument flow and thematic coherence in the letter. One of these macro-features is discourse analysis. Following is a brief introduction to DA and an attempt to apply it to the text of Philippians.

Discourse Analysis

The discipline of discourse analysis (DA), often referred to as text-linguistics, deals with the analysis of whole texts or discourses, while not neglecting the micro-features of the text. It involves a linguistic study of how the "parts" of a discourse function together to convey the message of the text as a whole. In this section, I will briefly survey some attempts at a discourse analysis of Philippians and conclude with my own discourse approach to the epistle.

A 1995 volume, *Discourse Analysis and Other Topics in Biblical Greek*, edited by Porter and Carson, contains a number of essays on DA in general and on Philippians in particular. Porter's introductory survey (14–35) provides the foundation for the studies that follow. Porter suggests that "the emphasis of discourse analysis is upon language as it is used," meaning that DA "has attempted to integrate into a coherent model of interpretation the three traditional areas of linguistic analysis: semantics ... syntax ... and pragmatics" (18). Further, "the distinctiveness of discourse analysis and the concern of discourse analysts is to be able to provide as comprehensive a description as possible of the various components of a given discourse, including its meaning and structure, and the means by which these are created and conveyed" (19). Essays by Guthrie (36–59), Levinsohn (60–74), and Reed (75–101) attempt to define a linguistic basis for a thematic analysis of Philippians. In his final essay (107–16), Porter favors Reed's analysis, arguing that it stresses two of the three major concerns of DA, namely prominence and coherence.

Other publications on DA include the book by Holmstrand (88–141), who argues for the key role of "discourse markers" such as καί, δέ, οὖν, μέν, ἀλλά, and γάρ in helping to segment a discourse and to enable its information flow. *Discourse Grammar of the Greek NT* by Runge (2010), building on the contributions of Levinsohn, has also brought to our attention the important roles of word order and the function of these small but important transitional markers in analyzing discourse.

In his book on linguistics for NT students (1995b, 170–94), Black elaborates on a previous article on Philippians (1995a) by again tracing through the use of "discourse markers," the "primary text sequences" of the book. He argues that Paul's chief concern is for unity and sees the special role of 2:1–4 in this regard. His following (abbreviated) discourse structure of the book can also be taken as my own approach to its overall structure:

1. Letter Opening/Epistolary Prescript: Greetings to All (1:1–2)
2. Letter Body: The Need for Unity in the Cause of the Gospel (1:3–4:20)
   A. Body Opening: Thanksgiving and Prayer for All (1:3–11)
   B. Body Proper: Argument for Ecclesial Unity (1:12–4:9)
      1. Body Head / Primary Development of the Argument: Exhortation to Unity in the Cause of the Gospel (1:12–2:30)
      2. Body Subpart/Secondary Development of the Argument: Warning Against Pride in Human Achievements (3:1–4:9)
   C. Body Closing: Renewed Expression of Gratitude for the Philippians' Cooperation in the Spread of the Gospel (4:10–20)
3. Letter Closing/Epistolary Postscript: Greetings from All (4:21–23)

Introduction

As my contribution to this subject, I suggest that there are four key features of DA, especially as they are applied to the text of Philippians.

Thinking Beyond the Clause and the Sentence

The most distinguishing principle of DA is to examine language at a level beyond the sentence. Much traditional biblical exegesis, while nodding its approval to the importance of context, has often ignored this principle in practice. The analysis of words and clauses is vastly important, but their importance is constrained by the larger discourse in which they are found. It is helpful to view all the linguistic elements of a text as comprising different "levels of discourse," with individual words on the bottom level and then phrases, clauses, clause complexes, sentences, paragraphs, and the entire discourse on ascending levels, similar to a pyramid (see Porter, 1994, 298). A full DA ignores neither a bottom-up nor a top-down analysis. Both must be done for a full analysis of any discourse.

Cohesion and Coherence

The second principle of DA is the role of cohesiveness in a text. The word coherence is also mentioned in close connection with a text's cohesiveness. Cohesion is a means of linking clauses and sentences into larger syntactical units while coherence is a semantic dimension and refers to the several ways in which readers make sense of a text. Cohesion refers to the linguistic devices by which the speaker can signal the interpersonal coherence of the text and is a textual phenomenon that points to features of the text which serve a cohesive function. Coherence, on the other hand, is in the mind of the writer and reader and thus is a mental phenomenon that cannot be identified and quantified in the same way as cohesion. A text that exploits the cohesive resources of the language effectively should be perceived as coherent. Frankly, most treatments of DA are simply discussions of cohesion/coherence.

There are many ways by which an author can establish the cohesion of a biblical text, but here only two will be mentioned. Lexical cohesion is the use of the same word or of similar words from the same semantic domain. In Philippians, the use of a lexeme like the verb φρονέω as well as Paul's intentional use of inclusios provide cohesion for the surface structure of his argument. Relational cohesion is signaled by conjunctions and other connectives. These often-overlooked connectives and particles (see Holmstrand and Runge) play a significant role in the cohesiveness and logical sequencing of the text of Philippians.

Prominence

The third feature of DA is the function of linguistic prominence. While lexical and grammatical ties function as a cohesion of *similarity*, prominence functions as cohesion of dissimilarity. In other words, an author uses language to set apart certain entities from other entities of the discourse. The reader's attention is drawn to important topics in the discourse, then supported by less prominent material. Prominence functions to set apart certain ideas as more semantically significant than others.

Some information in a discourse is less prominent and some is more prominent. Those items in thematic prominence provide information that is central to the author's "message." In non-narrative text, thematically prominent elements, when first appearing in a discourse, are expected to appear again. While background and thematic elements can appear across the discourse at all levels—clause, sentence, paragraphs, and discourse—the more focused elements can be prominent at the level of paragraph and fall out of this level of prominence in the next.

Discourse Peak as Foreground Prominence

As the fourth feature of DA, I suggest that prominence plays a key role in focusing attention on the main "theme" of Philippians. This type of prominence is marked by surface features in the text but also conveys a semantic macro-theme that can be traced throughout the text. Robert Longacre has termed this greatest prominence the peak of a discourse. Longacre's oft-quoted comment about a discourse without prominence is appropriate here. "Discourse without prominence would be like pointing to a piece of black cardboard and insisting that it was a picture of black camels crossing black sands at midnight" (38). Peak has features peculiar to itself and the marking of such features takes precedence over the marking of the mainline.

I suggest that Philippians 2:1–4 serves as the discourse peak of the entire text. This paragraph develops the call to unity first mentioned in 1:27. We encounter in 2:1 an intensive concentration of four successive protases ("if clauses") followed by a 2nd person aorist imperative in the apodosis (only one more in the conclusion, 4:21). These concentrated grammatical features are followed by an intense focus on unity with the Apostle's joy fulfilled if his readers will "think" hard about being one, which he again reinforces by clausal repetition in 2:2. After this stylistic reinforcement, Paul describes in a series of repetitive clauses in 2:3–4 how that unity will not and will be attained—by not looking out for yourselves but in caring more for others. ME (284) states that when an author "changes the length of sentences through significant expansion," as Paul does here, he indicates greater prominence. After this intense paragraph, he then offers in 2:5–30 at least three exemplars of this selfless attitude that is the key to unity: Jesus in 2:5–8; Timothy in 2:19–23; and Epaphroditus in 2:25–30 (and possibly himself in 2:17). In 2:1–4, therefore, by means of both the surface features of the text and the semantic "message" found there Paul conveys the theme that is stamped on almost every paragraph—unity through selflessness. Even the theme of "joy," which many commentators have discerned as the main theme, becomes a by-product of unity through selflessness as well as the by-product of strength to face persecution, another theme in the discourse. For a further explanation and application of this approach to DA, see Varner (13–40).

Space does not permit an attempt at a rhetorical analysis of Philippians; for a balanced treatment of the socio-rhetorical features of the book, see Witherington. We now turn to the details of the text, namely, its micro-features: text-critical issues, the subject of verbal aspect, and some basic observations about the vital topic of semantics.

Text-Critical Issues

Philippians has a relatively stable textual tradition and most of the different readings do not seriously impact the interpretation of the text. The Greek text in this volume follows the NA[28], which lists variant readings in approximately 100 places, with about 20 places having more than two alternate readings. I have chosen to mention the evidence for 21 of the places where there is uncertainty because these cases involve a choice in translation. In most of these I favor what has been called the Alexandrian family of readings, most often represented in 𝔓[46] and the fourth/fifth-century uncials ℵ, A, and B. This choice is especially appropriate when the Alexandrian reading is shared by the Western family represented by D, F, G, and the Latin manuscripts over against the Majority Text or Byzantine family of readings (𝔐). While recent scholarship has questioned the idea of "text-types" in favor of "text-clusters" of similar readings, such a preference does not significantly alter our process in choosing the best reading. After this *external* evidence, I have considered the *internal* evidence of the reading which most likely gave rise to the other readings, which is also usually the more difficult reading (*lectio difficilior*) and often also the shorter reading (*lectio brevior*). Thus, I have followed the method that has been called Reasoned Eclecticism. I am aware of other approaches to making textual choices (e.g., Thorough Eclecticism and the Coherence-Based Genealogical Method or CBGM), but my own "documentary" approach still has the broad support of NT scholarship and is the approach favored by the recently published Tyndale House Greek New Testament (THGNT). We must await the results of the CBGM in the Pauline epistles that will be found in future editions of the *Editio Critica Maior*. The present *ECM*, however, does not in the published Catholic Epistles depart seriously from the textual decisions of earlier editions of the NA/UBS texts. The THGNT (2017) has also been consulted, although there are very few differences in the text of Philippians from the NA[28] / UBS[5] texts.

The earliest copy of Philippians is found in 𝔓[46], an early (ca. 200 CE) collection of the Pauline epistles that is part of the Chester Beatty collection. This early witness has been given special attention in the comments because of its occasionally singular readings. This is particularly evident in 1:8, 11, 23, 30; 3:12, 18; and 4:16.

Through the courtesy of Bible Works, the Center for the Study of NT Manuscripts, and photographer Brian Morley, I have also included images of the beginning and the end of Philippians in the 4th century codices Vaticanus and Sinaiticus. These images illustrate such textual features as the *nomina sacra*, itacism, and scribal corrections.

Verbal Aspect and Aktionsart

The last quarter century has seen a renewed discussion of the Greek verb. The modern phase of the discussion owes its inception to McKay (1985), but the formal articulations of verbal aspect as distinct from *Aktionsart* are credited to the works of Porter (1989) and Fanning (1990). Porter's further thesis is that the semantic value of Greek tense was aspect in distinction from time. For the most recent defense of his approach to verbal aspect and other linguistic issues, see Porter (2015). While not all have affirmed his argument (e.g., Runge, 2014; Runge and Fresch, 2016), the overall greater attention to aspect vis-a-vis time in the Greek tenses has been a welcome contribution to the study of the Greek verb.

Verbal aspect is the way a writer grammaticalizes his view of the situation by the selection of a particular verb form in the verbal system. This view is either perfective, imperfective, or stative and is expressed by the tense forms aorist, present/imperfect, and perfect/pluperfect respectively. *Perfective* aspect views the situation as a complete event without regard for its progress. *Imperfective* aspect views the situation as in progress without regard for its beginning or end. *Stative* aspect depicts a state of affairs that exists with no reference to any progress. These aspects are the writer's view of the situation. They are sometimes determined by several factors (vocabulary, grammar, context, etc.) and at other times are the speaker's reasoned choice of a viewpoint that best expresses the nuance he desires to communicate (see Decker, *Mark*, xxviii).

Campbell (2008, 106–7) has offered additional insight into verbal aspect. He suggests that perfective aspect is an external viewpoint while the internal viewpoint is known as imperfective aspect. Perfective aspect views an action "from a distance" and as a whole without reference to how it happened and without viewing it as though happening. Imperfective aspect views an action "up close," from within it, and is often used to present an action as unfolding or in progress without reference to the whole action. McKay and Porter view the verbal aspect of the perfect tense as stative, while Fanning describes it as perfective, and Campbell describes it as imperfective. I generally affirm Porter's approach to verbal aspect. Campbell has advanced the discussion, especially in his book on recent advances in Greek study (2015). I am concerned, however, that his view that the perfect tense conveys imperfective aspect confuses the aspect of the perfect tense with the imperfect tense.

Aktionsart is a description of the action-related features of the verb as to the way in which it happens or exists. It is not a grammatical category based on the form of the verb but is a pragmatic category based on the semantics of the word as it is used in a particular context. Although still debated, the view here is that temporal reference is not expressed grammatically but is an implicature. Although the aorist form may not always grammaticalize past time, it can be used to describe events in the past, but the temporal reference comes from other contextual factors. Aspect expresses a view of the process grammatically, *Aktionsart* expresses it lexically and contextually (see Decker, *Mark*, xxviii).

It is inaccurate to call verbal aspect a "theory," since it is a widely recognized feature of the Greek verb, with only its details being debated. At the same time, we should not overemphasize the exegetical takeaway of verbal aspect. Silva's observation (11) reminds us "that the significance of such (aspectual) distinctions for biblical interpretation has been greatly overestimated. Aspectual choices are usually restricted by factors of a grammatical or contextual nature, and so only seldom do they reflect a conscious semantic motivation (probably in 3:7–8). In short, no reasonable Greek author, when wishing to make a substantive point, is likely to have depended on his readers' ability to interpret subtle syntactical distinctions." These cautions should not be ignored, but the above contributions on verbal aspect should also not be overlooked.

Since the immediate benefit of verbal aspect, in this writer's opinion, is more evident in narrative literature, observations about aspectual decisions will be few in my comments on the Philippians. There will be times, however, when we can detect Paul's purpose in his careful choice of verbal aspect (e.g., 2:1; 3:8).

Semantic Analysis

A work of this nature that focuses on identifying individual words and their meaning can run the risk of isolating the meaning of those words in an artificial way from the context in which they were originally written. Therefore, I have tried to follow three generally acknowledged linguistic principles that too often have been slighted in traditional Biblical semantics. First, semantics is not a prescriptive but a descriptive enterprise. In other words, the NT period usage of the word (synchronics) takes priority in deciding semantic issues over its historical usage (diachronics). I have thus limited the historical evolution of a lexeme in pre-Christian "classical" authors unless the word is a *hapax legomenon* or has few other appearances in the NT. Second, meaning resides not at the level of individual words but at the level of the collocations of these words in clauses, sentences, and ultimately in the overall discourse. This points to the often mentioned but often neglected role of *context* as the most important determiner of meaning. Third, the meaning of individual words is best expressed not in a single word gloss but in the semantic field of that lexeme. Translation most often demands a one-word gloss, but an effort will be made to provide a more complete definition of the word as well.

Spiritual Value

In a linguistic commentary such as this, with the expected emphasis on word meanings and grammatical functions, we should not overlook the deeply spiritual value of this letter. Philippians is one of the Pauline epistles that best reveals both its author's own struggles and his ongoing relationships with a church that he founded (Acts 16:6–40). The letter is marked by some very personal expressions of love and concern while also including some serious concerns about the church's unity, as well as the influence of false teaching in its midst. Readers have noticed the numerous expressions of "joy" and "rejoicing" in its contents. It contains some of the best known and most quotable statements that express Paul's unbounded optimism. For example: "To me to live is Christ and to die is gain" (1:21) and "I can do all things through the one who strengthens me" (4:13). While exuding an infectious optimism, there is also a deep seriousness about it since it is written by one who is facing the possibility of his own death. "He basically wants them to live in unity, faithfully representing Christ and the gospel to their community, as they eagerly await his second coming" (Moore, 57).

1

Analysis of Philippians One

Philippians 1:1–2

¹ Paul and Timothy, servants of Christ Jesus, to all the holy ones in Christ Jesus at Philippi, together with the overseers and assistants. ² Grace and peace to you from God our Father and the Lord Jesus Christ.

Paul and Timothy, slaves of Christ Jesus,
¶ To all the saints in Christ Jesus who are in Philippi, with the overseers and deacons: Grace to you and peace from God our Father and the Lord Jesus Christ. (LSB)

Summary: Paul begins his letter in his usual way, mentioning author, recipients, and a greeting. A well-known example of this model with its twofold structure, including a greeting in the form of a direct address, is the edict of Nebuchadnezzar: 'King Nebuchadnezzar to all peoples, nations, and languages that dwell in all the earth; peace be multiplied to you!' (Dn. 3:31). By the Hellenistic period the standard opening in the letters consisted of three components: the name of the sender (nominative case), the name of the addressee(s) (dative case), and the infinitive χαίρειν ('greeting'). Occasionally there were minor variations, including strengthening the greeting with a wish for good health (3 John 2). Although Paul's opening addresses are consistent with the letters of the period, they are far from being stereotyped introductions (see Weima, 11–50). He adapts his self-description and his credentials to the circumstances of each letter, employs phrases to describe his Christian readers, and pours Christian content into his greetings (adapted from Fee).

1:1 Παῦλος καὶ Τιμόθεος δοῦλοι Χριστοῦ Ἰησοῦ πᾶσιν τοῖς ἁγίοις ἐν Χριστῷ Ἰησοῦ τοῖς οὖσιν ἐν Φιλίπποις σὺν ἐπισκόποις καὶ διακόνοις,

Παῦλος καὶ Τιμόθεος. Nominative absolute. These nominatives appear in introductory material, such as the opening salutation of a letter, and do not constitute a sentence (Wallace, 49–51). As mentioned above, the ancient Greek letter opened with a standard formula: Addressor (in nominative case) – Addressee (in dative case) – Greeting (often the infinitive χαίρειν). Only the Letter from James (1:1) and two letters in Acts (15:23; 23:26) strictly maintain this minimal formula for the salutation of a letter. Although the mention of two names has led some to propose a dual authorship of this and other epistles (Richards, 32–35), Paul's immediate switch to the first person singular (see 1:3–9 and the rest of the letter) suggests that Timothy is mentioned simply as an associate or possibly as a secretary/amanuensis.

δοῦλοι. Nominative in apposition to Παῦλος καὶ Τιμόθεος. A δοῦλος denotes literal ownership by another, a "slave" (BDAG, 260.1; see also Josephus, *Ant.* 16.126; *J.W.* 7.336). An abundant amount of evidence in nonbiblical literature clearly describes a δοῦλος as a person who was owned by another free person (NIDNTTE, 1:767–68; GE, 551–52). In canonical Jewish literature, however, עֶבֶד (*eved*, regularly translated δοῦλος in the LXX) often indicates a special relationship between God and a person defined in terms of possession (by God) and service (by the person). The religious description of slavery as a complete dedication to God often is mentioned in the Psalms (LXX Pss 118:38, 76; 122:2; 133:1; 134:1; 142:12). Isa 42:19 utilizes the plural οἱ δοῦλοι τοῦ θεοῦ ("slaves of God") to convey the singular "servant of the Lord," the only occurrence of this Greek phrase in the LXX. The term δοῦλος also was applied to those leaders who were mediators between God and His people, such as Joshua (Josh 24:30), David (2 Sam 7:8, 25, 29), and Moses (Ps 104:26; Mal 3:24). It is often used of the prophets as messengers of the Lord (Amos 3:7; Joel 3:2;

Jonah 1:9; Zech 1:6; Jer 7:25; Ezek 38:17). While in the NT the term can apply to Jesus (Phil 2:7) or to Christians (1 Pet 2:16; Acts 2:18; 4:29; Rev 10:7; 19:5), their adversaries described Paul and Silas as "slaves (δοῦλοι) of the Most High God" (Acts 16:17) because they recognized their prophetic preaching. Johnson (168–69) has a helpful discussion of δοῦλος which has informed my own observations. Interestingly, the CSB[17] altered its previous HCSB translation from "slaves" to "servants."

Χριστοῦ Ἰησοῦ. Genitive of possession. Χριστός is a substantival adjective, derived from the verb χρίω, "to anoint" (BDAG, 1091). For early Christians, Χριστός retained much more of its original titular meaning, namely "the anointed one" or "Messiah," especially when preceding the personal name "Jesus." Novenson (*Christ Among the Messiahs*) argues that Χριστός in Paul is neither a name, nor simply a title, but an "honorific," like "Augustus" in the triple phrase *Imperator Caesar Augustus*, where *Imperator* is a title, Caesar is the personal name, and Augustus an honorific, adding an extra circle of meaning. Novenson's suggestion would be particularly appropriate for Gentile Christians because for Jewish Christians an idea of "Messiah" would naturally come to mind.

πᾶσιν τοῖς ἁγίοις. Dative of recipient (Wallace, 148). Because of the later ecclesiastical usage of the English word "saints," the translation "holy ones" is preferred (BDAG, 11.2.d.β). Montonari, tracing Attic substantives as "holy, righteous, pure," suggests the NT application to people as simply "the faithful" or "believers" (GE, 13). See also LN (11.27): "God's people." The article nominalizes the adjective to mark it as a substantive and also particularizes it (ME, 76–77).

ἐν Χριστῷ Ἰησοῦ. Locative. The metaphorical nature of the language cautions against dogmatic grammatical categories. It is best to take this language of indwelling as an idiomatic way of highlighting the intimate nature of the relationship.

τοῖς οὖσιν. Pres act ptc masc dat pl εἰμί (attributive).

ἐν Φιλίπποις. Locative. In Pauline salutations where the destination follows ἐν, only the letters to Philippians and Colossians have the destination in the plural. Polycarp to the Philippians also uses the plural (Pol. *Phil.* pr.). Robertson calls this an "idiomatic plural" (480). See also Campbell (2013, 2).

σὺν ἐπισκόποις καὶ διακόνοις. Accompaniment. In secular Greek, the word ἐπίσκοπος referred to a "guardian, overseer" (LSJ, 657) or a "watcher, protector" (GE, 789) and διάκονος was a "servant, attendant" (LSJ, 398). This is the only verse in the NT where these two terms for early Christian leaders appear together, although 1 Tim 3:1–7 discusses ἐπίσκοποι and 3:8–13 discusses διάκονοι. BDAG (379.2) describes an ἐπίσκοπος as an "overseer or supervisor, with special interest in guarding the apostolic tradition." The translation "bishop" carries too many later ecclesiastical overtones to be an appropriate term today. BDAG (230–31.2) defines διάκονος as "attendant, assistant, aide" and adds, "the Eng[lish] derivatives 'deacon' and 'deaconess' are technical terms, whose m[ea]n[in]g varies in ecclesiastical history and are therefore inadequate for rendering the NT usage of δ[ιάκονος]." The textual variant συνεπισκοποις replaces the two separate words in the correctors of B and D and in K, P, 075, 33, 1241, 1739, and 1881. This is a patently late reading since the word has no pre-history to the NT and does not appear elsewhere until the 4th century Fathers (PGL, 1323).

Codex Vaticanus at Philippians 1:1

Notice the attempted "correction" by the scribe mentioned above (the nu is "attached" to the beginning of ἐπισκόποις on line 5). Also note other features such as the *nomina sacra* in lines 2 and 3; the itacism of Τειμόθεος in line 1; the diaresis in the right margin of line 3 indicating the variant reading of "Jesus Christ" in later manuscripts. Another fascinating item concerns the itacism in line 1, where the medieval scribe who "strengthened" the letters did NOT strengthen the epsilon (ε) indicating that the original manuscript did not contain it. He then marked the correct reading (ι only) with a diaresis over it. The previous image is a photograph of the facsimile of Codex Vaticanus in the School of Biblical Studies, The Master's University. The following is an image of 1:1 from the digital facsimile of Codex Vaticanus (Courtesy of the Center for the Study of New Testament Manuscripts, http://www.CSNTM.org).

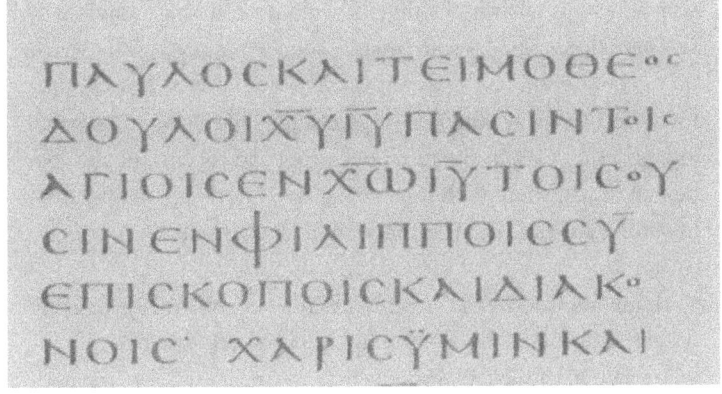

1:2 χάρις ὑμῖν καὶ εἰρήνη ἀπὸ θεοῦ πατρὸς ἡμῶν καὶ κυρίου Ἰησοῦ Χριστοῦ.

χάρις . . . καὶ εἰρήνη. Nominative absolutes. Paul (see also 1 Cor 1:3) along with other NT writers replaces the typical verbs of greeting in a Greek letter (χαίρειν or one of its cognates) with nouns rich in both Jewish (εἰρήνη/ שָׁלוֹם) and Christian (χάρις) meaning. 1 Peter, 2 Peter, and Jude use the aor pass opt of πληθύνω in their salutatory "wish prayer." The optative πληθυνθείη, therefore, may also be the implied verb in Paul's greeting. The sense would then be: "May grace and peace be multiplied to you from God our Father."

ὑμῖν. Dative of advantage.

ἀπὸ θεοῦ . . . καὶ κυρίου Ἰησοῦ Χριστοῦ. Source. The one pronoun ἀπὸ governing both persons indicates that both God and Jesus Christ are the source of grace and peace.

πατρὸς. Genitive in apposition to θεοῦ.
ἡμῶν. Genitive of relationship.
Ἰησοῦ Χριστοῦ. Genitive in apposition to κυρίου. For the nuanced meaning of Χριστοῦ as either a name or title ("Messiah") in an early Christian letter, see 1:1 on Χριστοῦ Ἰησοῦ.

Philippians 1:3–8

> ³ I always thank my God in all my remembrance of you, ⁴ in all my prayers for all of you, praying with joy, ⁵ because of your partnership in the gospel from the first day until now, ⁶ being confident of this very thing, that he who began a good work in you will carry it on to completion on the day of Christ Jesus. ⁷ Just as it is right for me to feel this way about all of you, since I have you in my heart and, whether I am in chains or defending and confirming the gospel, all of you share with me in his grace. ⁸ God can testify how I long for all of you with the affection of Christ Jesus.

> ¶I thank my God in all my remembrance of you, always offering prayer with joy in my every prayer for you all, because of your fellowship in the gospel from the first day until now. *For I am* confident of this very thing, that He who began a good work in you will perfect it until the day of Christ Jesus. For it is only right for me to think this way about you all, because I have you in my heart, since both in my chains and in the defense and confirmation of the gospel, you all are fellow partakers with me in this grace. For God is my witness, how I long for you all with the affection of Christ Jesus. (LSB)

Summary: Paul has a special affection for the first of his churches planted on European soil. This thanksgiving section (1:3–11) is the longest of any Pauline letter (Weima, 55). He assures them that they have a special place in his heart and that he has a longing for them because of their sharing in his apostolic work and suffering (1:7–8). Note that these summaries are sometimes adapted from the commentaries in the Bibliography.

1:3–6 is best read as one sentence. Some English versions break up

Analysis of Philippians One 23

this long sentence into two or more sentences. The verb Εὐχαριστῶ initiates the sentence and every following clause and phrase either complements or is subordinate to those complements. Following is a visual display of the structure of this sentence.

Εὐχαριστῶ τῷ θεῷ μου
   ἐπὶ πάσῃ τῇ μνείᾳ ὑμῶν
      πάντοτε ἐν πάσῃ δεήσει μου ὑπὲρ πάντων ὑμῶν,
      μετὰ χαρᾶς τὴν δέησιν ποιούμενος,
   ἐπὶ τῇ κοινωνίᾳ ὑμῶν εἰς τὸ εὐαγγέλιον
      ἀπὸ τῆς πρώτης ἡμέρας ἄχρι τοῦ νῦν,
   πεποιθὼς αὐτὸ τοῦτο,
      ὅτι ὁ ἐναρξάμενος... ἐπιτελέσει ἄχρι ἡμέρας Χριστοῦ Ἰησοῦ
      ἐν ὑμῖν ἔργον ἀγαθὸν

This "sentence flow analysis" displays visually the conviction that there are three things for which Paul thanks God and then elaborates on further details about each of those three.

1:3 Εὐχαριστῶ τῷ θεῷ μου ἐπὶ πάσῃ τῇ μνείᾳ ὑμῶν

Εὐχαριστῶ. Pres act ind 1st sg εὐχαριστέω.
τῷ θεῷ. Dative complement of Εὐχαριστῶ.
μου. Genitive of subordination.
ἐπὶ πάσῃ τῇ μνείᾳ. Cause (Wallace, 376). With the dative case, the translation "for" is probably the best translation with the preposition expressing "ground, reason or motive" (Abbott-Smith, 166, who cites BDF §235 in ET). The meaning of πάσῃ with the article τῇ is not "every" but "in the whole of" (BDF §235.3). The sense is "in all my remembrance," not "on every remembrance," which would point to isolated and intermittent prayers (Lightfoot, 82).
ὑμῶν. Objective genitive (so NIV, NET, CEB; Silva; Fee, 76–80; contra O'Brien 1991, 58–61, who takes it as a subjective genitive: "your remembrance of me"). In the next verse Paul uses ὑμῶν in an objective sense ("prayer for all of you"), and every use of "remembrance" in Pauline letter openings has "you" as the object (Rom 1:9; 1 Thess 1:2; Philm 4).

1:4 πάντοτε ἐν πάσῃ δεήσει μου ὑπὲρ πάντων ὑμῶν, μετὰ χαρᾶς τὴν δέησιν ποιούμενος,

πάντοτε. Temporal adverb, modifying the main verb Εὐχαριστῶ. There is an abundance of πας-words in verses 3–4: πάσῃ (3), πάντοτε, πάσῃ, πάντων (4). This makes it difficult to arrive at a smooth translation but is a rhetorically powerful description of Paul's all-consuming prayer for all his readers. The adjective πᾶς appears 33 times in Philippians (28% of its verses; only 2 Thess uses it more frequently at 29%) and the adverb πάντοτε 4 times ("a studied repetition"; Lightfoot, 83). This reflects Paul's concern for wholeness and supports his exhortations to unity in the face of strife, which is one of the major themes in the letter (1:27; 2:1–4; 4:2–9).

ἐν πάσῃ δεήσει. Means. The repetition of this idea from the previous verse (πάσῃ τῇ μνείᾳ) is best explained as a parenthetical comment. The sense would be: "I thank my God for every remembrance of you, always making petition with joy (that is, by every petition) for you all." The involved syntax of 1:3–7 has caused many translators and commentators to isolate 1:3 as an independent statement and then make 1:4–7 as a separate sentence. The main verb, however, is still the initial εὐχαριστῶ of 1:3 and the following clauses in 1:4–7 are all subordinate. I have attempted to maintain the entire passage as one complex sentence, but to do that demands that at least part of 1:4 is parenthetical.

ὑπὲρ πάντων ὑμῶν. Representation. This PP should be taken as an adjunct of the original verb εὐχαριστῶ rather than the preceding δεήσει, since the stress is on the author's thanksgiving for all rather than prayer for all. Paul has been dwelling on their good actions and in the parallel passages cited above he is giving thanks ὑπὲρ ὑμῶν.

μετὰ χαρᾶς. Manner. Joy (χαρά) is one of the main themes of the epistle (1:18, 25; 2:2, 17, 18, 29; 3:1; 4:1, 4, 10). Bengel (4:121) remarks: "Summa epistolae, 'gaudeo gaudete'" ("The sum of the epistle is, *I rejoice, rejoice ye*"). Whether the most prominent theme in the discourse is unity or joy has been addressed in the Discourse Analysis section of the Introduction.

τὴν δέησιν. Accusative direct object of ποιούμενος. The article functions anaphorically, referring back to the preceding anarthrous δεήσει.

Oftentimes the first mention of a noun (or a person) in a discourse will be anarthrous, with subsequent references to the same subject being arthrous (Levinsohn 2000, 148–67). The noun δέησις may be used in the broad sense of "prayer" as a synonym for προσευχή or in a narrow sense as a synonym of αἴτημα (request). Note the fine distinctions between words for "prayer" maintained by Trench (176–80). "The likelihood (is) that δέησις is being used in its more general sense ... indeed, the notion of 'thanksgiving' is thereby included in that of 'prayer.' The emphasis on joy seems more easily associated with the idea of thanksgiving than with that of petition" (Silva, 55). Two majuscules that often share the same readings, F and G, along with Ψ, 2495 plus a handful of Vulgate mss and one Syriac version add a καί, or its equivalent, before τὴν δέησιν. This appears to be a scribal attempt to smooth out the syntax of the clausal relationships in the long sentence.

ποιούμενος. Pres mid ptc masc nom sg ποιέω (manner, because of the adjunct expression μετὰ χαρᾶς). The imperfective aspect indicates a continuous action. The middle voice "expresses more direct participation, specific involvement ... of the subject doing the action" (Porter 1994, 67), or "calls attention to the whole subject being concerned with the action" (Moule, 24; see also Wallace, 414–15). The coupling of this specific verb and noun complement is also found in Luke 5:33 and 1 Tim 2:1.

1:5 ἐπὶ τῇ κοινωνίᾳ ὑμῶν εἰς τὸ εὐαγγέλιον ἀπὸ τῆς πρώτης ἡμέρας ἄχρι τοῦ νῦν,

ἐπὶ τῇ κοινωνίᾳ. Cause. The preposition ἐπί echoes its previous usage in 1:3. With the dative it is "giving the grounds for his joy" (GAGNT, 592). While this preposition is used to express the grounds of thanksgiving here and in 1 Cor 1:4, Paul more often uses a causal participle (Col 1:4; 1 Thess 1:3; Phlm 5) or ὅτι (Rom 1:8; 2 Thess 1:3). In Attic, the word κοινωνία describes an "association" or "partnership" such as a human society or marriage (LSJ, 969; GE, 1150). While in Acts 2:42 it describes the "sharing" of the early believers both spiritually and materially, here it conveys the spiritually close relations with God and his son. In this regard, see 1 John 1:3: "so that you have fellowship with us; but our fellowship is also with the Father and with his Son, Jesus

Christ," and also 1 John 1:6, 7: κοινωνίαν ἔχομεν. Paul also uses κοινωνία for the collection for the church in Jerusalem (Rom 15:26). He is thankful for the Philippians' "close participation" in the gospel, but it would be wrong to limit this to their monetary sharing. The noun conveys their entire "close participation" both in the gospel and in its outward ministry. Its usage in 2:1 and in 3:10 is describing the believers' spiritual "participation" in the Spirit and in Christ's sufferings.

εἰς τὸ εὐαγγέλιον. Locative. The classical meaning of the preposition εἰς, stressing a relationship "to" or "towards" or "unto" its object, is also often found in the NT. In later Greek, however, εἰς began encroaching on ἐν with the dative, so much so that the latter has been wholly displaced in Modern Greek (Abbott-Smith, 133–34; Robertson, 594; "Hellenistic use=εν" in CGELNT, 112). Other examples of εἰς with the object τὸ εὐαγγέλιον are in Phil 2:22; 2 Cor 2:12; and 9:13. The noun τὸ εὐαγγέλιον appears 9 times in Philippians, each time with the article. Wallace calls this the "monadic," i.e., "one of a kind" or "unique" article (223–24). "In our lit[erature εὐαγγέλιον is used] only in the sense of good news relating to God's action in Jesus Christ" (BDAG, 402). Recent attempts to view the "good news" against the imperial "good news" of the Roman emperor's reign may be overreading the linguistic evidence. The "good news" is better viewed in light of the Isaianic LXX references such as 40:9; 52:7 and 60:6.

ἀπὸ τῆς πρώτης ἡμέρας. Temporal. The preposition ἀπὸ is more often used as a spatial marker, but its usage here as a temporal marker can be found both in the Gospels (Matt 11:12; Luke 7:45; 13:25; 24:21) and in Pauline literature (Rom 1:20; 2 Cor 8:10; Col 1:6, 9). This entire phrase (τὸ εὐαγγέλιον ἀπὸ τῆς πρώτης ἡμέρας) corresponds to ἐν ἀρχῇ τοῦ εὐαγγελίου ("in the beginning of the gospel") in Phil 4:15.

ἄχρι τοῦ νῦν. Temporal. The article τοῦ nominalizes the adverb νῦν, changing it into the object of the preposition ἄχρι.

1:6 πεποιθὼς αὐτὸ τοῦτο, ὅτι ὁ ἐναρξάμενος ἐν ὑμῖν ἔργον ἀγαθὸν ἐπιτελέσει ἄχρι ἡμέρας Χριστοῦ Ἰησοῦ·

πεποιθώς. Prf act ptc masc nom sg πείθω. The participle is probably causal (Wallace, 631–32; O'Brien 1991, 63) and is thus dependent on the initial verb Εὐχαριστῶ in 1:3. Fee (85) sees it as related more to the preceding ποιούμενος in 1:4 (Sumney, 9–10). The persuasion expressed in the participle, however, is best viewed as another reason for which Paul gives thanks rather than as a further elaboration of his praying. The "state of affairs" conveyed by the verbal aspect of the perfect participle underscores Paul's present persuasion (Porter 1989, 279, 426).

αὐτὸ τοῦτο. An intensive personal pronoun (αὐτός) and a demonstrative pronoun (οὗτος), each in the accusative case and neuter gender and functioning as the complements of πεποιθώς. The pronoun αὐτό is defined by BDAG (152.1) as an "intensive marker, setting an item off fr[om] everything else through emphasis and contrast." The pronoun τοῦτο functions either anaphorically to recall something just mentioned or cataphorically to point out something about to be said. In this verse this "forward pointing" demonstrative "can accomplish the task of attracting extra attention to a target" (Runge, 66). In this case it calls attention to the following ὅτι clause. The collocation of these two pronouns with the prominent perfect aspect of πεποιθώς intensifies the emphatic pointing ("this very thing"). The usage of this expression in Rom 9:17; Eph 6:22; and Col 4:8 further illustrates this cataphoric/pointing forward function (although its use in 2 Pet 1:5 appears to be anaphoric). On the other hand, BDF (§154; §290) calls this construction an "accusative of content" and gives the expression an adverbial function ("I am sure"). This approach, however, emphasizes the case of the words over the function of the intensive marker and the demonstrative pronoun.

ὅτι. Introduces a content clause that is either appositional or epexegetical to the demonstrative pronoun τοῦτο (Wallace, 458–60).

ὁ ἐναρξάμενος. Aor mid ptc masc nom sg ἐνάρχομαι (substantival). This participle with its following complements (ἐν ὑμῖν ἔργον ἀγαθόν) functions as the subject of the verb ἐπιτελέσει. Lightfoot suggests that this verb contains a "sacrificial metaphor" (84). This idea, however, was drawn from its use in Euripides (LSJ, 557) and Polybius (GE, 686), but no such idea is contained in any of its eleven LXX usages or in any known papyri (MM, 211), nor in its only other NT occurrence (Gal 3:3). The verb ἐνάρχομαι by NT times simply conveyed the transitive sense of "to begin" (see BDAG, 331). This does not imply that Paul never utilizes sacrificial language; see, for example, Phil 2:17: εἰ καὶ σπένδομαι ἐπὶ τῇ θυσίᾳ καὶ λειτουργίᾳ τῆς πίστεως ὑμῶν; but there the sacrificial language is clearly drawn from the LXX.

ἐν ὑμῖν. Locative.

ἔργον ἀγαθόν. Accusative direct object of ἐναρξάμενος. The attributive adjective follows the noun, and the construction is anarthrous (Sumney, 10). Wallace calls this the "fourth attributive position" of the adjective (310–11). Both orders (adjective-noun and noun-adjective) are quite common in the NT.

ἐπιτελέσει. Fut act ind 3rd sg ἐπιτελέω. Embedded in the verb is an unexpressed complement such as the accusative αὐτό or τοῦτο ("will finish it", i.e., the good work). Any effort to make this verb (10 times in the NT) stronger than τελέω (28 times) because of its prefix ἐπι- is doomed to frustration. Both verbs mean "bring to an end, finish, complete" (BDAG, 383, 997; GE, 796–97, 2096–97).

ἄχρι ἡμέρας. Temporal. The improper preposition ἄχρι usually means "until" (BDAG, 160), but here it must have the meaning of "at" or "on" the day of Christ Jesus, because it specifies the day that God will perfect his purposes for the believer (Fee, 86). The use of "day" with "Jesus," "Christ," or "Lord" is a common way to refer to the Parousia (1:10; 2:16; 2 Cor 1:14).

Χριστοῦ Ἰησοῦ. Possessive genitive, in sense of "belonging to" (Wallace, 81); see also 1:10 and 2:16. This order of title-name is favored by Paul in this book (13/7 times), but it is difficult to conclude from these occurrences what motivated him to choose the order. The ratio of these two orders in the entire NT is 90/139. The "semi-colon" that ends verse six in the NA[28] and THGNT expresses the conviction of the editors that this is the end of the sentence beginning with 1:3. For Χριστός as a title, see 1:1.

1:7 Καθώς ἐστιν δίκαιον ἐμοὶ τοῦτο φρονεῖν ὑπὲρ πάντων ὑμῶν διὰ τὸ ἔχειν με ἐν τῇ καρδίᾳ ὑμᾶς, ἔν τε τοῖς δεσμοῖς μου καὶ ἐν τῇ ἀπολογίᾳ καὶ βεβαιώσει τοῦ εὐαγγελίου συγκοινωνούς μου τῆς χάριτος πάντας ὑμᾶς ὄντας.

Καθώς. Causal (BDAG, 494.3; BDF §453.2; Robertson, 968, 1382; as in Rom 1:28; 1 Cor 1:6; 5:7; Eph 1:4; 4:32). This adverb appears often in Pauline thanksgiving paragraphs (Rom 1:13; 1 Cor 1:6; 2 Cor 1:5; Eph 1:4;

Analysis of Philippians One

Col 1:6; 1 Thess 1:5; 2:13; 2 Thess 1:3).

ἐστιν. Pres act ind 3rd sg εἰμί.

δίκαιον. Predicate adjective: "To think this is right." When adjectives appear as predicates with an infinitive subject, they are neuter in gender.

ἐμοί. Dative of advantage.

τοῦτο. Accusative direct object of φρονεῖν. The demonstrative pronoun is anaphoric, referring back to the previous expressions.

φρονεῖν. Pres act inf φρονέω. The infinitive could be viewed as epexegetical, explaining the adjective δίκαιον. Syntactically, however, the infinitive is functioning as the subject of ἐστιν. This is the first of ten occurrences of this prominent verb in Philippians (see also 2:2[x2]; 2:5; 3:15[x2]; 3:19; 4:2; 4:10[x2]).

ὑπὲρ πάντων. Representation/advantage. The marker ὑπέρ indicates "that an activity or event is in some entity's interest, in behalf of" (BDAG, 1030). ME (108) suggests "concerning" or "about" with the genitive. Paul continues with a number of πας- cognates. See note on 1:4.

ἔχειν. Pres act inf ἔχω (used with διὰ τό to indicate cause).

με. Accusative subject of the infinitive (Porter 1994, 202–3). The clause could mean either "because I (με) hold you (ὑμᾶς) in my heart" (Silva, 56–57, and most commentators), or "because you (ὑμᾶς) hold me (με) in your heart" (NRSV, Hawthorne 22–23; Witherington, 38). Three factors favor the former approach: "(i) in Greek syntax the first accusative following the infinitive normally represents the subject and the second the object (cf. 2 Cor 2:13, 8:6; Fee, 90; Porter 1994, 197); (ii) the 'for' (*gar*) of v. 8a virtually requires such a reading (Lightfoot, 84); and (iii) John Chrysostom and Theodore of Mopsuestia, as native Greek speakers, see no ambiguity but invariably understand Paul to be describing his affection for the Philippians" (Bockmuehl, 63).

ἐν τῇ καρδίᾳ. Locative. The article τῇ functions here as a possessive pronoun ("my") if με is the subject of the infinitive (Wallace, 215–16).

ὑμᾶς. Accusative direct object of the infinitive ἔχειν (see above and Porter 1994, 202–3).

ἔν τε τοῖς δεσμοῖς. The enclitic particle τε balances with the following καί as "correlative conjunctions" (Wallace, 672). They express the pairing "both . . . and" as a declining Attic form being favored more in the Koine καί . . . καί construction (Turner, 335, 338). The plural noun δεσμοῖς ("bonds") is a synecdoche—a figurative extension of meaning—for "imprisonment," a quite common figure of speech in the NT (Phil 1:13; Acts 20:23; Col 4:18; Phlm 13; BDAG, 219, "to be in prison, imprisonment," LN 37.115).

καὶ ἐν τῇ ἀπολογίᾳ καὶ βεβαιώσει. The omission of ἐν by A D F G K L Ψ and a few Vulgate mss appears simply to be a scribal omission that entered the tradition. Some translations render the τε ... καὶ as "whether I am in chains or defending and confirming the gospel" (NIV), although most versions prefer a "both ... and" translation. As an indication that functional equivalence is not just a modern trend, note the rendering by Tyndale: "even in my bondes as I defende and stablysshe the gospell." One may possibly see a hendiadys with both nouns connected by καὶ and both governed by ἐν τῇ, but that option has not proved attractive to commentators. Other choices are to see the two substantives connected by καὶ as an example of the Granville-Sharp Rule (Wallace, 270–90). Wallace further nuances the relationship between the words in this example of an "impersonal construction" as "first entity being the subset of the second" (287). Lightfoot's simple observation, "The two words, being connected by the same article, combine to form one idea" (85), does not mention a possible hendiadys, but his language possibly describes such a figure.

ἀπολογίᾳ ... βεβαιώσει. These two nouns are set firmly within a legal context in their various appearances in the NT; see the entry on ἀπολογίᾳ in BDAG (117), and the entry on βεβαίωσις in BDAG (173) for "legal" usages in extra-biblical literature. Note the legal examples of ἀπολογίᾳ associated with Paul in 1:16; Acts 22:1; 25:16; and 2 Tim 4:6. The only other occurrence of βεβαίωσις in the NT is Heb 6:16. "The last passage esp[ecially] is a reminder that β[εβαίωσις] is a legal t[echnical] t[erm] for guaranteeing, furnishing security" (BDAG, 173). The cognate adjective βέβαιος does appear 8 times (note Heb 6:19 in same context as βεβαίωσις in 6:16), and means "certain, sure" (LN 71.15). What are the similarities and the differences between these two substantives? "As ἀπολογίᾳ implies the negative or defensive side of the Apostle's preaching, the preparatory process of removing obstacles and prejudices, so βεβαίωσις denotes the positive or aggressive side, the direct advancement and establishment of the Gospel. The two together will thus comprise all modes of preaching and extending the truth" (Lightfoot, 85). These two words "may well constitute a hendiadys" (Silva, 48) and convey a general sense: "You have supported me not only during those times when I have been able to set forth openly the defense that confirms the gospel, but even during this period of confinement" (see also 1:16).

τοῦ εὐαγγελίου. Objective genitive functioning as the complement to the verbal head nouns ἀπολογίᾳ and βεβαιώσει. The "good news" (see comments on 1:5) dominates this chapter (see also 1:12, 16, 27[2]; 2:22; 4:3, 15). These nine occurrences of εὐαγγέλιον in Philippians (in 8.6% of the verses) are matched only by its nine occurrences in the much longer epistle to the Romans. Therefore, the ratio to the total number of verses is higher in Philippians (8.6% to 2%).

συγκοινωνούς. Predicate accusative of the participle ὄντας and its subject ὑμᾶς. The four appearances of the preposition συν (1:1, 23; 2:22; 4:21) along with its 13 compounds (1:7, 23, 27; 2:2, 17–18, 25; 3:10, 17, 21; 4:3, 14) is another characteristic of this letter's emphasis on unity.

μου. Genitive of association. This usage, however, is not derived from the case but from the συν- prefix of the head noun. The pronoun, therefore, should be understood to go with συγκοινωνούς, not with the following τῆς χάριτος. The context stresses Paul's relationship with the Philippians. The more common Pauline usage is that μου is associated with its preceding noun (as in 1:8: μάρτυς γάρ μου ὁ θεός). See Bockmuehl (63) for a similar use by Chrysostom.

τῆς χάριτος. Objective genitive, serving as the complement of the verbal head noun συγκοινωνούς. A simpler explanation of the case is that the head noun is used "with genitive of the thing in which one shares" (BDAG, 952). This is also the case in the three other occurrences of the word in the NT: Rom 11:17 (τῆς ῥίζης); 1 Cor 9:23 (αὐτοῦ); and Rev 1:9 (τινος implied). Many commentators affirm the traditional meaning of χάρις as "the absolute grace of God" (Vincent, 10) or the "grace-gift" from the Philippians (Fee, 92). Paul, however, also uses χάρις in reference to his apostolic ministry (Rom 1:5; see also Rom 12:3; 15:15; 1 Cor 3:10; Gal 2:9), and it is that ministry that the verse has in view: "the defense and confirmation of the gospel." Note also the semantic parallel to Paul's ministry in 1 Cor 9:23, "And I do all things for the sake of the gospel that I may become a partaker (συγκοινωνός) of it." The meaning of συγκοινωνός also parallels the description of

Clement as a συνεργός in 4:3. Paul then has in view not divine grace in general but the Philippians' specific identification with his gospel ministry and their support of it (Silva, 47). The article τῆς is used as a possessive pronoun (Wallace, 215–16).

πάντας ὑμᾶς. This is a "a repetition of v. 4; note also πάντας ὑμᾶς, v. 7, which is then reiterated in the following verse" (O'Brien 1991, 66).

ὄντας. Pres act ptc masc acc pl εἰμί (adjectival). The participle echoes 1:1 (οὖσιν), but here the referent is the accusative ὑμᾶς, the previous accusative subject of the infinitive ἔχειν.

1:8 μάρτυς γάρ μου ὁ θεὸς ὡς ἐπιποθῶ πάντας ὑμᾶς ἐν σπλάγχνοις Χριστοῦ Ἰησοῦ.

μάρτυς. Predicate nominative. See comment below on ὁ θεὸς regarding the subject and predicate nominative in this type of construction.

γάρ. The first use of this coordinating conjunction, which is used 13 times in the book (1:18, 19, 21, 23; 2:13, 20, 21, 27; 3:3, 18, 20; 4:11). "Background material introduced by γάρ provides explanations or expositions of the previous assertion. ... The presence of γάρ constrains the material that it introduces to be interpreted as *strengthening* some aspect of the previous assertion, rather than as distinctive information" (Levinsohn 2000, 91). Runge (52) adds: "γάρ like καί, οὖν, and διὰ τοῦτο, signals close continuity with what precedes. However, it differs from the latter two in that it does not mark development. It differs from καί by adding the semantic constraint of strengthening/support. It does not advance the mainline of the discourse but rather introduces offline material that strengthens or supports what precedes. Γάρ can introduce a single clause that strengthens, or it may introduce an entire paragraph." Strengthening what precedes is its function here.

μου. Modifies μάρτυς, not the following ὁ θεὸς. Manuscripts containing a "Western" text (D F G), supported by two later majuscules and five minuscules, have the dative μοι instead of the genitive μου. 𝔓[46] and one Old Latin manuscript (9th cent.) omit the pronoun. Accidental omissions in 𝔓[46] are common. The addition of εστιν after μου (ℵ corrector, A D 𝔐) probably is evidence of a scribal attempt to clarify the grammar of the text.

ὁ θεός. Nominative subject of the implied equative verb. When two substantives are connected by an equative verb, either expressed or implied, the substantive with the article is the subject (Porter 1994, 109, on "Colwell's Rule"). The same expression is also used in Rom 1:9, although with an expressed verb (μάρτυς γάρ μού ἐστιν ὁ θεός).

ὡς. The overwhelming majority of the uses of this common adverb, which appears 504 times in the NT, focus on its comparative meaning, "as" or "just as." Eight occurrences, however, "focus on an aspect of an activity or event, *how*" (CGELNT, 389–90). This is its meaning here as well as in Luke 6:4; 24:6, 35; Acts 10:28; Rom 1:9; 11:2; 2 Cor 7:15; and 1 Thess 2:11.

ἐπιποθῶ. Pres act ind 1st sg ἐπιποθέω. Paul uses the same expression in 2:26, although the verb there is periphrastic, to describe Epaphroditus' similar longing for the Philippians. The verb is always used positively in the NT (except for its problematic usage in Jas 4:5). Older writers (Vincent, 10; Ellicott, 25; Thayer, 241) stressed that the prefix ἐπι- was "directed, not intensive." This was opposed to the opinion of another older writer, "It is a significant fact, pointing to the greater intensity of the language, that, while the simple words πόθος, ποθεῖν, etc. are never found in the New Testament, the compounds ἐπιποθεῖν, ἐπιποθία, ἐπιπόθησις, ἐπιπόθητος, occur with tolerable frequency" (Lightfoot, 85). The usage of the verb in the NT is very clear in conveying a strong desire or longing for something or someone. Current lexicons and commentators rarely mention the issue. The verb means "to have a strong desire for someth[ing], with implication of need, long for, desire" (BDAG, 377; GE, 784). The more fervent intensity of the verb is conveyed not by its prefix but more by its collocation with the following deeply expressive noun, σπλάγχνα.

πάντας. Attributive adjective, modifying ὑμᾶς.

ὑμᾶς. Accusative direct object of ἐπιποθῶ.

ἐν σπλάγχνοις. Means or manner. Although the metaphorical meaning of this substantive appears in Attic Greek, the literal meaning "entrails" dominated in secular Greek prior to the LXX (LSJ, 1628; GE, 1947). The metaphorical meaning of "mercy" and "compassion" is the dominant usage in later Biblical Greek, even in the LXX (Prov 12:10; Wis 10:5; see Muraoka, 631.2). In Hebrew thought, the entrails were the seat of רַחֲמִים (*rahamim*) "mercies" or "compassion" (Gen

43:30; 1 Kings 3:26; Jer 31:20). The Greek word group, including the verb σπλαγχνίζομαι, appears exclusively in its metaphorical sense in the Gospels, both about Jesus (nine times) and his followers. The σπλάγχνα of the Corinthians are constricted, those of Titus are open and go out to the believers (2 Cor 6:12; 7:15); Philemon has refreshed the σπλάγχνα of Christians under trial (Phlm 7, 20). The apostle loves Onesimus as his own σπλάγχνα (Phlm 12), hence as his own child. So here in 1:8 he loves the believers with the σπλάγχνα of Christ.

Χριστοῦ Ἰησοῦ. Subjective genitive or genitive of source.

Philippians 1:9–11

> [9] And this I am praying: that your love may abound more and more in knowledge and depth of insight, [10] so that you may be able to discern what is best, and that you may be pure and blameless for the day of Christ, [11] being filled with the fruit of righteousness that comes through Jesus Christ—to the glory and praise of God.

> And this I pray, that your love may abound still more and more in full knowledge and all discernment, so that you may approve the things that are excellent, in order to be sincere and without fault until the day of Christ, having been filled with the fruit of righteousness which *comes* through Jesus Christ, to the glory and praise of God. (LSB)

Summary: The final element in the introductory paragraph is also its climax. There had been a sort of interruption in 1:7–8, so that instead of praying, he spoke directly to the church in the second person with warmth and feeling. He now resumes that prayer by expressing the specific contents of his interceding for them. The prayer is an outward expression of those feelings he had just mentioned, although the opening "I pray" recalls his earlier reference to prayer in 1:4. He prays that divine love will increase beyond measure, and that as it increases it will show itself first in knowledge, that personal relationship with God through Christ, and second with all insight for all situations that involve practical conduct.

A sentence flow diagram will help to decide on the number of requests in this prayer on how each relates to the others:

Καὶ τοῦτο προσεύχομαι,
   A. **ἵνα** ἡ ἀγάπη ὑμῶν ἔτι μᾶλλον καὶ μᾶλλον **περισσεύῃ** ἐν ἐπιγνώσει καὶ πάσῃ αἰσθήσει
      B. εἰς τὸ δοκιμάζειν ὑμᾶς τὰ διαφέροντα,
   A'. ἵνα ἦτε εἰλικρινεῖς καὶ ἀπρόσκοποι εἰς ἡμέραν Χριστοῦ,
      B'. πεπληρωμένοι καρπὸν δικαιοσύνης τὸν διὰ Ἰησοῦ Χριστοῦ εἰς δόξαν καὶ ἔπαινον θεοῦ.

Based on the two ἵνα clauses, there are two main requests (A A'). There are then two intended results of those requests if granted (B B'). This is based on the idea that the two content ἵνα clauses carry the mainline requests and the two subordinate clauses (εἰς τὸ ... and πεπληρωμένοι ...) elaborate the result of each request. Both subordinate BB' constructions can convey result. This is most often the case with a present participle following the verb (Wallace, 637–39) as here. Εἰς τὸ + infinitive following the verb can convey either purpose or result (94–590). Paul probably uses different constructions in BB' because the first one better conveys purpose (the purpose of discernment is that we can distinguish correctly the more excellent things), while the second one conveys result (the result of being pure and blameless is that we are filled with the fruit of righteousness).

1:9 Καὶ τοῦτο προσεύχομαι, ἵνα ἡ ἀγάπη ὑμῶν ἔτι μᾶλλον καὶ μᾶλλον περισσεύῃ ἐν ἐπιγνώσει καὶ πάσῃ αἰσθήσει

Καὶ. While 1:9 is usually marked as a new paragraph, this connective does not signify a new topic or development. This prayer, therefore, is an expression of Paul's fervent desire and compassion in the previous verses. "The καί . . . of v. 9 should probably be viewed as resumptive, picking up the reference to Paul's prayer in v. 4" (Silva, 49).

τοῦτο. Accusative direct object of προσεύχομαι. Most commentators see a cataphoric functioning of this demonstrative pronoun to point out the prayer that follows. Its fronting before the verb (contrasted with its placement and cataphoric function in 1:6) points back (anaphoric function) to the prayer mentioned in 1:4 but not described there. "In a rhetorically skillful manner, Paul hinted at the prayer report in v. 4, but has suppressed it until vv. 9–11 so that it can serve as the climax of this section of the discourse" (Witherington, 64).

προσεύχομαι. Pres mid ind 1st sg προσεύχομαι.

ἵνα. Introduces a "clause denoting content" (Moule, 145–46; see also BDF §394); the clause thus expresses the initial "content" or request of the prayer. Wallace further defines this usage with ἵνα as a "substantival apposition clause" (Wallace, 474–76). While not the major usage of a ἵνα clause, there are a number of examples of this in the NT (e.g., Luke 1:43; John 15:8, 12; 17:3; 1 John 3:11, 23; 4:17, 21; 5:3; 3 John 4). The same construction also appears in 1:10. See the sentence flow diagram above for the implications of these two "content clauses" for discerning the structure of Paul's prayer.

ἡ ἀγάπη. Nominative subject of the verb περισσεύῃ. Although the book is filled with many expressions of affection, ἀγάπη appears only three additional times (1:16; 2:1, 2). The word draws its special significance from the following adjunct expression that includes ἐπιγνώσει and αἰσθήσει.

ὑμῶν. Possessive genitive.

ἔτι μᾶλλον καὶ μᾶλλον. While Paul will use the adverb μᾶλλον four additional times in Philippians (1:12, 23; 2:12; 3:4), this is its only doublet among the 81 uses of the word in the entire NT. This is an example of "an accumulation of words to denote superabundance, as below ver. 23" (Lightfoot, 86), a characteristic also witnessed in 2 Cor 4:17 (ὑπερβολὴν εἰς ὑπερβολήν).

περισσεύῃ. Pres act subj 3rd sg περισσεύω. With the preceding ἵνα this verb comprises a content clause that conveys the purpose of the prayer that love may "abound." Paul does not specify for whom he desires their love to abound. "Likely he is speaking of love in a comprehensive sense, i.e., love for God, for one another, and for all people" (Moore, 70).

ἐν ἐπιγνώσει καὶ πάσῃ αἰσθήσει. Means/manner. Some older writers held that ἐπιγνώσις "compared with γνῶσις . . . [is] sufficient to say that ἐπί must be regarded as intensive, giving to the compound word a greater strength than the simple possessed" (Trench, 285). A more accurate contrast is that ἐπίγνωσις means "knowledge, recognition in our lit[erature] limited to transcendent and moral matters" (BDAG, 369). The noun αἴσθησις is a NT *hapax legomenon*, but it is part of a cognate word group in the same semantic domain. The cognate noun αἰσθητήριον is also a *hapax legomenon* (Heb 5:14) as is the cognate verb αἰσθάνομαι (Luke 9:45). Louw and Nida describe the word's semantic domain: "αἰσθάνομαι; αἴσθησις, εως f; αἰσθητήριον, ου n: to have the capacity to perceive clearly and hence to understand the real nature of something" (32.28).

1:10 εἰς τὸ δοκιμάζειν ὑμᾶς τὰ διαφέροντα, ἵνα ἦτε εἰλικρινεῖς καὶ ἀπρόσκοποι εἰς ἡμέραν Χριστοῦ,

δοκιμάζειν. Pres act inf δοκιμάζω (used with εἰς τὸ to indicate purpose).

ὑμᾶς. Accusative subject of the infinitive δοκιμάζειν.

τὰ διαφέροντα. Pres act ptc masc acc pl διαφέρω (substantival direct object of the infinitive δοκιμάζειν). GE (515) defines its intransitive meaning as "to stand out" or "be superior." Hence my translation of the substantival ptcp as "what is best."

ἵνα. Introduces a purpose clause.

ἦτε. Pres act subj 2nd pl εἰμί.

εἰλικρινεῖς καὶ ἀπρόσκοποι. Predicate nominative complements of ἦτε.

εἰλικρινεῖς. Elsewhere only in 2 Peter 3:1: "pertaining to being sincere in the sense of having pure motivation – 'sincere, without hidden motives'" (LN 88.41). BDAG (282) rightly warns: "the etym[ology] 'judge in the light of the sun' is dubious."

ἀπρόσκοποι. This adjective can mean either "blameless" or "not giving offense" (BDAG, 125–26). While either fits the context, the first meaning better complements εἰλικρινεῖς.

εἰς ἡμέραν Χριστοῦ. Temporal. The addition of the article τὴν before ἡμέραν in $\mathfrak{P}^{46}$ is another of the manuscript's peculiarities.

1:11 πεπληρωμένοι καρπὸν δικαιοσύνης τὸν διὰ Ἰησοῦ Χριστοῦ εἰς δόξαν καὶ ἔπαινον θεοῦ.

πεπληρωμένοι. Prf pass ptc masc nom pl πληρόω (result). While all translations take the participle as simply circumstantial ("filled" or "being filled"), it fits the characteristics of a result participle (Wallace, 637–39). Bockmuehl calls this a "divine passive" (69), although this is evident from the context, not from the voice of the verb.

καρπὸν. Accusative direct object of πεπληρωμένοι. Since the verb is passive, it is more accurate to call this an "accusative of retained object" (Wallace, 197) or, conversely, a "passive with an accusative object" (Wallace, 438–39; Porter 1994, 66; Robertson, 485).

δικαιοσύνης. Epexegetical genitive (BDF §167). The fruit is righteousness. Note 3:6 and 3:9 for a different (negative) nuance of this word (see NIDNTTE 1:733–36 for its use in Paul's writings).

τὸν. The article functions as an adjectivizer, changing the PP διὰ Ἰησοῦ Χριστοῦ into an attributive modifier of καρπὸν δικαιοσύνης.

διὰ Ἰησοῦ Χριστοῦ. Agency.

εἰς δόξαν καὶ ἔπαινον. Purpose. The two substantives connected by καὶ may be a hendiadys. See a similar genitive expression in Eph 1:6, also conveying a "single idea" (BDF §168).

θεοῦ. Objective genitive. "In an objective genitive, the genitive represents a deep structure object and the verbal noun once again represents a deep structure verb" (Young, 31). The purpose of the fruit, therefore, would be to praise God. NA[28]/UBS[5] read δοξαν και επαινον θεου with strong external support of Greek mss and versions (ℵ A B D[2] I Ψ 𝔐 it syr cop). There are three textual variants, however: (1) δοξαν και επαινον Χριστου ("glory and praise of Christ") in D*₁ (2) δοξαν και επαινον μου ("my glory and praise") in F G; and (3) δοξαν θεου και επαινον εμοι ("glory of God and my praise") in 𝔓[46] (itg). The first is a simple change from "God" to "Christ." The second, which omits θεου, appears to be a scribal attempt to avoid a too close juxtaposition between God and Paul (Silva, 58). The third, found in 𝔓[46], has found an occasional supporter on transcriptional and exegetical grounds (Comfort, 605). This reading, however, may be another example of many singular readings for which 𝔓[46] is known. Metzger (546) refers to δοξαν και επαινον μου as "remarkable" for having no parallel in Paul and δοξαν θεου και επαινον εμοι as "astonishing" because of its clearly conflate character and Pauline self-praise. It is better to remain with the θεοῦ reading in NA[28]/UBS[5], as well as THGNT, because of its strong external support which is also affirmed by the parallel expression in Eph 1:6.

Philippians 1:12–18a

¹² Now I want you to know, brothers, that what has happened to me has served rather to advance the gospel. ¹³ As a result, it has become clear throughout the whole palace guard and to everyone else that I am in prison for Christ. ¹⁴ And because of my imprisonment, many more of the brothers, becoming confident in the Lord, dare all the more to proclaim the word without fear. ¹⁵ It is true that some proclaim Christ out of envy and strife, but others out of goodwill. ¹⁶ The latter do so out of love, knowing that I am put here for the defense of the gospel. ¹⁷ The former preach Christ out of selfish ambition, not sincerely, supposing that they can stir up trouble for me while I am in chains. ^{18a} For what does it matter? The important thing is that in every way, whether from false motives or true, Christ is preached. And in this I rejoice.

¶ Now I want you to know, brothers, that my circumstances have turned out for the greater progress of the gospel, so that my chains in Christ have become well known throughout the whole praetorian guard and to everyone else, and that most of the brothers, having become confident in the Lord because of my chains, have far more courage to speak the word of God without fear. Some, to be sure, are preaching Christ even from envy and strife, but some also from good will; the latter *do it* out of love, knowing that I am appointed for the defense of the gospel; the former proclaim Christ out of selfish ambition rather than from pure motives, thinking to cause me affliction in my chains. What then? Only that in every way, whether in pretense or in truth, Christ is proclaimed, and in this I rejoice. (LSB)

Summary: Although in prison, Paul never ceased his evangelistic efforts. Being chained to a soldier gave him many opportunities for private and prolonged conversations. When people gathered to hear Paul speak (Acts 28), the guard listened, and when they left, the soldier and Paul must have talked about the Jewish Messiah. Through these individuals, the message was carried through the whole camp of soldiers. Even outside his prison walls and through the whole city, the brothers were emboldened by Paul's success to preach Christ. Strangely some did this through faction and strife but others through love. Paul rejoiced that in either case the gospel was preached, whether by jealous enemies or by zealous allies. He was large-hearted enough to tolerate differences in method among brothers for the sake of the larger purpose of the gospel.

1:12 Γινώσκειν δὲ ὑμᾶς βούλομαι, ἀδελφοί, ὅτι τὰ κατ' ἐμὲ μᾶλλον εἰς προκοπὴν τοῦ εὐαγγελίου ἐλήλυθεν,

Γινώσκειν δὲ ὑμᾶς βούλομαι ἀδελφοί. This clause marks a new discourse direction. Mullins identifies this as a "disclosure" and lists its characteristics as (1) the use of θέλω (or βούλομαι), (2) identification of the person addressed, (3) a noetic verb in the infinitive, and (4) the information, usually introduced by a ὅτι (Mullins, 50). Runge (121–22) identifies the clause as a "metacomment." Γινώσκειν. Pres act inf γινώσκω (complementary). The fronting of the infinitive renders it as emphatic. THGNT adopts the ancient scribal spelling Γεινώσκειν.

δὲ. Signals development to a new section of discourse and is better translated as "Now" (Wallace, 674).

ὑμᾶς. Accusative subject of the infinitive.

βούλομαι. Pres mid ind 1st sg βούλομαι.

ἀδελφοί. Nominative plural of direct address (Porter 1994, 86–87), the vocative plural sharing the same endings as the nominative plural. The noun is used "in the collective sense of *brothers and sisters*" (CGELNT, 6). Combined with δὲ, it is evidence of a new paragraph.

ὅτι. Introduces the clausal complement of Γινώσκειν.

τὰ. The article functions as a nominalizer, changing the PP κατ' ἐμὲ into the subject of ἐλήλυθεν. "This means that the article alerts the reader to the fact that something other than a substantive is coming where a substantive is expected" (Funk, 715).

κατ' ἐμὲ. Reference.

μᾶλλον. Adverb, meaning not its usual "more" but "rather" (Abbott-Smith, 277). "The comparative (adverb) is often used without mention of the standard of comparison" (Vincent, 16); cf. 2:28; Rom 15:15; 1 Cor 7:38, 12:31; 2 Cor 7:7, 13.

εἰς προκοπὴν. Purpose. The noun, occurring elsewhere only in 1:25

Analysis of Philippians One 41

and 1 Tim 4:15, means "a movement forward to an improved state, progress, advancement, furtherance" (BDAG, 871).

τοῦ εὐαγγελίου. Objective genitive.

ἐλήλυθεν. Prf act ind 3rd sg ἔρχομαι. The verbal aspect is stative: "the action is conceived of by the language user as reflecting a given (often complex) state of affairs" (Porter 1994, 21–22), not imperfective aspect (Campbell 2013, xxvii).

1:13 ὥστε τοὺς δεσμούς μου φανεροὺς ἐν Χριστῷ γενέσθαι ἐν ὅλῳ τῷ πραιτωρίῳ καὶ τοῖς λοιποῖς πᾶσιν,

ὥστε. Indicates result, with infinitive γενέσθαι.

τοὺς δεσμούς. Accusative subject of the infinitive γενέσθαι. See 1:7 for its figurative extension of meaning for "imprisonment."

φανεροὺς. Predicate accusative of γενέσθαι; the accusative case agrees with δεσμούς (Porter 1994, 84).

ἐν Χριστῷ. Cause. The preposition ἐν is "used to mark causality or reason for someth[ing], because of, on account of" (CGELNT, 126.5).

γενέσθαι. Aor mid inf γίνομαι (used with ὥστε to indicate result).

ἐν ὅλῳ τῷ πραιτωρίῳ καὶ τοῖς λοιποῖς πᾶσιν. Locative. The single preposition implies that "all the rest" were associated somehow with the τῷ πραιτωρίῳ.

τῷ πραιτωρίῳ. A Latin loan word (*praetorium*). In the NT it is used for the procurator's palace in Jerusalem (Matt 27:27; Mark 15:16; John 18:28ab, 33; 19:9) and the Herodian palace in Caesarea (Acts 23:35). LSB adds the footnote: "Or *governor's palace.*" Its specific location here cannot be determined linguistically but depends on whether Paul wrote from Caesarea or Rome or even Ephesus. Lightfoot (99–104) argues for the Rome location from the sole meaning of the Latin *praetorium* as the "Praetorian Guard." "If the letter was written fr[om] Rome, the words ἐν ὅλῳ τῷ πραιτωρίῳ are best taken to mean *in the whole praetorian* (or *imperial*) *guard*. If it belongs to a non-Roman imprisonment, τὸ πραιτώριον beside οἱ λοιποί includes those who live in the governor's palace" (BDAG, 859). For the suggestion of Ephesus, see the introductory discussion of "Provenance." "We know that the 'imperial guard' was present in other cities, perched like frogs on the bank of the Mediterranean" (Roetzel, 128 n27). Roetzel's eloquence must be tempered by the lack of evidence for the Praetorian Guard actually being stationed in Ephesus.

τοῖς λοιποῖς πᾶσιν. The plural may include members of the Praetorian Guard or those who ran the prison (O'Brien 1991, 93; Sumney, 20).

1:14 καὶ τοὺς πλείονας τῶν ἀδελφῶν ἐν κυρίῳ πεποιθότας τοῖς δεσμοῖς μου περισσοτέρως τολμᾶν ἀφόβως τὸν λόγον λαλεῖν.

τοὺς πλείονας. Comparative adjective of πολύς, "many more" (LN 59.1). Accusative subject of the infinitive τολμᾶν.

τῶν ἀδελφῶν. Partitive genitive.

ἐν κυρίῳ. This language of indwelling is an idiomatic way of highlighting the intimate nature of the relationship. This PP is related to the following participle πεποιθότας rather than to the preceding ἀδελφῶν, fronted for emphasis.

πεποιθότας. Prf act ptc masc acc pl πείθω (adjectival, modifying πλείονας). This also avoids an accumulation of causal constructions. Sumney (20) observes that the order of ἐν plus dative before a participle is "a unique construction in the undisputed Paulines." Paul uses the verb 22 times, 20 in the perfect tense, and so in all 5 occurrences in Philippians (see also 1:6, 25; 2:24; 3:3, 4).

τοῖς δεσμοῖς. While Wallace (167–68; also BDF §196; Funk, 892.4) labels this dative as "causal," some prefer dative of means because the ultimate cause may also be the means of an action (Porter 1997, 98–99).

μου. Possessive genitive. This enclitic loses its accent to the *ultima* of the preceding word.

περισσοτέρως. Adverb, modifying τολμᾶν.

τολμᾶν. Pres act inf τολμάω (result). It is possible to see this infinitive functioning in a parallel manner with the infinitive γενέσθαι in 1:13 so that both are governed by ὥστε.

ἀφόβως. Adverb, modifying λαλεῖν.

τὸν λόγον. Accusative direct object of λαλεῖν. Two variants (του θεου ℵ A B D P Ψ 33 syr; and του κυριου F G) appear to be scribal attempts to make explicit what τὸν λόγον means. Some English versions (ASV, NASB, NLT), impressed with the testimony of ℵ A B D* in support of the first variant, followed WH, Tregelles, and earlier editions of the

Nestle text (prior to NA²⁶). The editors of NA²⁸ / UBS⁵ and the THGNT considered the variant readings as expansions and adopted the shorter text in 𝔓⁴⁶ and 𝔐.

λαλεῖν. Pres act inf λαλέω (complementary).

Introduction to the structure of 1:15–17:

The LSB along with most modern versions preserves the chiasm of the four clauses in 1:15–17. The KJV, however, follows the Textus Receptus and transposes 1:16 and 17, presumably to keep the sequence parallel with the order in 1:15. But the chiastic literary structure, in which item one is paired with item four while two is paired with three, appears elsewhere in the NT (e.g., Matt 7:6 and Philm 5). The ultimate sense of the passage is the same in either sequence.

1:15 τινὲς μὲν καὶ διὰ φθόνον καὶ ἔριν, τινὲς δὲ καὶ δι' εὐδοκίαν τὸν Χριστὸν κηρύσσουσιν·

τινὲς. Indefinite pronoun, subject of κηρύσσουσιν. It is also an enclitic, normally without an accent and not initiating a clause. Here, however, the enclitic pronoun begins a sentence (BDF §301; Moule, 125).

μὲν. This post-positive particle has been explained by Runge (75): "In spite of the multiplicity of senses claimed, μέν signals the presence of one common constraint: anticipation of a related sentence that follows. I contend that μέν simply creates anticipation of a related clause, most often introduced by δέ." The related sentence that follows is the clause beginning with τινὲς δὲ, offering a "point-counterpoint set" (Runge, 73–100).

καὶ ... καὶ. The conjunction καὶ appears in each clause, after τινὲς μὲν and τινὲς δὲ and before δι(ὰ), and signifies more than "and" or "but" (BDF §442). Silva (63) states that the initial καὶ has "a transitional but emphatic force." English translations attempt to convey this by "indeed" (KJV, ESV); "to be sure" (NASB, NET, CSB); or "it is true" (NIV).

διὰ φθόνον καὶ ἔριν. Cause. This PP is further qualified by the PP ἐξ ἐριθείας in 1:17. The words φθόνον καὶ ἔριν are always negative (φθόνος in Jas 4:5 disputed) and often appear together along with ἐριθεία (1:17) in other Pauline vice lists (Rom 1:29; 1 Cor 3:3; 2 Cor 12:20; Gal 5:20).

τινὲς. Indefinite pronoun, subject of κηρύσσουσιν; see above.

δὲ. Introduces the "counterpoint" to the preceding μὲν clause.

δι' εὐδοκίαν. Cause. The loss of the final vowel –α in the preposition δι' is due to the initial vowel in εὐδοκίαν. "Elision is most common with διά" (Robertson, 208). Standard lexicons translate εὐδοκίαν as "good will" (of humans) (Abbott-Smith, 185; BDAG, 404.1). Bockmuehl (79) argues from the references to divine εὐδοκία (Matt 11:26; Luke 10:21; Eph 1:5, 9; Phil 2:13) that it is not just a matter of sincerity or goodwill toward Paul but involves an orientation to God and the gospel (also Reumann, 179), but this is probably "alien to the context" (Silva, 66).

τὸν Χριστὸν. Accusative direct object of κηρύσσουσιν. While the presence of the article may suggest that the title "the Messiah" is meant, the titular use of this term in a Jewish sense is doubtful (Reumann, 176). See the explanation in 1:1.

κηρύσσουσιν. Pres act ind 3rd pl κηρύσσω. The predicate of two subjects, the twice-occurring τινὲς. This is the only example in Philippians of κηρύσσω (or κήρυγμα), a common Greek word (EDNT 2:288) meaning "to proclaim aloud" by a herald (κῆρυξ).

1:16 οἱ μὲν ἐξ ἀγάπης, εἰδότες ὅτι εἰς ἀπολογίαν τοῦ εὐαγγελίου κεῖμαι,

οἱ. The article functions as a nominalizer, changing the PP ἐξ ἀγάπης into the subject of the implied verb κηρύσσουσιν. The article points back to the people described at the end of 1:15.

ἐξ ἀγάπης. Source. The switch in preposition from διά in 1:15 should not be viewed as significant, although Silva (66) suggests that "the preposition ἐκ more clearly than διά calls attention to attitudes as sources of behavior." The genitive after ἐκ (ἐξ because ἀγάπης begins with a vowel) expresses "origin, cause, motive, reason" (BDAG, 296.3).

μὲν. See comments on 1:15.

εἰδότες. Prf act ptc masc nom pl οἶδα (causal). GAGNT (593) says: "causal, because they know." The perfect tense is best translated as a present: "knowing." Fee (120, n17) suggests that there is a balanced contrast with οἰόμενοι (1:17).

ὅτι. Introduces the content clause that is the clausal complement of εἰδότες.

εἰς ἀπολογίαν. Purpose (BDAG, 117.2.b).

τοῦ εὐαγγελίου. Objective genitive.

κεῖμαι. Pres mid ind 1st sg κεῖμαι. According to BDAG (537.3.a), this verb means "be appointed, set, destined." Robertson states that the present "serves as perf. pass. for τίθημι, 'be placed, put, appointed'" (316, 357, 813). Silva (64) discerns a "predestinarian motif" as in Gal 1:15–16. The theological rendering of O'Brien (1991, 97) is "I am divinely appointed." 𝔐 transposes the order of verses 16 and 17 (reflected in KJV and NKJV), following the order set forth in 1:15: preachers from rivalry are mentioned first; then those of goodwill. Not only does the overwhelming manuscript evidence, both early and diverse, support the order in the NA[28], but the transposition ignores the chiastic order:

A. τινὲς μὲν καὶ διὰ φθόνον καὶ ἔριν

B. τινὲς δὲ καὶ δι' εὐδοκίαν τὸν Χριστὸν κηρύσσουσιν·

B'. οἱ μὲν ἐξ ἀγάπης, εἰδότες ὅτι εἰς ἀπολογίαν τοῦ εὐαγγελίου κεῖμαι,

A'. οἱ δὲ ἐξ ἐριθείας τὸν Χριστὸν καταγγέλλουσιν, . . . τοῖς δεσμοῖς μου.

"Such chiasms are typically Pauline; the reversal of these may promote clarity, but it destroys the poetry" (Comfort, 605).

1:17 οἱ δὲ ἐξ ἐριθείας τὸν Χριστὸν καταγγέλλουσιν, οὐχ ἁγνῶς, οἰόμενοι θλῖψιν ἐγείρειν τοῖς δεσμοῖς μου.

οἱ δὲ. The counterpoint to οἱ μὲν in 1:16.

ἐξ ἐριθείας. Source; see 1:16. This is another member of the Pauline vice lists (see 1:15; also Jas 3:14, 16). "A derivation fr[om] ἔρις is not regarded w[ith] favor by recent NT linguistic scholarship . . . since ἔρις and ἐριθεῖαι are both found in these lists; yet for Paul and his followers, the m[ea]n[in]g *strife, contentiousness* (so Ltzm., MDibelius, JSickenberger) cannot be excluded" (BDAG, 392).

τὸν Χριστὸν. Accusative direct object of καταγγέλλουσιν; see 1:15.

καταγγέλλουσιν. Pres act ind 3rd pl καταγγέλλω. Paul has switched to a different verb from that used for "preaching" in 1:15 (κηρύσσουσιν). While the verb κηρύσσω can be used of Christian preaching, it occasionally retains its general sense (Mark 1:45; 7:36; Rom 2:21). After this passage, καταγγέλλω is used solely for the proclamation of the Christian message (Abbott-Smith, 233.1).

οὐχ. The negative particle οὐχ, spelled this way before a word beginning with vowel and rough breathing.

ἁγνῶς. Adverb from the adjective ἁγνός (4:8: "pure"). See also ἅγιοι (1:1; 4:21) and the entire word group (TDNT 1:88, 122). The adverb is a *hapax legomenon* meaning "purely, sincerely," and the expression is: "(not) from pure motives" (BDAG, 13–14). The cognate adjective ἁγνος is used 8 times in the NT.

οἰόμενοι. Pres mid ptc masc nom pl οἴομαι. The verb means "to consider someth[ing] to be true but with a component of tentativeness, think, suppose, expect" (BDAG, 701), and denotes "a belief or judgment based principally upon one's own feelings" (Vincent, 21). The participle is usually understood as causal (Reumann, 182) and contrasts with the confident εἰδότες of the other group (1:15). The other NT occurrences of the verb (John 21:25; Jas 1:7) offer illustrative semantic parallels.

θλῖψιν. Accusative direct object of ἐγείρειν. Paul refers to his "trouble" again in 4:14.

ἐγείρειν. Pres act inf ἐγείρω (complementary or indirect discourse). "The basic idea is to move from an inert state or position, in general rise, raise. In extended sense Phil 1:17 (tr. cause trouble)" (CGELNT, 106). Lightfoot (90) suggests "to make my chains gall me" by noting that Paul combines the two metaphors of θλίψις and δεσμός.

τοῖς δεσμοῖς. Dative of indirect object (Robertson, 538) or disadvantage (Porter 1994, 98). See the figurative extension of this word in 1:14.

μου. Possessive genitive. This enclitic loses its accent to the *ultima* of the preceding word.

1:18a Τί γάρ; πλὴν ὅτι παντὶ τρόπῳ, εἴτε προφάσει εἴτε ἀληθείᾳ, Χριστὸς καταγγέλλεται, καὶ ἐν τούτῳ χαίρω.

Τί. Neut sg interrogative pronoun (BDAG, 1007.1.a.β.ℸ).

γάρ. Conjunction indicating a cause or reason, often in questions (BDAG, 1.f). The expression Τί γάρ is an ellipsis. While Paul uses it as the subject of a clause in Rom 4:3; 1 Cor 5:12; 7:16; and 2 Cor 12:13, the closest parallel elliptical usage is in Rom. 3:3 τί γάρ; εἰ ἠπίστησάν τινες, μὴ ἡ ἀπιστία αὐτῶν τὴν πίστιν τοῦ θεοῦ καταργήσει; These occurrences are all in a diatribal context. In light of Rom 3:3, the best translation is "What difference does it make?" or "What does it matter?" (BDF §299.3; Fee, 124 n36).

πλήν. The adverb, used here as a conjunction, which with the following ὅτι introduces the content of Paul's conclusion.

ὅτι. Introduces the clausal complement of the implied verb in the preceding clause, Τί γάρ.

παντὶ τρόπῳ. Manner.

εἴτε... εἴτε. Variant of the conditional particle εἰ. Combined with the enclitic τε, it gains an accent (BDF §446; §54.3); "whether . . . or" (BDAG, 279.6.0).

προφάσει. Dative of manner. The noun means "falsely alleged motive, pretext, ostensible reason, excuse" (BDAG, 889.2).

ἀληθείᾳ. Dative of manner.

Χριστὸς. Nominative subject of καταγγέλλεται. The fronting of the subject, differing from the default verb-subject-object order, emphasizes the subject being proclaimed.

καταγγέλλεται. Pres pass ind 3rd sg καταγγέλλω. For significance of this verb, see 1:17.

ἐν τούτῳ. Cause (e.g., NIV "because of this"). The presence of the preposition ἐν indicates the reason for the intransitive verb χαίρω. O'Brien (1991, 106 n46) adds, "ἐν τούτῳ is neuter, signifying 'in this (fact)', namely that Christ is proclaimed."

χαίρω. Pres act ind 1st sg. See comment on μετὰ χαρᾶς in 1:4. This is the first verb of the sixteen χαίρω-cognates in Philippians. The basic sense is "rejoice, be glad" (BDAG, 1074.1), not necessarily a "joy in martyrdom" (TDNT 9:369).

Philippians 1:18b–26

[18b] But I will also continue to rejoice, [19] for I know that through your petition and the provision of the Spirit of Jesus Christ this (what has happened to me) will turn out for my salvation. [20] In keeping with my eager expectation and hope that I will in no way be ashamed but with all boldness so also now as always Christ will be made great in my body, whether by life or by death. [21] For to

me, living is Christ and to die is gain. ²² If I am to go on living in the body, this will be fruitful labor for me. And I am not making known what I will prefer. ²³ I am torn between the two, because I desire to depart and be with Christ, which is better by far; ²⁴ but to remain in the body is important for you. ²⁵ Convinced of this, I know that I will remain, and I will continue with all of you for your progress and joy in the faith, ²⁶ so that what you can be proud of in Christ Jesus will abound because of me through my coming to you again.

Yes, and I will rejoice, for I know that THIS WILL TURN OUT FOR MY SALVATION through your prayers and the provision of the Spirit of Jesus Christ, according to my earnest expectation and hope, that I will not be put to shame in anything, but *that* with all boldness, Christ will even now, as always, be magnified in my body, whether by life or by death. For to me, to live is Christ and to die is gain. But if *I am* to live *on* in the flesh, this *will mean* fruitful labor for me; and I do not know what I will choose. But I am hard-pressed between the two, having the desire to depart and be with Christ, for *that* is very much better, yet to remain on in the flesh is more necessary for your sake. And convinced of this, I know that I will remain and continue with you all for your progress and joy in the faith, so that your reason for boasting may abound in Christ Jesus in me, through my coming to you again. (LSB)

In traditional verse divisions, the end of 1:18 is the word χαρήσομαι. The NA/UBS, WH, and SBL Greek texts, however, attach the last clause to 1:19, concluding that the fronting of the conjunction supports its beginning a new sentence with 1:19 as a supporting clause to the main clause in 1:18b. However, the editors of the Tyndale House GNT, along with the TR, retain the clause as ending the sentence in 1:18, following the example of the scribe in Vaticanus. Note the "new paragraph" marker in the LSB.

Summary: While regretful that some do not see situations as he does, Paul still rejoices if they glorify Christ, and he will not put any hindrance in their way. One writer has observed that Paul could adapt an American patriot's words uttered facing his death: "Give me liberty or give me death; it will be Christ either way." To live is to work for Christ; to die is to be with Christ. This is Paul's soliloquy as he faces either martyrdom or further missionary labors. Paul weighs blessings against blessings and chooses the lesser blessings in pure unselfishness. While the aged apostle would rather die than live because he will be with the Lord, he would also rather live than die before his work for the Lord is done.

1:18b Ἀλλὰ καὶ χαρήσομαι,

Ἀλλά. "Although there are several contrastive or adversative particles, ἀλλά adds the unique constraint of correcting some aspect of what precedes" (Runge, 93).

καί. The context demands an adjunctive meaning ("also"), "indicating a key addition" (Wallace, 671).

χαρήσομαι. Fut mid ind 1st sg χαίρω. This is the first of two verbs in 1:18b–19 (also ἀποβήσεται) that retain the middle in the future (see BDF §77 for nine additional NT verbs).

1:19 οἶδα γὰρ ὅτι τοῦτό μοι ἀποβήσεται εἰς σωτηρίαν διὰ τῆς ὑμῶν δεήσεως καὶ ἐπιχορηγίας τοῦ πνεύματος Ἰησοῦ Χριστοῦ

οἶδα. Prf act ind 1st sg οἶδα.

γάρ. "Γάρ introduces explanatory material that strengthens or supports what precedes. This may consist of a single clause, or it may be a longer digression" (Runge, 54).

ὅτι. Introduces the clausal complement of οἶδα.

τοῦτο. Nominative subject of ἀποβήσεται. Neut sg of demonstrative pronoun οὗτος.

μοι. Dative of advantage.

ἀποβήσεται. Fut mid ind 3rd sg ἀποβαίνω. See the comment on the middle voice of χαρήσομαι in 1:18b. While used literally of disembarking a boat (Luke 5:2; John 21:9), BDAG (107.2) defines the figurative use of this verb as "to result in a state or condition, turn out, lead (to)." Both senses have a pre-history in Greek (GE, 242).

εἰς σωτηρίαν. Result. NT examples of σωτηρία as "deliverance" from danger are Acts 7:25; 27:34; Heb 11:7. BDAG (986.2) lists the remaining occurrences as referring to "salvation, w[ith] focus on transcendent aspects." Eternal deliverance is consistent with the word's use in 1:28 and 2:12. LXX Job 13:16a is exactly parallel: τοῦτό μοι ἀποβήσεται εἰς σωτηρίαν. LSB reads "FOR I KNOW THAT THIS WILL TURN OUT FOR MY SALVATION" to mark this as an OT quotation. Since Job expected eschatological vindication (13:18; 19:25–27), so did Paul, even if he may never have been released (1:20). He still believed, however, that he could be released (1:26). The CSB17 altered its previous HCSB translation from "deliverance" to "salvation."

διὰ τῆς ὑμῶν δεήσεως καὶ ἐπιχορηγίας τοῦ πνεύματος Ἰησοῦ Χριστοῦ. Means.

τῆς ὑμῶν δεήσεως καὶ ἐπιχορηγίας τοῦ πνεύματος Ἰησοῦ Χριστοῦ. The Granville Sharp Rule provides no insight here since neither of the nouns are personal. At the most, the one article governing both nouns indicates the close relation in which the two stand in Paul's mind; the two words "are treated as one for the purpose in hand" (Robertson, 787). ME suggests that in this type of construction "there will still be some conceptual link between the substantives" (83).

δεήσεως. See comments on δέησιν (1:4).

ἐπιχορηγίας. The noun elsewhere is only in a bodily metaphor (Eph 4:19) and here means spiritual "provision, support" (LN 35.31). While the word group has a Greco-Roman "cultural background of generous public service" (BDAG, 387), the NT noun simply means "a supply" (Abbott-Smith, 177) or "provision" (NIV).

τοῦ πνεύματος. Objective genitive. Their prayer will help to provide the Spirit.

Ἰησοῦ Χριστοῦ. Source. The Spirit comes from Jesus Christ.

1:20 κατὰ τὴν ἀποκαραδοκίαν καὶ ἐλπίδα μου, ὅτι ἐν οὐδενὶ αἰσχυνθήσομαι ἀλλ' ἐν πάσῃ παρρησίᾳ ὡς πάντοτε καὶ νῦν μεγαλυνθήσεται Χριστὸς ἐν τῷ σώματί μου, εἴτε διὰ ζωῆς εἴτε διὰ θανάτου.

κατὰ τὴν ἀποκαραδοκίαν καὶ ἐλπίδα μου. Standard. Κατὰ serves as "marker, w[ith] acc[usative], of a standard or aspect of perception . . . in line with, in accordance with, in keeping with" (CGELNT, 188.4.a). The first noun, also in Rom 8:19, was possibly coined by Paul, although the cognate verb does appear in the historians Polybius and Josephus

(BDAG, 112; GE, 251). The noun denotes a keen anticipation of the future. The two nouns are probably a hendiadys like "my eager expectation" (Silva, 77) or are another example of two different nouns "treated as one for the purpose in hand" (Robertson, 787).

μου. Possessive genitive.

ὅτι. Introduces the clausal complement of ἐλπίδα μου (Fee, 135; O'Brien 1991, 113).

ἐν οὐδενί. Manner (Wallace, 372).

αἰσχυνθήσομαι. Fut pass ind 1st sg αἰσχύνω. Paul uses the same form in 2 Cor 10:8, although in a different context.

ἀλλ'. Conjunction that corrects an aspect of what precedes (see Ἀλλά in 1:18b). The contraction is due to the rough breathing in the next word.

ἐν πάσῃ παρρησίᾳ. Manner.

ὡς πάντοτε καὶ νῦν. Comparative particle ὡς plus the adverb πάντοτε ("as always") introduces a comparison with an adverbial καὶ and νῦν (BDAG, 496, 2.b, "so also now"). The adverb νῦν refers to Paul's imprisonment. Note also the alliteration with the previous phrase: πάσῃ παρρησίᾳ ... πάντοτε.

μεγαλυνθήσεται. Fut pass ind 3rd sg μεγαλύνω. The passive voice conveys "to be made great, grow" (GE, 1282). The two future passives (with αἰσχυνθήσομαι) provide an effective rhetorical balance. "I will not be ashamed by anything that happens to me. Christ shall be made great by anything that happens to me."

Χριστός. Nominative subject of μεγαλυνθήσεται.

ἐν τῷ σώματί. Instrumental. Paul also uses the expression ἐν τῷ σώματί in this way in 1 Cor 6:20 and 2 Cor 4:10. "Christ shall be magnified with my body, whether it is through life or death."

μου. Possessive genitive.

εἴτε ... εἴτε. The second of three times Paul uses this construction (1:18, 20, 27). The disjunctive conjunctions introduce subordinate clauses but with the ellipsis of a finite verb (BDF §446). The translation is "whether ... or." The construction is uniquely Pauline (Rom 12:7; 1 Cor 3:22; 8:5; 10:31; 12:13, 26; 13:8; 14:7; 15:11; 2 Cor 5:9, 10, 13; 8:23; 12:2, 3; Eph 6:8; Col 1:16, 20; 1 Thess 5:10; 2 Thess 2:15).

διὰ ζωῆς. Means.

διὰ θανάτου. Means.

1:21 Ἐμοὶ γὰρ τὸ ζῆν Χριστὸς καὶ τὸ ἀποθανεῖν κέρδος.

Ἐμοί. Dative of reference or ethical dative (Wallace, 147). The dative pronoun is fronted for emphasis.

γὰρ. As in 1:18a and 1:19a, this conjunction links 1:21 with the preceding verse, but more likely with the last phrase of v. 20, εἴτε διὰ ζωῆς εἴτε διὰ θανάτου (Fee, 139-40).

τὸ ζῆν. Pres act inf ζάω (substantival, subject of a verbless equative clause; see Porter 1994, 195). The subject infinitive can be either arthrous or anarthrous (Robertson, 1058-59). The article's presence with ζῆν and ἀποθανεῖν indicates that these infinitives are the subjects in a subject-predicate nominative construction (Black 1998, 46).

Χριστός. Predicate nominative of a verbless equative clause. In this type of construction, the anarthrous substantive is the predicate nominative.

τὸ ἀποθανεῖν. Aor act inf ἀποθνήσκω (substantival, subject of a verbless equative clause). Some English translations render the infinitives like gerunds: "Living is Christ and dying is gain" (NRSV, NET), but this neglects the tense difference. Lightfoot (92) and Wallace (601) call attention to the aspectual distinction between the present ζῆν and the aorist ἀποθανεῖν, a difference between imperfective aspect (process) and perfective aspect (event). Such differences are not always easily conveyed through translation. Demurring from most commentators (e.g., Fee, 140-41 n9), Silva (77) observes, "There is probably no semantic significance in the tense." If choice implies meaning, however, Paul's choice of these verbal nouns with their distinctive aspects may explain why he chose to use them rather than the simple nouns ζωή and θάνατος.

κέρδος. Predicate nominative of a verbless equative clause. "Paul no doubt meant that for any man or woman in Christ to die would be **gain**, whatever form the death took. But the death that he has specially in mind for himself in the present situation is execution in consequence of an adverse judgment in an imperial court. If such a death in the service of Christ crowned a life spent in the service of Christ, it would be **gain** not to Paul alone but to the cause of Christ throughout the world" (Bruce, 50). The fact that we are still reading this statement nearly two thousand years after he wrote it is testimony to this meaning.

1:22 εἰ δὲ τὸ ζῆν ἐν σαρκί, τοῦτό μοι καρπὸς ἔργου, καὶ τί αἱρήσομαι οὐ γνωρίζω.

εἰ. Conditional particle introducing the protasis of a first class conditional sentence.

δὲ. In keeping with its function elsewhere, δὲ is not adversative but signals development of thought from 1:21 (Fee, 143–44).

τὸ ζῆν. Pres act inf ζάω (substantival, subject of an implied equative verb); see 1:21.

ἐν σαρκί. Locative. Parallel to ἐν τῷ σώματί (1:20).

τοῦτό μοι καρπὸς ἔργου. Apodosis of the conditional clause.

τοῦτό. Nominative subject of an implied equative verb. Neut sg of demonstrative pronoun οὗτος, which refers anaphorically to the articular infinitive clause τὸ ζῆν ἐν σαρκί (BDAG, 740.1.a.ε).

μοι. Dative of advantage. The dative pronoun goes with the substantive ἔργου, not with the assumed verb (Robertson, 537).

καρπὸς. Predicate nominative.

ἔργου. Zerwick (155) calls this genitive epexegetical, while BDF (§167) calls it apposition: Paul's fruit is the work itself (TLNT 1:57, n12). BDF (§165) suggests a genitive of quality: "work-fruit" or "ministry fruit." It is probably best to regard this as attributed genitive: "fruitful work" (Wallace, 90) or "fruitful labor" (Bockmuehl, 89; ESV, NIV).

καὶ. Introduces a new sentence.

τί. Neut sg interrogative pronoun.

αἱρήσομαι. Fut mid ind 1st sg αἱρέω. The three occurrences of this verb are usually defined as "choose" (Abbott-Smith, 13). BDAG (28.2), however, translates the combination of αἱρέω with the accusative as "prefer." $\mathfrak{P}^{46}$ B 2464 read αἱρήσωμαι (aor mid subj). BDF (§336) calls this a deliberative subjunctive: "What should I choose?" Although this reading is early, it is represented in only three mss and blunts the decisive attitude expressed in the context.

οὐ γνωρίζω. An indicative statement is possible in an indirect question (BDF §366.2, §368, §442.8; Turner, 117; Robertson, 875), "I do not know what I will prefer."

γνωρίζω. Pres act ind 1st sg γνωρίζω. Verbs ending in -ίζω are normally causative, as are the other 24 NT occurrences of γνωρίζω (BDAG, 203.1; Abbott-Smith, 93–94). Because of this and its causative meaning in 4:7, I have translated it causatively: "And I am not making known what I will prefer" (BDF §108.3; Bockmuehl, 90; O'Brien 1991, 128: "nothing to declare"; NKJV: "I cannot tell").

1:23 συνέχομαι δὲ ἐκ τῶν δύο, τὴν ἐπιθυμίαν ἔχων εἰς τὸ ἀναλῦσαι καὶ σὺν Χριστῷ εἶναι, πολλῷ [γὰρ] μᾶλλον κρεῖσσον·

συνέχομαι. Pres pass ind 1st sg συνέχω ("to cause distress by force of circumstances, seize, attack, distress, torment," BDAG, 971.5). The passive verb describes the distress of being torn between two options. TLNT (3:338) paraphrases: "to be on the horns of a dilemma."

δέ. Signals development describing the emotional distress of his choice in 1:22.

ἐκ τῶν δύο. Preposition with a genitive plural article and genitive δύο (indeclinable in genitive and accusative). BDAG (297.3.g) defines ἐκ as a marker "denoting origin, cause, reason . . . the source from which something flows." "The δύο are the two horns of the dilemma, stated in verses 21, 22" (Lightfoot, 93). The KJV is quaint but elegant: "For I am in a strait betwixt two . . . ."

τὴν ἐπιθυμίαν. Accusative direct object of ἔχων.

ἔχων. Pres act ptc masc nom sg ἔχω. Causal, describing the reason for his distress.

εἰς τὸ ἀναλῦσαι. Aor act inf ἀναλύω (epexegetical to τὴν ἐπιθυμίαν). The verb is intransitive and means "depart, return" (BDAG, 67.2). While εἰς τό with the infinitive usually introduces a purpose or result clause, Wallace (611) argues that this epexegetical function of εἰς τό + infinitive is rare. BDF (§402.2) calls this a "freer use." Jas 1:19 (ταχὺς εἰς τὸ ἀκοῦσαι, βραδὺς εἰς τὸ λαλῆσαι) presents the only other possible examples.

σὺν Χριστῷ. Accompaniment. Unlike this future focus, the other uses of this expression refer to past death σὺν Χριστῷ (Rom 6:8; Col 2:20).

εἶναι. Pres act inf εἰμί (epexegetical to τὴν ἐπιθυμίαν). Because of the preceding καί, it is parallel to ἀναλῦσαι.

πολλῷ. "The comparative [that follows] is heightened as in classical by the addition of πολύ, πολλῷ" (BDF §246; see Reed 1997, 360), which functions as an adverb. See 2:12.

γάρ. Marks material supporting the previous statement. The word is bracketed in the NA[28]/UBS[5] texts because it is lacking in many Western and Byzantine witnesses, but its presence in 𝔓[46] Clement of Alexandria 0278 A B C led the editors to include it in brackets. THGNT includes it without brackets. Its lack in the TR requires a relative pronoun to smooth the syntax: "which is far better" (NKJV).

μᾶλλον. Comparative of the adverb μάλα.

κρεῖσσον. Comparative of ἀγαθός. The Attic form κρείττων (e.g., Heb 11:40; 12:24) began to give way to the Hellenistic κρεῖσσον found in Paul (BDF §34.1). The manuscript tradition continued to fluctuate in many places between ττ and σσ. The double comparative μᾶλλον κρεῖσσον, literally "more better" (Robertson, 278, 546), is redundant in English, but still acceptable in Greek.

1:24 τὸ δὲ ἐπιμένειν [ἐν] τῇ σαρκὶ ἀναγκαιότερον δι' ὑμᾶς.

δέ. Marks the development of a contrast to being "with Christ" in 1:22.

τὸ ἐπιμένειν. Pres act inf ἐπιμένω (substantival, subject of an implied equative verb). Although infinitives do not have gender, when they are substantival a neuter article is often attached. This explains why the following predicate adjective (ἀναγκαιότερον) is neuter (Wallace, 588).

ἐν τῇ σαρκί. Locative. The article functions anaphorically to recall ἐν σαρκί in 1:22. The bracketed ἐν is missing from ℵ A and C, and it is omitted in the THGNT. Sumney (31) defends the omission but wrongly states that the dative τῇ σαρκὶ is thus the direct object of the infinitive, something that is grammatically anomalous with an intransitive verb! The inclusion of the preposition is supported by both early (𝔓[46] and B) and widespread (D, Western, and Byzantine) evidence and thus was supported by the majority of the NA/UBS committee.

ἀναγκαιότερον. Comparative of ἀναγκαῖος ("necessary"), functioning as a predicate adjective describing the substantival infinitive. A comparative in the NT can sometimes function as a "positive" (Turner, 30), so it could be simply an emphatic word reflecting Paul's desire to reassure the Philippians (Silva, 78). I suggest the translation "important" (CGELNT, 23).

δι' ὑμᾶς. Cause. BDAG (225.B.2.a) translates διά with the accusative as "because of, for the sake of," as in 1:15.

1:25 καὶ τοῦτο πεποιθὼς οἶδα ὅτι μενῶ καὶ παραμενῶ πᾶσιν ὑμῖν εἰς τὴν ὑμῶν προκοπὴν καὶ χαρὰν τῆς πίστεως,

καί. Provides additional information to the preceding verse.

τοῦτο. Accusative direct object of πεποιθὼς. This demonstrative pronoun is fronted to point back (anaphorically) to the claim made in the previous verse.

πεποιθώς. Prf act ptc masc nom sg πείθω (causal). "Adverbial perfect participles almost always belong in this category" (Wallace, 631). See 1:6.

οἶδα. Prf act ind 1st sg οἶδα. This perfect verb (see 1:19; 4:12, 15), preceded by a perfect participle, reflects aspectually the current state of Paul's conviction and knowledge. He expresses the same convictions by the two verbs in Rom 14:14 (οἶδα καὶ πέπεισμαι).

ὅτι. Introduces the clausal complement of οἶδα.

μενῶ. Fut act ind 1st sg μένω. BDAG (631, 2.a) translates this verb as "remain, last, persist, continue to live."

παραμενῶ. Fut act ind 1st sg παραμένω. BDAG's definition of μένω (769, 1.b) is similar to παραμένω: "stay or remain with someone," offering the following translation of the clause μενῶ καὶ παραμενῶ πᾶσιν: "I will remain and continue with you all." In addition to "stay," παραμενῶ can also mean "continue in an occupation/office" or simply "serve" (BDAG, 769.2). MM (487–88) lists papyrus evidence for service of slaves and examples of a manumitted slave staying on in voluntary service. Some translations do not distinguish clearly between the two verbs. Instead of attempting to distinguish between the two words by adding a semantic component to παραμενῶ, Silva (75) regards the repetition as an example of stylistic reinforcement. "The function of such reinforcement is to aid the communication process by emphasizing his assurance that he will remain with them" (Snyman, 107).

πᾶσιν ὑμῖν. Dative of association.

εἰς τὴν ὑμῶν προκοπὴν καὶ χαρὰν τῆς πίστεως. Purpose. See 1:12.

τὴν ὑμῶν προκοπὴν καὶ χαρὰν. O'Brien (1991, 140) observes: "Here, towards the end of the paragraph, as an example of *inclusio*, προκοπή turns up again, this time in connection with the Philippians' progress." The one article τὴν before two substantives connected by καί does not reflect their identity but probably another hendiadys, "your joyful progress in the faith" (GAGNT, 594).

τῆς πίστεως. Objective genitive. The presence of the article (as in 1:27; 2:17; and 3:9b) suggests "the faith," i.e., the body of faith (Hawthorne, 52; O'Brien 1991, 140).

1:26 ἵνα τὸ καύχημα ὑμῶν περισσεύῃ ἐν Χριστῷ Ἰησοῦ ἐν ἐμοὶ διὰ τῆς ἐμῆς παρουσίας πάλιν πρὸς ὑμᾶς.

ἵνα. Introduces a result clause (Porter 1994, 235: "so that your boasting might multiply in Christ Jesus"). Wallace (473–74) observes that purpose and result cannot always be neatly distinguished. BDAG (477.1.a.δ) indicates purpose but adds that "in many cases purpose and result cannot be clearly differentiated" (BDAG, 477.3).

τὸ καύχημα. According to BDAG (537.1), this noun could be used "to denote the thing of which one is proud." The ten occurrences in Paul, like the English word, can be either negative/sinful boasting (Rom 4:2; 1 Cor 5:6) or positive/godly boasting, i.e., in the Lord, as here and in 2:16, which is preferred here.

ὑμῶν. Subjective genitive. The Philippians do the boasting (O'Brien 1991, 141; Fee, 154 n19).

περισσεύῃ. Pres act subj 3rd sg περισσεύω. Subjunctive with ἵνα. According to BDAG (805.1.a.β), this verb here means "be present in abundance."

ἐν Χριστῷ Ἰησοῦ. This language of indwelling is an idiomatic way of highlighting the intimate nature of the relationship. The PP relates to περισσεύῃ, i.e., where they abound.

ἐν ἐμοί. If Christ is the sphere of boasting, ἐν ἐμοί is the occasion. "In Christ, through me, i.e., through my ministry." On the repetition of ἐν, Lightfoot (94) says, "The first denotes the sphere in which their pride lives; the second the object on which it rests." Another possible usage is cause, as in "because of me" (NET; Turner, 253; Wallace, 372).

διὰ τῆς ἐμῆς παρουσίας. Means. While "presence" is often the meaning of παρουσία (BDAG, 780.1), its collocation with the preposition πρός points to the active sense of "coming" (780.2.a).

ἐμῆς. The possessive adjective/pronoun is feminine because it agrees with the noun it modifies (παρουσίας). The use of this pronoun for emphasis (Reumann, 231) is difficult to maintain since Paul refers to his παρουσία in 2:12 with the pronoun μου (BDF §285.1).

πάλιν. The use of the adverb "again" presupposes Paul's earlier visits to the congregation (see Acts 16).

πρὸς ὑμᾶς. Direction.

Philippians 1:27–30

> ²⁷ Conduct yourselves only in a manner worthy of the gospel of Christ, so that whether I come and see you or only hear about you in my absence, I may know that you stand firm in the one Spirit, striving together as one soul for the faith which is the gospel ²⁸ without being frightened in any way by those who oppose you. This is a sign to them of their destruction, but to you of salvation—and this comes from God. ²⁹ For it has been granted to you on behalf of Christ not only to believe in him, but also to suffer for him, ³⁰ since you are going through the same struggle as you saw in me, and you now hear that is still in me.

> Only live your lives in a manner worthy of the gospel of Christ, so that whether I come and see you or remain absent, I will hear about your circumstances, that you are standing firm in one spirit, with one mind contending together for the faith of the gospel, in no way alarmed by *your* opponents—which is a sign of destruction for them, but of salvation for you, and that *too*, from God. For to you it has been granted for Christ's sake, not only to believe in Him, but also to suffer for His sake, having the same struggle which you saw in me, and now hear *to be* in me (LSB).

Summary: Paul was a Roman citizen and so were his readers. He tried to live in a manner worthy of his citizenship and so must they. He had a still higher ambition, however, that he and they might live as citizens worthy of the gospel of Christ. He fought as a good soldier, stood fast in the faith, and was in no way afraid of his adversaries. They should then follow his example, since they were engaged in the same conflict. To them it had been granted to believe and to suffer on the behalf of Christ. Their faith was not of themselves since it was the gift of God, so their suffering also was not self-chosen because it too was a gift of God.

1:27 Μόνον ἀξίως τοῦ εὐαγγελίου τοῦ Χριστοῦ πολιτεύεσθε, ἵνα εἴτε ἐλθὼν καὶ ἰδὼν ὑμᾶς εἴτε ἀπὼν ἀκούω τὰ περὶ ὑμῶν, ὅτι στήκετε ἐν ἑνὶ πνεύματι, μιᾷ ψυχῇ συναθλοῦντες τῇ πίστει τοῦ εὐαγγελίου

Μόνον. According to BDAG (659.2), μόνος is "a marker of limitation, *only, alone,* the neut[er] μόνον being used as an adv[erb]." It emphasizes what follows (Reumann, 262). From a discourse perspective, it marks off a new unit (Reed 1997, 266).

ἀξίως. Adverb, meaning "worthily" (Robertson, 505, 637), used with a genitive. BDAG (94) suggests the translation "in a manner worthy of."

τοῦ εὐαγγελίου. Genitive after certain adjectives and adverbs (Wallace, 134).

τοῦ Χριστοῦ. Objective genitive, "about Christ" (BDAG, 402–3.1.b.β.ℵ). For the subjective genitive, "from Christ," see TDNT (2:731 n70), which concludes that "Christ is . . . the object and the author of the proclamation." TLNT (2:89, n35) prefers a "comprehensive genitive."

πολιτεύεσθε. Pres mid impv 2nd pl πολιτεύομαι. This verb, along with its cognate noun πολίτευμα (3:20), has generated an intense discussion. The following comments will focus on the Greek usage. MHT (2:399) mentions πολιτεύομαι in a group of verbs ending in -εύω and -εύομαι that "mean 'to play the part of' or 'to act as' the person denoted by the corresponding noun." LSJ (143), GE (1701) and BDAG (846.1.2.3) define the verb as "be a citizen" and "administer a corporate body, conduct one's life." The verb carries a metaphorical meaning of living in a certain way (Acts 23:1). LSB adds the footnote: "to lead one's life as a citizen." Lightfoot (105) comments about πολιτεύομαι: "It was natural that, dwelling in the metropolis of the empire, St Paul should use this illustration. The metaphor moreover would speak forcibly to his correspondents; for Philippi was a Roman colony, and the Apostle had himself obtained satisfaction, while in this place, by declaring himself a Roman citizen: Acts 16:12, 37, 38." For a thorough discussion of the word group in Philippians, see Fee (161–62), as well as NIDNTTE 4:95–97.

ἵνα. Introduces a purpose clause.

εἴτε ... εἴτε. See 1:18 and 1:20.

ἐλθών. Aor act ptc masc nom sg ἔρχομαι (conditional). It agrees with the subject "I" of ἀκούω.

ἰδών. Aor act ptc masc nom sg ὁράω (conditional). Doublet with ἐλθών.

ὑμᾶς. Accusative direct object of ἰδών.

ἀπών. Pres act ptc masc nom sg ἄπειμι (conditional). See ἐλθών.

ἀκούω. Pres act subj 1st sg ἀκούω. Subjunctive with ἵνα. THGNT adopts the future ἀκούσω supported by the first corrector of ℵ plus A C D² and later uncials.

τά. The article functions as a nominalizer, changing the PP περὶ ὑμῶν into the direct object of ἀκούω.

περὶ ὑμῶν. Reference. "It does not sound as if he expected to be executed within the next few weeks: he was prepared for the possibility of execution but expresses himself as expecting to be around for some time yet" (Bruce, 57).

ὅτι. Introduces a substantival clause in apposition to the PP τὰ περὶ ὑμῶν.

στήκετε. Pres act ind 2nd pl στήκω. BDAG, 944.2: "to be firmly committed in conviction or belief." This metaphorical use of "stand firm" is uniquely Pauline in the NT (see 4:1; 1 Cor 16:13; 1 Thess 3:8; 2 Thess 2:15; Gal 5:1).

ἐν ἑνὶ πνεύματι. Manner. For similar usage, see 1:8 (ἐν σπλάγχνοις Χριστοῦ Ἰησοῦ). The term πνεύματι refers to the divine Spirit (contra "community spirit"), which is consistent with other references to πνεῦμα in 1:19; 2:1; 3:3; 4:23, and the exact expression in 1 Cor 12:13 (Martin, 83).

μιᾷ ψυχῇ. Dative of means, modifying the following participle. Lit. "as one soul."

συναθλοῦντες. Pres act ptc masc nom pl συναθλέω (manner). Related to στήκετε. The verb in 4:3 describes Euodias' and Syntyche's "struggle alongside" Paul in the gospel ministry. These are the only occurences of the verb apart from a 1st century BC writer named Diodorus Siculus (GE, 2018). Despite the verbal root, the image may be related to the military rather than to athletics (see BDAG, 964).

τῇ πίστει. Dative of advantage (BDAG, 964; also Bockmuehl, 99; Fee, 166 n47).

τοῦ εὐαγγελίου. This genitive has been viewed as (1) objective (BDAG, 402.1.a.β); (2) subjective (Hawthorne, 71); and (3) apposition or epexegetical, "the faith which is the gospel" (Vincent, 34; Silva, 89; Fee, 167). Number 3 is consistent with the earlier meaning of πίστις in 1:25 as "the body of faith."

1:28 καὶ μὴ πτυρόμενοι ἐν μηδενὶ ὑπὸ τῶν ἀντικειμένων, ἥτις ἐστὶν αὐτοῖς ἔνδειξις ἀπωλείας, ὑμῶν δὲ σωτηρίας, καὶ τοῦτο ἀπὸ θεοῦ·

μή. Negative particle used with non-indicative moods.

πτυρόμενοι. Pres pass ptc masc nom pl πτύρω (manner). *Hapax legomenon*. According to BDAG (895), this verb is "almost always pass[ive] and so in our lit[erature] to let oneself be intimidated, be frightened, terrified." It parallels structurally but contrasts semantically with the participle συναθλοῦντες in 1:27.

ἐν μηδενί. Manner. With previous μή, this constitutes a double negative common in Greek (BDF §431). "It excludes every type of intimidation" (Reumann, 269).

ὑπὸ τῶν ἀντικειμένων. Agency. Pres mid ptc masc gen pl ἀντίκειμαι "be in opposition to" (substantival, i.e., "adversary" BDAG, 88-89). The two successive prepositional phrases describe the degree to which (ἐν μηδενί) and by whom (ὑπὸ τῶν ἀντικειμένων) they are not to be scared. Jesus warned of these future enemies with the same substantival ptcp (Luke 21:15), and Paul was never free of them throughout his ministry (1 Cor 16:9; 1 Tim 1:10). He also warned his readers against the ultimate enemy behind all of these opposers (2 Thess 2:4; 1 Tim 5:14).

ἥτις. Relative pronoun (ὅστις). According to BDAG (729.2.b), this pronoun is used "to emphasize a characteristic quality, by which a preceding statement is to be confirmed" meaning "who (to be sure, by his very nature), in so far as." The feminine gender looks forward to ἔνδειξις as a "pointer" (Zerwick, 216), but it is difficult to discern the antecedent: (1) their fearlessness in 1:28a (Lightfoot, 106); (2) their faith in 1:27d (Hawthorne, 58–59); or (3) "the general idea of the preceding clause" (Robertson, 729).

ἐστίν. Pres act ind 3rd sg εἰμί.

αὐτοῖς. Dative of disadvantage.

ἔνδειξις. Predicate nominative in agreement with ἥτις. BDAG, 332.1: "something that points to or serves as an indicator of something, *sign, omen.*"

ἀπωλείας. Objective genitive. BDAG, 127: "destruction, ruin, opp[osite] to σωτηρία."

ὑμῶν. Possessive genitive, modifying σωτηρίας. There is apparent incongruity, since one might expect another dative to parallel αὐτοῖς. This has led some scribes to "improve" the syntax (see below) and some commentators to conclude that the syntax "is extraordinarily difficult to interpret" (Hawthorne, 72). Silva (89–90) explains Paul's relative lack of concern for strict syntax but also points out the conceptual parallel to 2 Thess 1:4–8 that "makes plain that 'destruction' and 'salvation' in Phil 1:28 should be understood in their strongest soteriological sense."

δέ. Signals development of a contrast with previous ἀπωλείας.

σωτηρίας. Objective genitive related to head noun ἔνδειξις. See note on 1:19 about Paul's use of this word in Philippians. The NA[28] reading of verse 28b (ἥτις ἐστὶν αὐτοῖς ἔνδειξις ἀπωλείας, ὑμῶν δὲ σωτηρίας) has strong external support (א A B C² P Ψ 33 1739). The first variant (ητις αυτοις μεν εστιν ενδειξις απωλειας, υμιν δε σωτηριας) is a scribal alteration in 𝔐 that balances the two statements with μεν . . . δὲ (KJV, NKJV). The second variant (ητις εστιν αυτοις ενδειξις απωλειας, ημιν δε σωτηριας), supported by some Western manuscripts (C* D* F G), makes the reading inclusive. These changes were probably introduced to make the two statements parallel, contradicting the reading in NA[28] that stresses the contrast between their destruction and your salvation. The THGNT affirms the NA[28] reading.

καὶ τοῦτο. Nominative demonstrative pronoun that looks back (anaphoric), probably to the entire clause beginning with ἥτις (Vincent, 35).

ἀπὸ θεοῦ. Source. A verb must be supplied, such as "is" or "comes from."

1:29 ὅτι ὑμῖν ἐχαρίσθη τὸ ὑπὲρ Χριστοῦ, οὐ μόνον τὸ εἰς αὐτὸν πιστεύειν ἀλλὰ καὶ τὸ ὑπὲρ αὐτοῦ πάσχειν,

ὅτι. Introduces causal clause for the preceding verse.
ὑμῖν. Dative indirect object of ἐχαρίσθη.
ἐχαρίσθη. Aor pass ind 3rd sg χαρίζομαι. BDAG (1078.1) suggests the following translation: "you have graciously been granted the privilege of."
τὸ. The article functions as a nominalizer, changing the PP ὑπὲρ Χριστοῦ into the subject of ἐχαρίσθη.
ὑπὲρ Χριστοῦ. Representation.
οὐ μόνον. Adverb preceded by a negative particle. Lightfoot (107) points out, "The sentence is suspended by the insertion of the after-thought," namely, the clause οὐ μόνον τὸ εἰς αὐτὸν πιστεύειν. It is then resumed with ἀλλὰ καί.
τὸ ... πιστεύειν. Pres act inf πιστεύω (substantival, appositional to τὸ ὑπὲρ Χριστοῦ).
εἰς αὐτὸν. Prepositional phrase that complements the substantival infinitive. According to BDAG (817.2.a.β), πιστεύω is frequently used with εἰς. The preposition εἰς indicates "the content of a process" (Reed 1997, 329).
ἀλλὰ. Conjunction that functions to correct the idea that only believing is granted.
καὶ. Adverbial use. "Frequent translational equivalents are 'indeed', 'even' and 'also'," (Porter 1994, 212). Robertson (1180) prefers calling it "the adjunctive use ('also')." "The original meaning of καί, before it became also merely a coordinating particle, was *also*" (Turner, 335).
τὸ ... πάσχειν. Pres act inf πάσχω (substantival, appositional to τὸ ὑπὲρ Χριστοῦ).
ὑπὲρ αὐτοῦ. Representation, modifying the substantival infinitive (CGELNT, 362.1.c).

This reminder is an encouragement to the afflicted people of God in Philippi and in all ages. To suffer on behalf of Christ is actually a privilege given by God. Christ himself identifies with the affliction of his followers, something Paul vividly recalled from a statement by the living Jesus to him during his Damascus Road encounter: "Saul, why are you persecuting me?" (Acts 9:4).

1:30 τὸν αὐτὸν ἀγῶνα ἔχοντες, οἷον εἴδετε ἐν ἐμοὶ καὶ νῦν ἀκούετε ἐν ἐμοί.

τὸν αὐτὸν ἀγῶνα. Accusative direct object of ἔχοντες. With ἀγῶνα, the athletic imagery of a "struggle" for the gospel (BDAG, 17.2) continues from the συναθλοῦντες of 1:27. 1 Thess 2:2 speaks of Paul's preaching the gospel in Thessalonica ἐν πολλῷ ἀγῶνι, "with much struggle." The word is used in Heb 12:1 to describe the Christian life as a race or competition. This was also one of the last words the apostle wrote as he looked back on his ministry: "I have fought the good ἀγῶνα" (2 Tim 4:7). The pronoun αὐτὸν is in the first attributive position (BDF §270), meaning "same."

ἔχοντες. Pres act ptc masc nom pl ἔχω (manner). Most grammarians (BDF §468.2; Moule, 31) and commentators (Silva, 90; O'Brien 1991, 161) consider this nominative participle ungrammatical since the antecedent ὑμῖν is dative. It is possible, however, that the antecedent is the subject of στήκετε in 1:27. The nominative participle, therefore, functions in the same way as the previous nominative participles συναθλοῦντες (1:27) and πτυρόμενοι (1:28).

οἷον. Relative pronoun masc acc, functioning as direct object of εἴδετε. According to BDAG (701), this pronoun can be translated as "of what sort (such)."

εἴδετε. Aor act ind 2nd pl ὁράω.

ἐν ἐμοί. Locative. BDAG (329.8), ἐν is a "marker denoting the object in which someth[ing] happens or in which someth[ing] shows itself."

καὶ νῦν. According to BDAG (681.1.a.β.ℷ), this expression can be translated as "and now." See 1:20.

ἀκούετε. Pres act ind 2nd pl ἀκούω. The difference is what they saw when he was with them and what they now (νῦν) are hearing about his situation.

ἐν ἐμοί. See above. 𝔓⁴⁶ MS 81 omit this phrase. Fee (159 n18), "The awkwardness (apparently) of this final ἐν ἐμοί caused it to be omitted."

𝔓⁴⁶ has a well-earned reputation for singular readings, despite its early date. THGNT also retains the words.

"We do not know what precise form was taken by the persecution to which the Philippian Christians were currently exposed. Paul had no need to enter into particulars that they knew only too well. What mattered was the spirit in which they accepted persecution" (Bruce, 59).

This church had personally witnessed the combination of both faith and suffering in Paul when he was at Philippi (Acts 16:29ff), and now they hear it from him, as Epaphroditus (2:25) could inform them. The difference is what they saw when he was with them and what they now are hearing about his situation. In Paul's catalogue of suffering in 2 Cor 11:23–27, he mentions that he was beaten with rods three times and one of those times was in Philippi (Acts 16:22–23). For both the apostle and for "his" church, there was the same fight and the same suffering on behalf of the same Christ.

2

Analysis of Philippians Two

Philippians 2:1–4

¹ Therefore, if there is any encouragement in Christ, if any consolation from love, if any sharing in the Spirit, if any affection and mercy, ² fulfill my joy by thinking the same way, having the same love, being united in spirit, thinking the one thing. ³ Do nothing selfishly or from empty conceit, but in humility consider others as more important than yourselves. ⁴ Everyone should look out not only for your own interests, but also for the interests of others.

Therefore if there is any encouragement in Christ, if there is any consolation of love, if there is any fellowship of the Spirit, if any affection and compassion, fulfill my joy, that you think the same *way*, by maintaining the same love, *being* united in spirit, thinking on one purpose, doing nothing from selfish ambition or vain glory, but with humility of mind regarding one another as more important than yourselves, not *merely* looking out for your own personal interests, but also for the interests of others. (LSB)

Summary: Paul expresses in one compound/complex sentence the same concern as the previous sentence unit (1:27–30). The similar imperative in both is to be fervent in unity: *stand firm in one Spirit, striving together with one accord for the faith of the gospel* (1:27); *being like-minded, having the same love, being one in spirit and of one mind*

(2:2). The first imperative emphasizes the need to remain united for the gospel in the face of opponents. This one focuses on the need to be one even with those who divide the church. Paul's concern is that we be one together so we can be able to endure suffering caused by those outside the body and also to heal any divisions caused by those inside the assembly. This is to be done by not insisting on our own interests but to regard others as more important.

See the Introduction for the important role this paragraph plays in the discourse structure of the epistle.

2:1 Εἴ τις οὖν παράκλησις ἐν Χριστῷ, εἴ τι παραμύθιον ἀγάπης, εἴ τις κοινωνία πνεύματος, εἴ τις σπλάγχνα καὶ οἰκτιρμοί,

Εἴ. Conditional particle introducing the protasis of a first class conditional sentence. The particle appears four times before the apodosis is stated in 2:2. First class conditional clauses assume the reality of the condition, not merely its possibility (Boyer 1981, 106). However, "one should resist the tendency to translate with 'since,' for this rendering weakens the rhetorical force of the passage" (Silva, 90).

τις. Feminine indefinite pronoun agreeing with παράκλησις. Each of the four indefinite pronouns function adjectivally modifying the following noun, and in each occurrence, there is an implied equative verb such as ἐστίν.

οὖν. The consequential conjunction is always postpositive. Sumney (60, who wrongly calls the indefinite pronoun τις a "relative pronoun") states about its location with οὖν: "This may have occurred because εἴ τις was viewed as a single word." A better explanation is that οὖν is placed third because it is not strictly limited to the second position but can be third (John 16:22, καὶ ὑμεῖς οὖν), and even fourth (1 Cor 8:4). The consequential conjunction οὖν either recalls 1:27–28 or more likely πολιτεύεσθε in 1:27, the only imperative thus far. On the discourse level, οὖν also indicates a shift in the discourse (Black 1995b, 35).

παράκλησις. Translators and commentators differ widely whether the nuance of "exhortation" or "encouragement" is appropriate here (see BDAG, 766, for examples of both). The tone of the letter, while containing many imperatives, is not the harsher admonition of an epistle like the Galatians; the qualifiers of these virtues (Χριστῷ, ἀγάπης, πνεύματος) also point toward the translation of "encouragement" rather than "exhortation." See Lightfoot (107) for a defense of "exhortation" and Fee (179–80), tying the word to 1:29–30, for a persuasive defense of "encouragement."

ἐν Χριστῷ. This language of indwelling is an idiomatic way of highlighting the intimate nature of the relationship.

εἴ. Conditional particle introducing the second protasis of a first class conditional sentence.

τι. Neuter indefinite pronoun agreeing with παραμύθιον.

παραμύθιον. *Hapax legomenon*. While Lightfoot (107) defends the more active translation of "incentive," he acknowledges that the meaning of the word outside the NT is "consolation." BDAG (769) affirms its meaning as "consolation, means of consolation, alleviation," thus the "solace afforded by love."

ἀγάπης. Genitive of source.

εἴ. Conditional particle introducing the third protasis of a first class conditional sentence.

τις. Feminine indefinite pronoun agreeing with κοινωνία.

κοινωνία. BDAG (552.1) classifies the word here, as also in 1:5, as "close association involving mutual interests and sharing, association, communion, fellowship, close relationship."

πνεύματος. Genitive of association or objective genitive. Wallace (129) notes that "some nouns and adjectives already embrace lexically the idea of 'in association with' and hence can take a genitive of association." A more familiar grammatical usage would be an objective genitive, i.e., "participation in the Spirit" (Vincent, 54; Martin, 86–87; O'Brien 1991, 174; Fee, 181 n40, "sharing in the Spirit").

εἴ. Conditional particle introducing the fourth protasis of a first class conditional sentence. The fourfold repetition of the conditional clauses is an example of stylistic reinforcement, sometimes called "iconic" reinforcement.

τις. This grammatical solecism, a singular pronoun modifying two plural nouns, is discussed in a number of grammars (BDF §137.2; Robertson, 130; Turner, 316). The explanations have been that it is either an authorial mistake or a scribal mistake (i.e., Paul originally wrote the neuter τι and an early scribe may have doubled the σ which initiates σπλάγχνα). BDF, however, comments that "the solecism was not so offensive" (§137.2). Perhaps the τις was original and the τινα was avoided simply for rhythmical considerations. We should be careful about calling this a breach of concord, since early scribes apparently did not feel a need to correct it (only one 11th century manuscript contains the neuter plural τινα which is also in the TR). These "anomalies" are more frequent than many realize, and they often have a discernible reason.

σπλάγχνα καὶ οἰκτιρμοί. These words have similar meanings like "affection and mercy." The words appear separately in virtue lists with different meanings, but Silva (90–91) offers a persuasive case for a hendiadys here ("compassionate mercy"), since these two nouns are joined grammatically in Col 3:12, σπλάγχνα οἰκτιρμοῦ. If this is the case, then a singular indefinite pronoun like τις would be appropriate.

2:2 πληρώσατέ μου τὴν χαρὰν ἵνα τὸ αὐτὸ φρονῆτε, τὴν αὐτὴν ἀγάπην ἔχοντες, σύμψυχοι, τὸ ἓν φρονοῦντες,

πληρώσατέ. Aor act impv 2nd pl πληρόω. Introduces the apodosis in the first class conditional sentence initiated in 2:1. Perfective aspect in the imperative mood implicates a specific command (Campbell 2013, xxiv). This is the first of only two aorist imperatives in the book (see also 4:21), while there are no less than 22 present imperatives. This singular aorist imperative also functions to mark the thematic peak of the discourse. This paragraph conveys the main theme of Philippians, namely the unity of the people of God, conveyed thematically by the abundance of words for "thinking" and "unity." It is furthermore marked by this special imperative usage. See the Introduction for further discussion of the role of this verse in a discourse analysis of Philippians.

μου. Possessive genitive.

τὴν χαρὰν. Accusative direct object of πληρώσατέ.

ἵνα. Introduces a substantival or content clause, which defines the χαρὰν just mentioned (Porter 1994, 239). Wallace (476) classifies it as an epexegetical substantival ἵνα clause.

τὸ αὐτὸ. Accusative direct object of φρονῆτε. Reed (1997, 390) perceptively observes: "Another interesting feature of prominence in this section is the use of OV (Object/Complement–Verb) word order in

2:2–5, where the complement occurs first in view of its thematic importance (namely, each complement concerns the idea of unity or 'oneness')."

φρονῆτε. Pres act subj 2nd pl φρονέω. Subjunctive with ἵνα. See 1:7.

τὴν αὐτὴν ἀγάπην. Direct object of ἔχοντες. The intensive pronoun in the first attributive position is translated "the same" (Wallace, 349–50).

ἔχοντες. Pres act ptc masc nom pl ἔχω (means). "This participle is the first of a string of seven participial clauses (with some implied) modifying the previous verb φρονῆτε" (Moore, 118).

σύμψυχοι. Hapax legomenon. BDAG (961) translates this adjective as "lit. 'united in spirit', harmonious." "Psychē terms in Philippians indicate 'church unity' and bind the Philippians to one another" (Reumann, 306). This substantival adjective is one of the 20 occurrences of συν or its compound nominals and verbals in the book, further underscoring the role of this passage in conveying the unity theme of the book. See comments on συγκοινωνούς in 1:7. The adjective has left no trace in LXX or Attic Greek and raises again the possibility of "Pauline coinage."

τὸ ἕν. The article functions as a nominalizer, changing the numerical adjective into the direct object of φρονοῦντες.

φρονοῦντες. Pres act ptc masc nom pl φρονέω (means). Some significant manuscripts (ℵ A C I Ψ 33) have the variant reading το αυτο φρονουντες "thinking the same thing," which has been adopted in the CSB and NET. The variant was probably the result of scribes conforming this phrase to the first phrase of the clause (τὸ αὐτὸ φρονῆτε). In addition to the strong external support (𝔓⁴⁶ B D F G 075 1739 𝔐), internally Paul probably made a general appeal for unity and then provided one specific focus that would unite their minds when he said τὸ ἕν φρονοῦντες ("thinking the one thing"). The THGNT affirms this reading. LSB renders it as "thinking on one purpose."

2:3 μηδὲν κατ' ἐριθείαν μηδὲ κατὰ κενοδοξίαν ἀλλὰ τῇ ταπεινοφροσύνῃ ἀλλήλους ἡγούμενοι ὑπερέχοντας ἑαυτῶν,

μηδέν. Accusative direct object of an implied verbal component, either a participle like πράσσοντες, "doing nothing," or an imperative like πρασσείτω (Lightfoot, 108; KJV, "Let nothing be done"; or NRSV, NIV, ESV, "Do nothing"). Vincent (55) suggested φρονοῦντες from 2:2d. Perhaps all these suggestions are unnecessary since the negated neuter adjective is rhetorically effective on its own (Reed 1997, 398) and since no early scribe tried to improve the syntax with an added verbal supplement.

κατ' ἐριθείαν. Standard. The usage of κατά here and in the next phrase is defined by BDAG (512.5) as "a marker of norm of similarity or homogeneity" and translated as "according to, in accordance with, in conformity with, according to." In this verse its combination with ἐριθείαν is "as a periphrasis for the adverb" (BDAG, 513.5.b). When combined with ἐριθεία, "selfishness" (BDAG, 392), the adverbial meaning of the expression would be "selfishly."

μηδέ. Point-counterpoint set with previous μηδέν.

κατὰ κενοδοξίαν. Standard. See discussion above for κατ' ἐριθείαν. The adverbial meaning would be "from empty conceit" (BDAG, 538). The noun κενοδοξία is a *hapax legomenon* with sparse LXX (Muraoka, 394) and Attic usage (GE, 1111).

ἀλλά. Conjunction that signals a correction of the preceding behavior.

τῇ ταπεινοφροσύνῃ. Dative of manner. Collange (79) calls attention to the assonance between the verb φρονέω and the noun ταπεινοφροσύνη. The usage of the ταπειν- root anticipates the reference in the following hymn (2:5–11) to Jesus' humbling himself (ἐταπείνωσεν ἑαυτόν, v. 8).

ἀλλήλους. Direct object of ἡγούμενοι in a double accusative object-complement construction. "This reciprocal pronoun brings out the *mutual* relations involved" (Robertson, 692).

ἡγούμενοι. Pres mid ptc masc nom pl ἡγέομαι (manner).

ὑπερέχοντας. Pres act ptc masc acc pl ὑπερέχω (substantival, complement in a double accusative object-complement construction). While not uniquely Pauline (see 1 Pet 2:13 [and Rom 13:1] for "authorities"), he uses the word in 3:8 and 4:7 also as participles. BDAG (1033.3) defines here as: "surpass" or "excel."

ἑαυτῶν. Genitive of comparison. The reflexive pronoun does not really differ in idea from the genitive reciprocal pronoun ἀλλήλων (Robertson, 690; see parallel usage in Col 3:13).

2:4 μὴ τὰ ἑαυτῶν ἕκαστος σκοποῦντες ἀλλὰ [καὶ] τὰ ἑτέρων ἕκαστοι.

μὴ. Negates the following τὰ ἑαυτῶν.

τὰ ἑαυτῶν. The first of two direct objects of the participle. The neuter plural article nominalizes the reflexive pronoun. Literally "the things of yourselves," but commonly rendered as "your own interests" (NRSV).

ἕκαστος. The singular form of this adjective is used with the plural σκοποῦντες (BDAG, 298.b). See other examples in John 16:32; Matt 18:35; Luke 2:3; Acts 11:29; Eph 4:25; Heb 8:11 (Jer 38:34); Rev 5:8; and 20:13.

σκοποῦντες. Pres act ptc masc nom pl σκοπέω (imperatival). This participle is plural like the verb and other participles in 2:2–3, but its function here is imperatival (BDF §468.2; Moule, 179–80; Lightfoot, 110), consistent with the verb's other appearances in the NT where it is clearly admonitory (Phil 3:17; Rom 16:17; 2 Cor 4:18; Gal 6:1). Most translations render it as an imperative, even if they do not follow 𝔐 and TR which replace the participle with σκοπεῖτε. The meaning is highly focused: "to pay careful attention to, look (out) for, notice" (BDAG, 931).

ἀλλὰ. Marker of contrast to what has just been expressed.

[καὶ]. If original, the conjunction is adverbial; with the preceding clause: "looking not only . . . but also." Silva (91), as well as THGNT, consider the brackets as unnecessary because καὶ is absent only in some Western witnesses.

τὰ ἑτέρων. The second direct object of σκοποῦντες. The neuter plural article nominalizes the adjective.

ἕκαστοι. See the discussion of ἕκαστος above. The plural of the word was nearly obsolete by NT times (BDF §64.6) and appears only here and in the TR of Rev 6:11. The plural balances the singular ἕκαστος in a point-counterpoint set, especially combined with the contrast marker ἀλλὰ (Runge, 98). Because of the difficulty in rendering the plural, many versions do not translate it (NASB, NET, ESV, CSB). The different forms of ἕκαστος led to attempts to unify the two words in the manuscript tradition. In the first occurrence in this verse, external evidence ($\mathfrak{P}^{46}$ ℵ C D K L P 𝔐 itd syr cop) favors ἕκαστος over ἕκαστοι (A B F G Ψ 33 81 104 462 it vg), which was probably the result of scribal conforming to the many plurals in the context. In its second occurrence in this verse, the singular ἕκαστος has weak support (𝔐 itd syr) in comparison to the plural ἕκαστοι (𝔓⁴⁶ ℵ A B D P Ψ 33 1739), which is clearly the more difficult reading, and is also favored by the THGNT. Lightfoot (109) recognized the difficulty of the plural and while retaining it as original, suggested the following: "Paul can hardly have written ἕκαστος in the first clause and ἕκαστοι in the second, intending the clauses as correlative. Therefore, if we retain ἕκαστος in the first case, it will be necessary to detach the following ἕκαστοι, and join it on with the next sentence." Commentators and translators have not followed this creative suggestion.

For a formal analysis of the Greek text of 2:1–4, see the article by Black (1985).

Philippians 2:5–8

> ⁵ Have the same mindset among you which was also in Christ Jesus, ⁶ who, although being in the form of God, did not consider being equal with God a prize to be grasped, ⁷ but rather emptied himself by taking the form of a slave, taking on the likeness of human beings. And when he was found in appearance as a human being, ⁸ he humbled himself by becoming obedient to the point of death, even death on a cross.

> Have this *way of* thinking in yourselves which was also in Christ Jesus, who, although existing in the form of God, did not regard equality with God a thing to be grasped, but emptied Himself, by taking the form of a slave, by being made in the likeness of men. Being found in appearance as a man, He humbled Himself by becoming obedient to the point of death, even death on a cross. (LSB)

Summary: Although most commentators focus on this passage, including 2:9–11, as an early hymn to Christ, many neglect seeing the connection of this passage and the ones that follow to their preceding context. Paul has just exhorted his readers to not think about themselves but to give up themselves for others. Here he offers the first exemplar of that self-giving, Jesus' giving up His glory for us. He will offer two more exemplars of this selfless attitude, Timothy (2:19–24) and Epaphroditus (2:25–30).

2:5 Τοῦτο φρονεῖτε ἐν ὑμῖν ὃ καὶ ἐν Χριστῷ Ἰησοῦ,

Τοῦτο. Accusative direct object of φρονεῖτε. The fronting of this demonstrative pronoun indicates that it functions anaphorically, pointing back to the mental attitude of self-giving described in the previous verses. It does not function cataphorically because that is what the following relative clause does in pointing the reader forward to verses 6–12.

φρονεῖτε. Pres act impv 2nd pl φρονέω. The present tense verb recalls the φρονῆτε and φρονοῦντες in 2:2 as well as the other present participles, ἡγούμενοι in 2:3 and σκοποῦντες in 2:4. The imperfective aspect highlights the process of thinking the way Jesus thought. Although the UBS[5] does not list it as a variant, 𝔐 and the TR have the third-person passive imperative φρονείσθω. Since the earliest support for this reading is from three ninth century uncials, the variant should be recognized as an attempt to smooth out a perceived grammatical irregularity.

ἐν ὑμῖν. Locative. The preposition means "among" as in 1:6 (BDAG, 326.1.d).

ὅ. This neuter nominative relative pronoun takes its gender from its antecedent, the neuter τοῦτο. Its case, however, is derived from its function in the relative clause, which is as the subject of an implied equative verb.

καὶ. Adverbial ("also"). Zerwick (156) argues that this is a case when καὶ after a relative pronoun is "otiose" and "without any special reason for its insertion." Citing also ὃς καὶ in 2 Cor 3:5, he suggests that the comparison is not between the sentiments of the faithful and those of Christ, but the sense is simply to "entertain among yourselves the sentiments which are ἐν Χριστῷ Ἰησοῦ." While most modern versions do not translate καὶ (except NASB and LSB), it is difficult to understand why, if the apostle thought it "otiose," he did not just omit it.

ἐν Χριστῷ Ἰησοῦ. This language of indwelling is an idiomatic way of highlighting the intimate nature of the relationship. It parallels the previous ἐν ὑμῖν and identifies the person in whom this attitude of humility is found.

2:6 ὃς ἐν μορφῇ θεοῦ ὑπάρχων οὐχ ἁρπαγμὸν ἡγήσατο τὸ εἶναι ἴσα θεῷ

ὅς. The relative pronoun functions as the subject (hence in the nominative) of all the following indicative verbs and participles in 2:6–8.

ἐν μορφῇ. Locative. "'Form' is an inadequate rendering of μορφή, but our language affords no better word" (Vincent, 57; see Abbott-Smith, 296; BDAG, 659). This word only appears twice in the NT, here and in 2:7. GE (1364) suggests "nature" or "essence."

θεοῦ. Possessive genitive.

ὑπάρχων. Pres act ptc masc nom sg ὑπάρχω (concessive). Some translations have the concessive "though" or "although" (NAB, NASB, CEB, ESV, NET; LSB) while others prefer a simple circumstantial participle, "being" (KJV, NJB, NIV, NLT) or "existing" (CSB). BDAG (1029.2) states that in Hellenistic Greek ὑπάρχω is simply a substitute for εἰμί and carries no special nuance (also Silva, 113). Abbott-Smith (457) thinks that here the verb retains its Attic meaning of "begin" and conveys the sense of "continuance of an antecedent state or condition," thus suggesting the translation "being originally." See also GE (2188.1).

οὐχ. Negative particle that negates ἡγήσατο.

ἁρπαγμόν. Complement of τὸ εἶναι ἴσα θεῷ in an object-complement double accusative construction (Wallace, 186, 220). BDAG (133.1&2) defines this *hapax legomenon* with both an active ("a violent seizure of property, robbery") and a passive ("someth[ing] to which one can claim or assert title by gripping or grasping, someth[ing] claimed") meaning. Since the first meaning "is next to impossible in Phil 2:6," the best functional equivalent translation is "a prize to be tenaciously grasped." As an illustration of the difficulty of this issue, the CSB[17] altered its HCSB translation from "something to be used for His own advantage" to "something to be exploited."

ἡγήσατο. Aor mid ind 3rd sg ἡγέομαι.

τὸ εἶναι ἴσα θεῷ. Infinitival clause that functions as direct object of ἡγήσατο in an object-complement double accusative construction.

εἶναι. Pres act inf εἰμί (substantival).

ἴσα. BDAG (480) identifies ἴσος ("equal") as an adjective that appears 8 times in the NT, but it is here used predicatively as an "adverbial neuter plural" (BDF §434; Abbott-Smith, 219). For the predicative use of ἴσα elsewhere, see LXX Job 11:12 and Thucydides, *Hist.* 3.14.

θεῷ. Dative complement of ἴσα. The closest linguistic and semantic parallel to ἴσα θεῷ is the charge against Jesus in John 5:18 that "you are making yourself equal to God" (ἴσον ἑαυτὸν ποιῶν τῷ θεῷ). Lightfoot (112) carefully observes: "Between the two expressions ἴσος εἶναι and ἴσα εἶναι no other distinction can be drawn, except that the former refers rather to the *person*, the latter to the *attributes*."

2:7 ἀλλ' ἑαυτὸν ἐκένωσεν μορφὴν δούλου λαβών, ἐν ὁμοιώματι ἀνθρώπων γενόμενος· καὶ σχήματι εὑρεθεὶς ὡς ἄνθρωπος

ἀλλ'. Conjunction that marks a correction of any idea of ἁρπαγμὸν in the previous verse. THGNT includes the word without eliding the final α.

ἑαυτὸν. Accusative direct object of ἐκένωσεν.

ἐκένωσεν. Aor act ind 3rd sg κενόω. The combination with ἑαυτὸν is "unparalleled in Greek" (Reumann, 347). Verb is used only 5 times in the NT, always by Paul and "to make empty" in a bad sense (1 Cor 1:17; Rom 4:14; 1 Cor 9:15; 2 Cor 9:3). LSB adds the footnote: "laid aside his privileges."

μορφὴν. Accusative direct object of λαβών. See comments on the same word in 2:6.

δούλου. Possessive genitive.

λαβών. Aor act ptc masc nom sg λαμβάνω. The context suggests that the participle conveys "instrument or means" (ME, 216).

ἐν ὁμοιώματι. Locative. Zerwick observes that "ὁμοίωμα *likeness* (Rom 8:3) denies nothing of the content of μορφή but of itself indicates simply that in every respect he was like a man" (GAGNT, 596).

ἀνθρώπων. Attributive genitive. The plural is used because Jesus represented not the individual man but the human race (Rom 5:15, 1 Cor 15:45–47).

γενόμενος. Aor mid ptc masc nom sg γίνομαι (means). The aorist participle describes "identical action" to ἐκένωσεν and λαβών and (Burton §145, citing Acts 25:13; Rom 4:19, 21; Heb 9:12 and 1 Pet 3:18 as parallel examples). The two subordinate participles define what Paul meant by ἐκένωσεν, i.e., Jesus took the form of a servant and took on the likeness of human beings. Theories about the "Kenosis" of Jesus often needlessly speculate beyond these participles. The language of the passage does not encourage such speculation but simply states that He was in the likeness of humankind rather than in His pre-incarnate form.

καί. Indicates additional information, not coincidental action.

σχήματι. Reference (Wallace, 144–46). The former verse described the contrast between what Jesus was and then became: λαβών (not ἔχων), ὁμοίωμα (not μορφῇ), γενόμενος (not ὤν), words describing a change. By the word σχῆμα the contrast is between what He is and what He appeared to humans: thus σχήματι (not μορφῇ), εὑρεθείς (not γενόμενος), ὡς ἄνθρωπος (for ἄνθρωπος), expressions describing external resemblance (see Lightfoot, 112–13; GE, 2069).

εὑρεθείς. Aor pass ptc masc nom sg εὑρίσκω (temporal). The participle is part of a temporal frame that introduces a new sentence setting the background for the indicative verb ἐταπείνωσεν that follows. Sumney (47) sees the participle as expressing means, like the previous two participles, but overlooks that εὑρεθείς backgrounds ἐταπείνωσεν in 2:8 and expresses time rather than means. "Of the 120 aorist participles in Paul, approximately 78 precede and 42 follow the main verb, with those preceding showing a definite tendency toward antecedent action and those following showing a definite tendency toward coincidental action" (Porter 1995b, 189, 383–84).

ὡς ἄνθρωπος. Comparative phrase completes the temporal frame that provides background for what follows. It was as a true "human being" that Jesus humbled Himself. Differing from the NA/UBS and THGNT texts, NIV, ESV, and NASB begin 2:8 with καὶ σχήματι εὑρεθείς ὡς ἄνθρωπος, returning to the verse numbering in the TR.

2:8 ἐταπείνωσεν ἑαυτὸν γενόμενος ὑπήκοος μέχρι θανάτου, θανάτου δὲ σταυροῦ.

ἐταπείνωσεν. Aor act ind 3rd sg ταπεινόω. Three aorist indicative verbs—ἡγήσατο (2:6), ἐκένωσεν (2:7), and ἐταπείνωσεν (2:8)—propel Jesus' main actions in the passage, while five adverbial participles qualify His actions. This word is one of the effective semantic links to 2:1–4. Compare ταπεινοφροσύνῃ (2:3) with ταπεινόω (2:8). For other links, compare φρονῆτε, φρονοῦντες (2:2), and ταπεινοφροσύνῃ (2:3) with φρονεῖτε (2:5); ἡγούμενοι (2:3) with ἡγήσατο (2:6); and ἑαυτῶν (2:4)

Analysis of Philippians Two

with ἑαυτὸν (2:7). Appropriately, the Philippians are associated with each of the attitudes and actions in 2:1–4 and Jesus is associated with each of the attitudes and actions in 2:5–8.

ἑαυτόν. Accusative direct object of ἐταπείνωσεν.

γενόμενος. Aor mid ptc masc nom sg γίνομαι (manner). While εὑρεθεὶς provides the temporal frame for ἐταπείνωσεν, this adverbial manner participle explains "how" He humbled himself.

ὑπήκοος. Predicate adjective.

μέχρι θανάτου. Temporal. Μέχρι is an uncommon preposition appearing only 17 times in the NT and only twice in Philippians, both times with θανάτου as its object (2:8, 30). Abbott-Smith (289) describes it as "properly an adverb" that has the adverbial meaning of "until" in Eph 4:13; Mark 13:30; and Gal 4:19. This temporal nuance may be indicating here the idea of "until the time of death." The genitive θανάτου, which functions as a complement of μέχρι, refers to death in general (BDAG, 443.1.b.β).

θανάτου. BDF (§447.8) describes the repetition of this noun as "intensification."

δέ. Marks development from death in general to a specific type of death.

σταυροῦ. Genitive of place ("death on a cross"), genitive of production ("death produced by a cross"), or genitive of means ("death by means of a cross") (see Wallace, 105).

Philippians 2:9–11

> [9] For this reason God highly exalted him by granting him the name that is above every name, [10] so that in the name of Jesus every knee will bow of those in heaven and on earth and under the earth, [11] and every tongue should confess, "Jesus Christ is Lord," to the honor of God the Father.

> Therefore, God also highly exalted Him, and bestowed on Him the name which is above every name, so that at the name of Jesus EVERY KNEE WILL BOW, of those who are in heaven and on earth and under the earth, and that EVERY TONGUE WILL CONFESS that Jesus Christ is LORD, to the glory of God the Father. (LSB)

Summary: Jesus' humiliation (2:5–8) was followed by His exaltation (2:9–11). In language reminiscent of Yahweh in Isaiah and other OT passages, Paul focuses on the lordship of Jesus over all the created order. Although this passage changes the direction from downward to upward, Jesus remains as the center, both as the earlier obedient slave on a cross and now as the Lord to be worshipped by all.

2:9 διὸ καὶ ὁ θεὸς αὐτὸν ὑπερύψωσεν καὶ ἐχαρίσατο αὐτῷ τὸ ὄνομα τὸ ὑπὲρ πᾶν ὄνομα,

διὸ. A new section is clearly marked by the transitional particle διὸ combined with a change of the grammatical subject, ὁ θεὸς.

καὶ. Adverbial ("also").

ὁ θεὸς. Nominative subject of ὑπερύψωσεν.

αὐτὸν. Accusative direct object of ὑπερύψωσεν.

ὑπερύψωσεν. Aor act ind 3rd sg ὑπερυψόω. *Hapax legomenon*. BDAG (1034) stresses that the prefix ὑπερ- strengthens this root to mean "to raise to a high point of honor, raise, exalt." BDF (§116.1.4) cautions that Koine Greek added prefixes to weakened verbs without adding any further meaning. The context, mentioning ἐπουρανίων, supports the strengthened meaning as do its over 100 appearances in the LXX to describe God (see LXX Ps 76:9; 96:9 and 35 times in the *Prayer of Azariah*). The verb anticipates the following ὑπὲρ πᾶν ὄνομα.

καὶ. The fact that the first καὶ is placed before θεὸς and not before the verb ὑπερύψωσεν discourages a "both . . . and" translation. The second καὶ is epexegetical (Silva, 128–29): "even."

ἐχαρίσατο. Aor mid ind 3rd sg χαρίζομαι. If the preceding καὶ is epexegetical, then the translation is "by granting Him." The verbs are "coincident" aorists (O'Brien 1991, 237, n26). Thus Lenski (793) describes the two verbs as "one act."

αὐτῷ. Dative indirect object of ἐχαρίσατο.

τὸ ὄνομα. Accusative direct object of ἐχαρίσατο. There is no article in D F G 𝔐 (KJV "a name"), but τὸ is in 𝔓⁴⁶ ℵ A B C. Some scholars suggest that the ὄνομα is κύριος mentioned in 2:11 (Silva, 129; Hawthorne, 93; O'Brien 1991, 238), while Fee (222–23) sees an intertextual connection with Isa 45:23: "Jesus is Lord." Others suggest "Jesus" (Moule, 270, because of 2:10); "Jesus Christ" (Vincent, 62); and θεὸς (Martin, 235).

τὸ ὑπὲρ πᾶν ὄνομα. The article in the second attributive position serves "to make the following prepositional phrase modify the preceding ὄνομα" (Sumney, 49). Some writers call this the "TNTA" (article-noun-article-adjective) position.

2:10 ἵνα ἐν τῷ ὀνόματι Ἰησοῦ πᾶν γόνυ κάμψῃ ἐπουρανίων καὶ ἐπιγείων καὶ καταχθονίων

ἵνα. Introduces a purpose clause. Wallace (473–74) cites this as a prime example of a "purpose-result clause" because "it indicates both the intention and its sure accomplishment." BDF (§391.5) asserts that "Jewish theology in general contributed to the blurring of the distinction between purpose and result." Such decisions are based not on ἵνα and the subjunctive verb, but on contextual and theological factors. In light of this, it is best to stay with the traditional definition of this construction as a purpose clause.

ἐν τῷ ὀνόματι. Moule (78) calls this an extended use of ἐν as "accompaniment, attendant circumstances," and translates the expression as "when the name of Jesus is spoken" or "at the name."

Ἰησοῦ. While possession is the simplest use of this genitive, it is also possible to see an epexegetical genitive at work here, i.e., "the name which is Jesus" (see Wallace, 95–100).

πᾶν γόνυ. Nominative subject of κάμψῃ. The adjective makes the reference universal. Eleven of the twelve NT uses of the noun are in conjunction with prayer and/or submission to a god.

κάμψῃ. Aor act subj 3rd sg κάμπτω. Subjunctive with ἵνα. TDNT (on γόνυ, 1:738–40) traces the Greco-Roman uses of "bowing the knee" to reverencing a person or deity. TDNT (3:594–95) cites a common LXX usage to "bend" the knee either before Baal (Rom 11:4/1 Kings 19:18) or before Yahweh (Rom 14:11/Isa 45:23).

ἐπουρανίων καὶ ἐπιγείων καὶ καταχθονίων. Genitives of place ("in the heavenly and earthly and subterranean places"), or more probably possessive genitives ("of those in heaven, etc."; see Wallace, 124–25). These substantival adjectives are anarthrous, which supports the idea that specific locales are not the focus of the words. The intent of this combination of places is simply to stress the universal extent of Jesus' lordship. Paul expresses the same idea with similar, although not identical, language in Col 1:16–20.

καταχθονίων. This *hapax legomenon* was used widely in Greek literature from Homer onward for "chthonic deities" (TDNT 3:633–34) and "infernal gods" (GE, 1091), and some see cosmic/spirit powers here (Cullman, 1964, 227–228). The rarity of the word in the NT discourages speculation about the specific identities involved. Paul expressed the same idea elsewhere with "Christ died and was raised that he might be Lord of both the dead and the living" (Rom 14:9).

Ignatius in *To the Trallians* 9:1 affirms that Jesus was crucified and died in the sight of "those in heaven and on earth and under the earth" (τῶν ἐπουρανίων καὶ ἐπιγείων καὶ ὑποχθονίων), probably alluding to this verse.

2:11 καὶ πᾶσα γλῶσσα ἐξομολογήσηται ὅτι κύριος Ἰησοῦς Χριστὸς εἰς δόξαν θεοῦ πατρός.

πᾶσα γλῶσσα. Nominative subject of ἐξομολογήσηται. BDAG (201.2.b) defines γλῶσσα as "language" and clarifies that the word "can be used as a synonym of φυλή, λαός, ἔθνος," citing as examples LXX Isa 66:18; Dan 3:4, 7; Jdt 3:8, and Rev 5:9; 7:9; 10:11; 11:9; 13:7; 14:6; 17:15. Fee (225, n36), demurs: "Paul is more likely picking up the sense of the LXX of Isa 45:23, that the 'tongue of every person shall confess' – which is also in keeping with the parallel 'knee.'"

ἐξομολογήσηται. Aor mid subj 3rd sg ἐξομολογέω. Parallel to the κάμψῃ in the previous verse and governed by the same ἵνα. The reading ἐξομολογήσηται ($\mathfrak{P}^{46}$ ℵ B Fc Clement of Alexandria) is replaced by εξομολογησεται (A C D F* G L P 33 1739), involving the change of only one letter, -ηται to -εται. The variant reading is future indicative, which is predictive ("every tongue will confess"). The aorist subjunctive indicates that all people should confess that Jesus Christ is Lord, but not that they actually will do so. One letter could easily be accidentally confused for the other, but it is possible that scribes intentionally changed the future to the subjunctive to avoid any notions of universalism or to make the verb parallel to the subjunctive verb of the previous verse, κάμψῃ ("should bend"). It is also possible that scribes changed the subjunctive to the future to conform the word to LXX Isa 45:23. The subjunctive has better external support, is included in the

THGNT, and avoids any universalist implication.

ὅτι. Introduces the clausal complement (direct discourse) of ἐξομολογήσηται. "The ὅτι is a ὅτι-recitativum (used to introduce a quote), thus indicating ... that these are the actual words of the confession" (Fee, 225, n37).

κύριος. Predicate nominative. This is a conscious allusion to Isa 45:23 where the Greek word κύριος translates the Hebrew יהוה. The LSB footnote reads: "In OT, Yahweh, cf. Isa 45:23–25." One of the strongest evidences for the deity of Jesus is the application to Him of OT texts mentioning Yahweh. See also Rom 10:9 (Joel 2:32).

Ἰησοῦς Χριστὸς. Nominative subject of an implied equative verb.

εἰς δόξαν θεοῦ. Purpose. Compare the expression in 1:11, also ending a section. BDAG (257.3) nuances the traditional "glory" translation as "honor as enhancement or recognition of status or performance, fame, recognition, renown, honor, prestige."

θεοῦ. Objective genitive.

πατρός. Genitive in apposition to θεοῦ. The two nouns are anarthrous, which is characteristic of formulaic expressions (BDF §252, §254, §257.3). Of the eighteen NT appearances of θεοῦ πατρός, only 2 Pet 1:17 does not occur in a salutation or benediction. "When divine honors are thus paid to the humiliated and exalted Jesus, the glory of God the Father is not diminished but enhanced. When the Son is honored, the Father is glorified; for none can bestow on the Son higher honors than the Father himself has bestowed" (Bruce, 75).

Philippians 2:12–18

[12] So then, my beloved, just as you have always obeyed, not only in my presence, but now even more in my absence, continue working out your own salvation with fear and trembling. [13] For God is the one who is working in you both the desiring and the doing for his good purpose. [14] Do everything without grumbling and arguing, [15] so that you may be blameless and pure, faultless children of God amid a crooked and perverted generation, among whom you shine like luminaries in the world, [16] holding firmly to the message of life, so that I can boast on the day of Christ that I did not run or labor for nothing. [17] But even if I am poured out as a drink offering

on the sacrifice and service of your faith, I am glad and I rejoice with all of you. [18] In the same way you should also be glad and rejoice with me.

So then, my beloved, just as you have always obeyed, not as in my presence only, but now much more in my absence, work out your salvation with fear and trembling; for it is God who is at work in you, both to will and to work for *His* good pleasure. ¶ Do all things without grumbling or disputing, so that you will be blameless and innocent, children of God without blemish in the midst of a crooked and perverse generation, among whom you shine as lights in the world, holding fast the word of life, so that in the day of Christ I will have reason to boast because I did not run in vain nor labor in vain. But even if I am being poured out as a drink offering upon the sacrifice and service of your faith, I rejoice and share my joy with you all. And you also, rejoice in the same way and share your joy with me. (LSB)

Summary: Paul resumes his exhortation by directly addressing the Philippians ("my beloved"), but the paragraph is still part of a larger hortatory section, 1:27–2:18, over which the imperative of 1:27 stands as a topic statement: "Live as citizens in a manner worthy of the gospel of Christ." Thematic links with 2:5–11 include the important theme of 'obedience' appearing first with the reference to Jesus (ὑπήκοος, 2:8) and then used of the Philippians (ὑπηκούσατε, 2:12). The exhortation to work out their own salvation (2:12–13) constitutes the main thought of the paragraph. It is followed by a more specific command to avoid dissension within the fellowship (2:14–16). Finally, by appealing to his own ministry (2:17–18) Paul describes the life of the congregation at Philippi as an acceptable offering in God's sight to which his own life may be added as a modest drink-offering (freely adapted from Fee).

2:12 Ὥστε, ἀγαπητοί μου, καθὼς πάντοτε ὑπηκούσατε, μὴ ὡς ἐν τῇ παρουσίᾳ μου μόνον ἀλλὰ νῦν πολλῷ μᾶλλον ἐν τῇ ἀπουσίᾳ μου, μετὰ φόβου καὶ τρόμου τὴν ἑαυτῶν σωτηρίαν κατεργάζεσθε·

Ὥστε. BDAG (1107.1.b) translates this conjunction as "so then." It appears also in 1:13 and 4:1, each time beginning a new unit and initiating a statement of some consequence.

ἀγαπητοί μου. Vocative, or more preferably, nominative of direct address (Porter 1994, 86–87), and the first direct address since 1:12 (ἀδελφοί). Paul uses this noun only twice in the letter, each time with the personal pronoun (see 4:1), following Ὥστε and preceding fervent imperatives (κατεργάζεσθε and στήκετε) about the readers' relationship with the Lord.

καθώς. With the following ὡς, this adverb sets up the comparison of past with present experiences.

πάντοτε. Adverb that references "always" in the past.

ὑπηκούσατε. Aor act ind 2nd pl ὑπακούω. The aorist is clearly not expressing a "punctiliar action" because of the implicature of πάντοτε (Porter 1989, 184, 187). In the comparative clause the aorist is background to the thrust of the following imperative κατεργάζεσθε.

μή. Negates μόνον. It is used instead of οὐκ because it does not refer back to the indicative ὑπηκούσατε but forward to the imperative κατεργάζεσθε (Burton §479).

ὡς. Repeats καθώς in an abbreviated way. The word is omitted by B 33 1241, probably because it is considered "as superfluous" (Metzger, 613; Silva, 141; Fee, 230 n3). Thus, it is often omitted in translations.

ἐν τῇ παρουσίᾳ μου. Temporal. In 1:26 (τῆς ἐμῆς παρουσίας), Paul referred to his future presence with them, while here τῇ παρουσίᾳ μου refers to his past presence with them.

μόνον. See above.

ἀλλά. Conjunction that indicates a switch from past to present.

νῦν. Adverb that shifts the focus from πάντοτε to "now."

πολλῷ μᾶλλον. μᾶλλον is comparative of the adverb μάλα. The simple form does not occur in the NT, but the comparative often occurs with another comparative (see 1:23) or with an adjective (Acts 20:35). "The comparative is heightened . . . by the addition of πολύ, πολλῷ" (BDF §246). These collocations often appear as part of the rhetorical argument, "from the lesser to the greater" (Heb 10:25; 12:9).

ἐν τῇ ἀπουσίᾳ μου. Temporal, contrasted with ἐν τῇ παρουσίᾳ. *Hapax legomenon.*

μετὰ φόβου καὶ τρόμου. Manner. The collocation of the two nouns became a stock expression in the LXX with approximate parallels in

Ps 2:11; Isa 19:16; and Gen 9:2, as well as combinations of cognates in Exod 15:16; Deut 2:25; 11:25; Job 4:13–14; and Isa 54:14. The LXX occurrences suggest "reverence and awe" (O'Brien 1991, 282–84). The phrase is equivalent to having a disposition of obedience to God in light of our weakness (ἐν ἀσθενείᾳ). The LXX use of the phrase illuminates the tone of solemnity that it lends to Paul's command. The phrase in this context is probably intended to have the same force as 1 Cor. 10:12, "therefore let him who thinks he stands take heed lest he fall." For other parallels with 1 Cor 10:1–13, see Silva (130).

τὴν ἑαυτῶν σωτηρίαν. Accusative direct object of κατεργάζεσθε. The reflexive pronoun "reflects the verbal process back on the subject of the verb" (ME, 46). As in 1:19, as well as in 1:28 and here, the transcendent aspects of "salvation" are intended (BDAG, 986.2).

κατεργάζεσθε. Pres mid impv 2nd pl κατεργάζομαι. The prefixed pronoun intensifies the verb's meaning suggesting "work out" emphasizing the carrying out of the work (ME, 93). The imperfective aspect also portrays salvation as a process of working at something until it is brought to completion and is preferred to a general admonition. This sense is best conveyed by the translation, "continue working out" (Bockmuehl, 151; Reumann, 386; Hawthorne, 140).

2:13 θεὸς γάρ ἐστιν ὁ ἐνεργῶν ἐν ὑμῖν καὶ τὸ θέλειν καὶ τὸ ἐνεργεῖν ὑπὲρ τῆς εὐδοκίας.

θεός. Nominative subject of ἐστιν.

γάρ. Introduces the reason why the Philippians can obey the previous imperative κατεργάζεσθε.

ἐστιν. Pres act ind 3rd sg εἰμί.

ὁ ἐνεργῶν. Pres act ptc masc nom sg ἐνεργέω (substantival). Predicate nominative. "He is the 'Great Energizer' who directs, empowers, operates, and accomplishes Christlike character and behavior in believers" (Moore, 145).

ἐν ὑμῖν. Locative.

καὶ ... καὶ. "both ... and" (CGELNT, 183.c: "with focus on inclusiveness").

τὸ θέλειν καὶ τὸ ἐνεργεῖν. Articular infinitives functioning as a compound direct object of ὁ ἐνεργῶν (Wallace, 235 n50).

τὸ θέλειν. Pres act inf θέλω (substantival).
τὸ ἐνεργεῖν. Pres act inf ἐνεργέω (substantival). Substantival infinitives (BDF §399.1) have been utilized as a stylistic feature in 1:21, 22, 24, and 2:6.
ὑπὲρ τῆς εὐδοκίας. Representation/advantage. BDAG (1031.2) interprets the preposition ὑπὲρ in this phrase as a "marker of the moving cause or reason" and translates it as "because of, for the sake of, for." The "good will" is either human, as it was used in 1:15, or divine ("good pleasure/purpose"), which is consistent with the previous words that show God as the actor (ὁ ἐνεργῶν ἐν ὑμῖν). If εὐδοκία is God's (the dominant view), the article is used as a possessive pronoun (Wallace, 215–16). If it is the Philippian's good will (Hawthorne, 101), then the article suggests "the well-known εὐδοκία," a sense of benefaction (Reed 1997, 320, 326).

2:14 Πάντα ποιεῖτε χωρὶς γογγυσμῶν καὶ διαλογισμῶν,

Πάντα. Accusative direct object of ποιεῖτε. The fronting of the direct object is intended to give it special prominence. "In Philippians VO occurs 64 times, OV 54 times and OVO 7 times" (Reed 1997, 379).
ποιεῖτε. Pres act impv 2nd pl ποιέω. Imperfective aspect conveys a general command, as is evidenced by πάντα.
χωρὶς. Fairly common NT preposition (41 times) but it occurs only here in Philippians.
γογγυσμῶν. Genitive required by χωρίς. Onomatopoetic noun like the English "murmur." The noun is rare in secular Greek (GE, 438) but appears eight times in the LXX (Muraoka, 135). It occurs only here in Paul, but the verb is in 1 Cor 10:10 where the Israelites "murmured" in the wilderness. Elsewhere this noun is not about Israel's grumbling, but it is directed more at leaders (John 7:12; Acts 6:1), who could also be the target here (ἐπίσκοποι καὶ διάκονοι in 1:1).
διαλογισμῶν. Another genitive required by χωρίς. This noun is more common in the NT (14 times), where the use is primarily negative (Luke 9:46; 1 Cor 3:20; Rom 1:21; 14:1). BDAG (232.3) translates this noun as "verbal exchange that takes place when conflicting ideas are expressed, dispute, argument." Fee (243–44) suggests arguments such as that between Euodias and Syntyche (4:1–3).

2:15 ἵνα γένησθε ἄμεμπτοι καὶ ἀκέραιοι, τέκνα θεοῦ ἄμωμα μέσον γενεᾶς σκολιᾶς καὶ διεστραμμένης, ἐν οἷς φαίνεσθε ὡς φωστῆρες ἐν κόσμῳ,

ἵνα. Introduces a purpose clause. Because it follows closely the two imperatives in 2:13–14, Moule (144–45) calls this an "imperatival ἵνα."
γένησθε. Aor mid subj 2nd pl γίνομαι. Subjunctive with ἵνα. While usually taken as equivalent to εἰμί, some prefer a more dynamic rendering such as BDAG (198.5), "to experience a change in nature and so indicate entry into a new condition, become someth[ing]." Compare GAGNT (597): "live (= conduct oneself)." So NKJV, NIV ("become") and NASB ("prove yourselves to be"). Some manuscripts ($\mathfrak{P}^{46}$ A D F G) have ητε because scribes may have thought that γίνομαι would imply that the Philippians were not yet children of God. Defending the better supported γένησθε, Comfort (609) observes that "the word γίνομαι describes the process of becoming blameless and pure, not the process of becoming a child of God." THGNT has γένησθε.

ἄμεμπτοι. Predicate adjective. Trench (204–9; 318–22; 379–82) suggest fine semantic distinctions between these three adjectives, ἄμεμπτοι, ἀκέραιοι, and ἄμωμα. Some scholars (Lightfoot, 117) also follow this effort, often basing their distinctions on etymological arguments. Silva (132), however, suggests that "we should here invoke the notion of stylistic reinforcement." These lexical distinctions are often neutralized in specific contexts where there is a need for stylistic reinforcement rather than making an additional semantic point. Paul's practice of grouping of synonyms (e.g., εὐχαριστέω, μνεία, δέησις in 1:3–4; ἄμεμπτοι, ἀκέραιοι, ἄμωμα in 2:15; λαμβάνω, καταλαμβάνω, τελειόω in 3:12) illustrates this iconic reinforcement. The translations "blameless ... pure ... faultless" convey the goal of the ἵνα clause collectively.

καὶ ἀκέραιοι. Predicate adjective.
τέκνα. Nominative plural in apposition to ἄμεμπτοι.
θεοῦ. Possessive genitive.
ἄμωμα. The three adjectives, ἄμεμπτοι, ἀκέραιοι, and ἄμωμα, are also alliterative, each with a negating *alpha* privative (BFD §117.1). 𝔐, supported by some "Western" manuscripts like D F G and Ψ, reads ἀμώμητα ("flawless") for ἄμωμα, which has the strong support of $\mathfrak{P}^{46}$ ℵ A B C 33. This later reading probably reflects an attempt to assimilate 2:15 to the referenced LXX text of Deut 32:5 (τέκνα μωμητά, γενεὰ σκολιὰ καὶ διεστραμμένη).

μέσον. An improper preposition used as an adverb (BDAG, 635.1.c, "amid"; BDF §215.3; Moule, 85). Nearly all improper prepositions govern the genitive case (Black 1998, 86).

γενεᾶς. Genitive object of μέσον. The noun appears 33 times in the Synoptics, 17 times as "this generation," often (as in Deut 32:5) with a pejorative adjective: "adulterous" (Mark 8:38), "faithless" (Mark 9:19), "faithless and perverse" (Matt 17:17/Luke 9:41). This usage may be informing its negative meaning here. BDAG (191.2) suggests "contemporaries."

σκολιᾶς. Descriptive adjective in the fourth attributive position (the anarthrous noun-adjective construction). It is used once in its literal sense of "crooked" (Luke 3:5), but it is employed metaphorically for "crooked behavior" here, in Acts 2:40 (τῆς γενεᾶς τῆς σκολιᾶς), and in 1 Pet 2:18.

διεστραμμένης. Prf pass ptc fem gen sg διαστρέφω (adjectival attributive). This participle with its head noun may be an adaptation of the Jesus *logion* in Matt 17:17/Luke 9:41 (ὦ γενεὰ ἄπιστος καὶ διεστραμμένη).

ἐν οἷς. Locative. Since there is no plural noun that is the antecedent of the relative pronoun, this is a *constructio ad sensum* – a plural according to the sense, "among whom."

φαίνεσθε. Pres mid ind 2nd pl φαίνω. Some prefer this as an imperative (Hawthorne, 103). An imperative, however, is awkward following a phrase like ἐν οἷς and an indicative is more likely. Silva (146–47) observes that the NT calls people to "become" (imperative) and "act" by emphasizing "what we already are" (indicative).

ὡς. Marking a simile.

φωστῆρες. Elsewhere only in Rev 21:11. The noun is not ἀστήρ, "star," but φῶς plus the ending -τήρ which conveys the agent (MHT 2:364–65; BDF §109.8), thus "light-bearers" or "luminaries" (Abbott-Smith, 477). The word had a limited pre-history to the NT, appearing as "light-bearer" only in Themistocles and eight times in the LXX (see GE, 2324).

ἐν κόσμῳ. Locative. The noun is anarthrous, but this is common in prepositional phrases with κόσμος (Turner, 175). Does the noun refer to the universe/sky or human beings? If Paul is drawing on Dan 12:3 (φωστῆρες τοῦ οὐρανοῦ), it is the sky. Note the change in the NIV from "stars in the universe" (1984) to "stars in the sky" (2011). Since illumination by the Philippians comes in the human realm, "the world" of people is preferable.

2:16 λόγον ζωῆς ἐπέχοντες, εἰς καύχημα ἐμοὶ εἰς ἡμέραν Χριστοῦ, ὅτι οὐκ εἰς κενὸν ἔδραμον οὐδὲ εἰς κενὸν ἐκοπίασα.

λόγον. Accusative direct object of ἐπέχοντες, with the sense of "message" (BDAG, 599.1.a.β).

ζωῆς. Objective genitive or epexegetical genitive ("the word, i.e., life").

ἐπέχοντες. Pres act ptc masc nom pl ἐπέχω (means). Does the verb connote "by holding on to" the word (NET) or "by holding forth" the word (KJV)? Of its five occurrences in the NT, only here is the verb transitive with a direct object (λόγον). Abbott-Smith (166) suggests "to hold out, offer." BDAG (362.1) suggests "hold fast" to its preceding accusative and cites several extra-biblical examples for support (see also LN 31.47). This meaning is attested by a singular variant reading in Codex D at Luke 4:42 where επειχον (with a following accusative) replaces κατεῖχον ("hold fast"). NIV correctly renders the phrase as "holding firmly to the word of life." See LSB: "Holding fast the word of life."

εἰς καύχημα. Purpose. The preposition εἰς is telic, "with a view to, so that" (Moule, 70; BDAG, 290.4.e; Fee, 248), similar to its use in 1:19, where it is also with a dative of possession (ὅτι τοῦτό μοι ἀποβήσεται εἰς σωτηρίαν). It is difficult to always finely discern the difference between "purpose" and "result." BDAG (537.1) defines καύχημα as "that which constitutes a source of pride" and paraphrases the expression, "as my pride (and joy) in the day of Christ."

ἐμοὶ. Dative of possession.

εἰς ἡμέραν. Temporal. BDAG (εἰς, 289.2.a.β), however, suggests "for" the day of Christ (Matt 6:34; 1 Tim 1:16; Acts 13:42). O'Brien (1991, 299) prefers "on" the day.

Χριστοῦ. Genitive of possession. See also "the day of Christ (Jesus)" in 1:6, 10. It is characteristically Pauline to replace numerous OT examples of the expression "the day of the Lord" with "the day of Christ (Jesus)."

ὅτι. Introduces the clausal complement of καύχημα ("that"; most versions; O'Brien 1991, 299), not a causal clause ("because"; BDF §456.2).

οὐκ... οὐδὲ. Point-counterpoint expression: "neither... nor."

εἰς κενὸν. This prepositional phrase has an adverbial force, "vainly" (Robertson, 550; see Jas 4:5).

ἔδραμον. Aor act ind 1st sg τρέχω. Paul employs the irregular verb τρέχω of "exertion" in life (Rom 9:16; 1 Cor 9:26) and of missionary labor (Gal 2:2, εἰς κενὸν τρέχω ἢ ἔδραμον). For the metaphor, see also Gal 5:7 and 2 Thess 3:1.

εἰς κενὸν. See above.

ἐκοπίασα. Aor act ind 1st sg κοπιάω. The verb appears 23 times in the NT for both secular and spiritual labor. TLNT (2:323–25) cites many LXX examples of "working hard," and MM (352) cites numerous papyri examples for the verb and cognate noun as "hard labor."

2:17 Ἀλλ' εἰ καὶ σπένδομαι ἐπὶ τῇ θυσίᾳ καὶ λειτουργίᾳ τῆς πίστεως ὑμῶν, χαίρω καὶ συγχαίρω πᾶσιν ὑμῖν·

Ἀλλ'. Adversative conjunction that indicates a different situation from the preceding.

εἰ καὶ. Introduces a first class conditional sentence. This condition assumes the reality of the protasis for the sake of the argument. The apodosis begins with the verb χαίρω. BDAG (278.6.e) translates εἰ with καὶ as "even if, even though, although." "This ... accounts for the contrastive ἀλλά: 'Yes, I have labored hard, but even death cannot take away my joy'" (Silva, 132).

σπένδομαι. Pres pass ind 1st sg σπένδω. The verb was used widely in extra-biblical literature as "offer a libation/drink-offering" (BDAG, 937; references in GE, 1944) but is used metaphorically for Paul's death in its two NT occurrences (see 2 Tim 4:6). The present tense form should not be interpreted that he is already undergoing death by referencing the more specific statement in 2 Tim 4:6. That statement is qualified by the adverb ἤδη (Ἐγὼ γὰρ ἤδη σπένδομαι) and reflects a time later than the imprisonment described in Philippians. A better approach is that the imperfective aspect portrays Paul's perception of the internal process he was experiencing during his imprisonment (Campbell 2008, 19–20).

ἐπὶ τῇ θυσίᾳ καὶ λειτουργίᾳ τῆς πίστεως ὑμῶν. Spatial. While the preposition ἐπὶ has a large number of uses, it appears that its most basic sense of "upon" fits the metaphor of a libation poured on the sacrifice. Vincent (71), O'Brien (1991, 306–7) and Fee (254 n62) prefer "in addition (to)," as in Num 28–29; the drink offering is an addition to the burnt offering or some other sacrifice. The metaphorical language combined with the flexibility of ἐπί make a decision about its specific meaning difficult.

τῇ θυσίᾳ καὶ λειτουργίᾳ. A hendiadys = sacrificial service. Hendiadys is a stylistic feature in Philippians (Robertson, 787; Zerwick, 60). See notes on 1:19; 1:20; 1:25. The extensive OT/LXX cultic usage is occasionally reflected in the NT (Luke 1:23; Heb 8:6; 9:21; 10:11). Paul mostly employs the noun λειτουργία in a practical and ministerial way. In 2 Cor 9:12 and Rom 15:27 it is the collection. In Phil 2:30 it is the ministry by Epaphroditus. Acts 13:2 reflects the new "service" of prophets and teachers at Antioch. Phil 2:17 combines both the cultic and priestly aspects to describe Paul's offering up the faith of the Philippians to God (NIDNTTE 3:552; TLNT 2:383).

τῆς πίστεως ὑμῶν. Objective genitive. See above for the Philippians' faith viewed as a "sacrificial service."

χαίρω καὶ συγχαίρω πᾶσιν ὑμῖν. Apodosis of the conditional sentence.

χαίρω. Pres act ind 1st sg χαίρω. The present tense form should not be described as iterative, repeated action (Reumann, 401). An aspectual approach recognizes that the imperfective aspect conveys Paul's internal view of the rejoicing process in both this and the next verb.

συγχαίρω. Pres act ind 1st sg συγχαίρω. The prepositional prefix is associative (Robertson, 627, 828). Lightfoot (119) suggests the translation "congratulate" (cf. Luke 1:58), but it does not seem appropriate in this context because it damages the parallel with συγχαίρετέ in 2:18.

πᾶσιν ὑμῖν. Dative of accompaniment.

2:18 τὸ δὲ αὐτὸ καὶ ὑμεῖς χαίρετε καὶ συγχαίρετέ μοι.

τὸ ... αὐτό. The article nominalizes the pronoun αὐτό. The phrase τὸ αὐτό functions as adverbial accusative (BDF §154; Robertson, 487) that can be translated "in the same way" (Moule, 34). Lightfoot (120):

"The accusative defines the character rather than the object of the action."

δὲ. Indicates a transition from first person singular to second person plural verbs.

καὶ. Adverbial ("also").

ὑμεῖς χαίρετε καὶ συγχαίρετέ μοι. This clause parallels the preceding clause in 2:17.

ὑμεῖς. Empathic use of pronoun, following the mild shift with δὲ.

χαίρετε. Pres act impv 2nd pl χαίρω. See χαίρω in 2:17. While the tense and aspect are the same, the mood differs. The imperative demands a translation like "you should rejoice" (see NIV).

καὶ συγχαίρετέ. Pres act impv 2nd pl συγχαίρω. See συγχαίρω in 2:17 and the preceding comment on χαίρετε.

μοι. Dative of accompaniment, as πᾶσιν ὑμῖν in 2:17.

Philippians 2:19–24

[19] Now I am hoping by the Lord Jesus to send Timothy to you soon so that I also may be encouraged when I learn about your affairs. [20] Because I have no one else like-minded who will genuinely care about your affairs, [21] for all seek their own interests, not those of Jesus Christ. [22] But you know his proven character, because he has served with me in the gospel ministry like a son with a father. [23] Therefore, I hope to send him as soon as I see how things go with me. [24] I am convinced by the Lord that I myself will also come quickly.

¶ But I hope in the Lord Jesus to send Timothy to you shortly, so that I also may be in good spirits when I learn of your circumstances. For I have no one *else* of kindred spirit who will genuinely be concerned about your circumstances. For they all seek after their own interests, not those of Christ Jesus. But you know of his proven worth, that he served with me in the furtherance of the gospel like a child *serving* his father. Therefore I hope to send him immediately, as soon as I evaluate my own circumstances, and I am confident in the Lord that I myself also will be coming shortly. (LSB)

Summary: There are verbal parallels between 2:19–24 and the christological confession of 2:5–11. He presents Timothy, who has served selflessly in the gospel (2:22; cf. 1:1, 7) and has a genuine concern for the interests of the Philippians (τὰ περὶ ὑμῶν, 2:20), as a godly example of the way the Philippians should imitate Christ. Thus, 2:19–24 as well as 2:25–30, does not simply inform the Philippians about Paul's plans for Timothy and Epaphroditus. The section also has a hortatory purpose by pointing to them as models of a selfless attitude that Paul wants the community to follow (adapted from Fee).

2:19 Ἐλπίζω δὲ ἐν κυρίῳ Ἰησοῦ Τιμόθεον ταχέως πέμψαι ὑμῖν, ἵνα κἀγὼ εὐψυχῶ γνοὺς τὰ περὶ ὑμῶν.

Ἐλπίζω. Pres act ind 1st sg ἐλπίζω.

δὲ. Combined with the shift to the indicative mood from the previous imperatives and the introduction of two new participants, Timothy and Epaphroditus, this δὲ signals a new development of the discourse.

ἐν κυρίῳ Ἰησοῦ. Sumney (59) states that the prepositional phrase "designates the sphere within which Paul expresses this hope." This PP is better understood as instrumental. The expression ἐν κυρίῳ (Ἰησοῦ) also forms an inclusio that brackets this section (2:19 and 24). Instead of κυρίῳ, some "Western" manuscripts (D F G), along with a few others, read Χριστῷ. Silva (140) suggests that this "may be due to the fact that Paul does not use the title 'Lord Jesus' as frequently as he uses other combinations."

Τιμόθεον. Accusative direct object of πέμψαι. This is the first mention of Timothy since 1:1.

ταχέως. Temporal adverb.

πέμψαι. Aor act inf πέμπω (complementary).

ὑμῖν. Dative indirect object.

ἵνα. Introduces a purpose clause.

κἀγὼ. Crasis for καὶ plus ἐγώ.

εὐψυχῶ. Pres act subj 1st sg εὐψυχέω. Subjunctive with ἵνα. *Hapax legomenon*. Paul's stated purpose is that he may gain encouragement. BDAG (417) translates this verb as "be glad, have courage, with implication of release from anxiety."

Analysis of Philippians Two

γνοὺς. Aor act ptc masc nom sg γινώσκω (temporal). To describe the aorist participle as "ingressive" (O'Brien 1991, 318) is to go beyond both its perfective aspect and the context.

τὰ. The article functions as a nominalizer, changing the PP περὶ ὑμῶν into the direct object of γνοὺς (see 1:27).

περὶ ὑμῶν. Reference. Moule (63) suggests "your affairs," which is followed by the NIV.

2:20 οὐδένα γὰρ ἔχω ἰσόψυχον, ὅστις γνησίως τὰ περὶ ὑμῶν μεριμνήσει

οὐδένα. Direct object of ἔχω in a double accusative object-complement construction.

γὰρ. This conjunction functions more as explanatory than as providing a reason (Reed 1997, 330).

ἔχω. Pres act ind 1st sg ἔχω. BDAG (420.1.c) translates this verb here as "have at one's disposal." In other words, Paul does not refer to all those whom he knows but to those available to him in his circumstances.

ἰσόψυχον. Complement in a double accusative object-complement construction. *Hapax legomenon*, appearing occasionally in Attic as "of equal soul" (GE, 990). The LXX usage in Ps 54:14 is informative: ἄνθρωπε ἰσόψυχε, "man of like mind" (Muraoka, 343).

ὅστις. Indefinite relative pronoun serving as the subject of μεριμνήσει.

γνησίως. This adverb is another *hapax legomenon*. The adjective appears in 4:3 to describe the "genuine" implied reader (γνήσιε σύζυγε).

τὰ. The article functions as nominalizer, changing the PP περὶ ὑμῶν into the direct object of μεριμνήσει (see 1:27 and 2:19).

περὶ ὑμῶν. Reference (see 2:19).

μεριμνήσει. Fut act ind 3rd sg μεριμνάω. Although μεριμνάω is often used intransitively (see 1 Cor 7:32–34), when it is transitive it takes the accusative as its direct object (BDAG, 632.2).

2:21 οἱ πάντες γὰρ τὰ ἑαυτῶν ζητοῦσιν, οὐ τὰ Ἰησοῦ Χριστοῦ.

οἱ πάντες. Substantival adjective, subject of ζητοῦσιν. The adjective does not imply universality but rhetorically functions as hyperbole to call attention to the role of Timothy (Collange, 117; Silva, 140).

γάρ. The conjunction again does not provide a reason but is simply continuative and explanatory, as in 2:20.

τὰ ἑαυτῶν. Direct object of ζητοῦσιν. The article nominalizes the reflexive pronoun that functions as a possessive pronoun. "The neuter plural is common for the notion of 'affairs' or 'things'" (Robertson, 767).

ζητοῦσιν. Pres act ind 3rd pl ζητέω. With τὰ ἑαυτῶν, the expression is equivalent to τὰ ἑαυτῶν σκοποῦντες in 2:4.

τὰ. The article functions as a nominalizer, changing the genitive phrase Ἰησοῦ Χριστοῦ into the second direct object of ζητοῦσιν. The negative particle οὐ before the article modifies the entire phrase into the negated direct object. These conflicting direct objects parallel 2:4.

Ἰησοῦ Χριστοῦ. Genitive of source.

2:22 τὴν δὲ δοκιμὴν αὐτοῦ γινώσκετε, ὅτι ὡς πατρὶ τέκνον σὺν ἐμοὶ ἐδούλευσεν εἰς τὸ εὐαγγέλιον.

τὴν δοκιμὴν. Accusative direct object of γινώσκετε. Like 2:20, the fronted direct object calls special attention to the role of Timothy.

δὲ. Signals development from discussing those who do not seek the things of Christ to discussing one who does.

αὐτοῦ. Objective genitive.

γινώσκετε. Pres act ind 2nd pl γινώσκω.

ὅτι. Introduces either the clausal complement of γινώσκετε ("that he") or a causal clause that provides reason for γινώσκετε ("because he").

ὡς. Introduces a simile.

πατρὶ. There is an ellipsis with no verb, but if the following clause provides the verb (ἐδούλευσεν), this could be a dative of the person served (see δουλεύω, BDAG, 259.2.a.α). Most interpreters and translators, however, view this as a dative of accompaniment. If this is the case, the preposition σὺν is also elided.

τέκνον. Nominative subject of the elided verb ἐδούλευσεν.

σὺν ἐμοὶ. Accompaniment, because of the preposition σὺν.

ἐδούλευσεν. Aor act ind 3rd sg δουλεύω. Paul has already described Jesus as taking the lowly position of a slave for others (2:5–8). "So he commends Timothy as one who has followed Jesus in taking the role of a slave" (Moore, 159).

εἰς τὸ εὐαγγέλιον. See comments on this expression in 1:5.

Analysis of Philippians Two

2:23 τοῦτον μὲν οὖν ἐλπίζω πέμψαι ὡς ἂν ἀφίδω τὰ περὶ ἐμὲ ἐξαυτῆς·

τοῦτον. Accusative direct object of πέμψαι. Fronted demonstrative pronoun referring back (anaphoric) to Timothy.

μὲν. Introduces a "point-counterpoint" set with δὲ in 2:24.

οὖν. Consequential conjunction that signals a conclusion that derives from what was written.

ἐλπίζω. Pres act ind 1st sg ἐλπίζω. The verb initiates the end of an inclusio that began in 2:19.

πέμψαι. Aor act inf πέμπω (complementary).

ὡς ἂν. The combination of particles (BDAG, 57.I.c.δ, "as soon as") plus a subjunctive conveys an event the speaker believes likely but cannot be assumed with certainty (MHT 1:167). Other examples of this combination are Rom 15:24 (ὡς ἂν πορεύωμαι) and 1 Cor 11:34 (ὡς ἂν ἔλθω).

ἀφίδω. Aor act subj 1st sg ἀφοράω. Subjunctive with ἄν. Literally, "look away" from the present to the future, "determine, see" (BDAG, 158.2).

τὰ. The article functions as a nominalizer, changing the PP περὶ ἐμὲ into the direct object of ἀφίδω.

περὶ ἐμὲ. Reference. The phrase τὰ περὶ ἐμέ, "my affairs," expresses the same idea as 2:20 τὰ περὶ ὑμῶν, "your affairs." The preposition with the accusative conveys the sense of "concerning/about me" (ME, 105).

ἐξαυτῆς. This is the only Pauline use of this adverb. The other occurrences (Mark 6:25; Acts 10:33; 11:11; 21:32; 23:30) stress the immediacy of the proposed action (BDAG, 346, "at once, immediately"). However, the translation "immediately" (NASB) may be misleading because Timothy cannot be sent right away. Paul will send him as soon as he knows about his own future (see NIV).

2:24 πέποιθα δὲ ἐν κυρίῳ ὅτι καὶ αὐτὸς ταχέως ἐλεύσομαι.

πέποιθα. Perf act ind 1st sg πείθω. BDAG (792.2.a) translates this verb as "depend on, trust in." The stative aspect conveys Paul's attitude of confidence in his state of affairs. Note previous πείθω participles: πεποιθώς (1:6), πεποιθότας (1:14), and πεποιθώς (1:25). Hawthorne (109) notes that this verb is a deliberate change from ἐλπίζω in 2:19 because

Paul's coming to them is in his view "more certain than the expected arrival of Timothy."

δέ. Signals development from discussion of Timothy's affairs to Paul's.

ἐν κυρίῳ. Locative, in a metaphorical sense. See comments on ἐν κυρίῳ Ἰησοῦ in 2:19.

ὅτι. Introduces the clausal complement of πέποιθα.

καί. Adverbial ("also").

αὐτός. Intensive pronoun.

ταχέως. Temporal adverb.

ἐλεύσομαι. Fut mid ind 1st sg ἔρχομαι. The addition of the words πρὸς ὑμᾶς after ἐλεύσομαι has some significant support (ℵ* A C and Latin versions), but this is probably a scribal effort to smooth out the sense by completing the verb.

The language of 2:24 parallels the language of 2:19 so clearly that these two verses serve as an inclusio of this pericope.

2:19 Ἐλπίζω δὲ   2:24 πέποιθα δὲ
2:19 ἐν κυρίῳ Ἰησοῦ   2:24 ἐν κυρίῳ
2:19 ταχέως πέμψαι   2:24 ταχέως ἐλεύσομαι

Philippians 2:25–30

> [25] But I considered it a necessity to send you Epaphroditus, my brother, coworker, and fellow soldier, as well as your messenger and minister to my need, [26] since he has been longing for all of you and was distressed because you heard that he was sick. [27] Indeed, he was so sick that he nearly died, but God had mercy on him, and not only on him but also on me, so that I would not have one grief on top of another. [28] For this reason, I am very eager to send him so that you may rejoice when you see him again and I may be less anxious. [29] Therefore, welcome him in the Lord with all joy and hold such people like him in honor, [30] because he was near to death for the work of Christ, risking his life to make up what was lacking in your ministry to me.

But I regarded it necessary to send to you Epaphroditus, my brother and fellow worker and fellow soldier, who is also your messenger and minister to my need; because he was longing for you all and was distressed because you had heard that he was sick. For indeed he was sick to the point of death, but God had mercy on him, and not on him only but also on me, so that I would not have sorrow upon sorrow. Therefore I have sent him all the more eagerly so that when you see him again you may rejoice and I may be less concerned. Receive him then in the Lord with all joy, and hold men like him in high regard because he came close to death for the work of Christ, risking his life to fulfill what was lacking in your service to me. (LSB)

Summary: Before Timothy sets out for Philippi, Epaphroditus, a messenger of the congregation who had been sent with a gift for Paul's need, is to return home immediately without waiting to learn the result of the trial. The apostle focuses on this member of the Philippian church, not only in order to inform them of what has happened to their brother and to explain his return with the letter itself, but to offer them still another striking example of the self-giving service that was originally exemplified by the Savior (2:5–8). Thus he provides still another godly example (in addition to Timothy) of the way the Philippians should imitate Christ in their selfless giving for others.

2:25 Ἀναγκαῖον δὲ ἡγησάμην Ἐπαφρόδιτον τὸν ἀδελφὸν καὶ συνεργὸν καὶ συστρατιώτην μου, ὑμῶν δὲ ἀπόστολον καὶ λειτουργὸν τῆς χρείας μου, πέμψαι πρὸς ὑμᾶς,

Ἀναγκαῖον. Substantival adjective functioning as the direct object of ἡγησάμην. As a substantive the adjective should be translated as "a necessity" (Sumney, 63).

δὲ. Signals development from discussing Timothy to discussing Epaphroditus. Its combination with the fronting of Ἀναγκαῖον and the switch to an aorist marks a new pericope through 2:30 (Reed 1997, 391).

ἡγησάμην. Aor mid ind 1st sg ἡγέομαι. BDAG (434.2) translates ἡγέομαι as "think, consider, regard." Paul used this verb in 2:3 with a double accusative and in 2 Cor 9:5 with the same accusative (ἀναγκαῖον) and an infinitive. The aorist tense form is often explained as "epistolary" (Burton §44; BDF §334), but Porter (1995b, 36–37) and

Young (124–25) suggest that Paul composed the letter within his own time frame and the readers interpreted it accordingly. It was a mental decision he had made.

Ἐπαφρόδιτον. Accusative direct object, not of the main verb ἡγησάμην, but of the infinitive πέμψαι.

τὸν ἀδελφὸν καὶ συνεργὸν καὶ συστρατιώτην μου. Accusative nouns in apposition to Ἐπαφρόδιτον. The three terms with a single article is a valid example of the Granville Sharp Rule (Wallace, 275). The addition of μου does not invalidate the rule but modifies all three nouns.

δὲ. Indicates development from Paul's relationship to Epaphroditus to the Philippians. The translation "as well as" is appropriate.

ἀπόστολον καὶ λειτουργὸν. Accusatives in apposition to Ἐπαφρόδιτον. A hendiadys is not the best choice since the following genitive is related more to λειτουργὸν than to ἀπόστολον.

ἀπόστολον. Hawthorne (163) suggests that Paul uses ἀπόστολος to stress Epaphroditus' equality with him. However, the non-technical sense of "messenger" (cf. 2 Cor. 8:23) is better suited to the context, because Epaphroditus is described as the Philippians' ἀπόστολος.

λειτουργὸν. The term was a familiar one from Greek civic life: "one engaged in personal service, aid, assistant" (BDAG, 592.2). The background in this context is not cultic but civic officials (Rom 13:6). When a cultic association is intended for this word, the context so indicates (Rom 15:16; Heb 1:7; 8:2; and 2:17). Sumney (64) suggests both cultic and personal connotations. While this may possibly have been in Paul's mind, cultic associations probably would not have come to his readers' minds.

τῆς χρείας. Objective genitive.

πέμψαι. Aor act inf πέμπω (epexegetical, explaining Ἀναγκαῖον).

πρὸς ὑμᾶς. Direction. The location of this infinitive and its complement at the end of the sentence is due to Paul's giving prominence not to his sending but to the one he sent, Epaphroditus.

2:26 ἐπειδὴ ἐπιποθῶν ἦν πάντας ὑμᾶς καὶ ἀδημονῶν, διότι ἠκούσατε ὅτι ἠσθένησεν.

ἐπειδὴ. Causal conjunction that is used only here in Philippians, because Paul will soon utilize the normally causal ὅτι as "that." See the following use of διότι.

Analysis of Philippians Two

ἐπιποθῶν. Pres act ptc masc nom sg ἐπιποθέω. With ἦν this forms a periphrastic construction. The verb is especially strong with the prefix ἐπι- augmenting the "desire." This verb can be translated as "to have a strong desire for someth[ing], with implication of need, long for, desire" (BDAG, 377) with the accusative of the person/thing longed for. Paul used the same verb to express his own longing for the Philippians in 1:8 (see also 2 Cor 5:2; 9:14; Rom 11:1; 1 Thess 3:6; 2 Tim 1:4).

ἦν. Impf act ind 3rd sg εἰμί.

πάντας ὑμᾶς. Accusative direct object of ἐπιποθῶν. THGNT mentions that ℵ* A C D I(vid) 69 1424 add ἰδεῖν. The LSB footnote here states: "An early ms reads *to see you all.*" This appears to be a scribal clarification (Metzger, 546–47).

ἀδημονῶν. Pres act ptc masc nom sg ἀδημονέω, with ἦν forming a second periphrastic construction. The participle is not adjectival (O'Brien 1991, 334 n31) because the preceding καὶ connects it to the first periphrastic participle. It is used only here and in reference to Jesus' being "distressed" and "troubled" in the garden (Matt 26:37/Mark 14:33).

διότι. Causal conjunction introducing a causal clause (ME, 250–51). It is used only here in Philippians instead of the more common ὅτι (21 times) since the next ὅτι is not causal but introduces a content clause ("that").

ἠκούσατε. Aor act ind 2nd pl ἀκούω.

ὅτι. Introduces the clausal complement of ἠκούσατε.

ἠσθένησεν. Aor act ind 3rd pl ἀσθενέω. While this verb can convey being "weak" (2 Cor 11:29; 12:10), here and in numerous other places it means "to suffer a debilitating illness, be sick" (BDAG, 142.1).

2:27 καὶ γὰρ ἠσθένησεν παραπλήσιον θανάτῳ· ἀλλ' ὁ θεὸς ἠλέησεν αὐτόν, οὐκ αὐτὸν δὲ μόνον ἀλλὰ καὶ ἐμέ, ἵνα μὴ λύπην ἐπὶ λύπην σχῶ.

καὶ γάρ. Ascensive καὶ and explanatory γάρ. BDF (§452.3) translates this phrase as "yes even, in which each particle retains its own force."

ἠσθένησεν. Aor act ind 3rd sg ἀσθενέω.

παραπλήσιον. *Hapax legomenon* adjective, although a similar *hapax legomenon* adverb παραπλησίως ("likewise") is in Heb 2:14.

Abbott-Smith (342) translates it as "coming near." With the neuter ending, the adjective functions improperly as a preposition (BDF §184).

θανάτῳ. Dative complement of παραπλήσιον (note μέσον γενεᾶς in 2:15). BDAG (770) and BDF (§184) cite several extra-biblical examples of this construction.

ἀλλ'. Conjunction that indicates the strong contrast between being near death and life. THGNT includes the word without eliding the final α.

ὁ θεὸς. Nominative subject of ἠλέησεν.

ἠλέησεν. Aor act ind 3rd sg ἐλεέω. There are over 400 ἐλεο-cognates in the LXX, most often associated with the Hebrew חֶסֶד (*hesed*) and חֵן (*hen*) meaning mercy/kindness. OT associations of this verb with God inform its meaning here.

αὐτόν. Accusative direct object of ἠλέησεν. The pronoun refers to Epaphroditus.

οὐκ αὐτόν . . . μόνον. Accusative direct object of ἠλέησεν preceded by a negative particle.

ἀλλὰ. Second strong adversative conjunction, marking a point-counterpoint set.

καὶ. Adverbial ("also").

ἐμέ. Accusative direct object of ἠλέησεν.

ἵνα. Introduces a result clause.

λύπην. Accusative direct object of σχῶ. Paul's only other "sorrow" is in Rom 9:2.

ἐπὶ λύπην. The preposition ἐπὶ serves as a "marker of addition to what is already in existence, to, in addition to" (BDAG, 365.7). BDF (§235.3; §208.2) suggests the meaning, "to follow without ceasing."

σχῶ. Aor act subj 1st sg ἔχω. Subjunctive with ἵνα. BDAG (421.7.a.β) proposes the translation, "experience something, have."

2:28 σπουδαιοτέρως οὖν ἔπεμψα αὐτόν, ἵνα ἰδόντες αὐτὸν πάλιν χαρῆτε κἀγὼ ἀλυπότερος ὦ.

σπουδαιοτέρως. Comparative of the adverb σπουδαίως. While BDAG (939.1) translates "with special urgency," the context may suggest "more hastily than I would have done otherwise," or "with the greater dispatch" (Vincent, 76), or "as promptly as I can" (Hawthorne,

119). The fronting of the adverb increases the intensity of the comparative. The adverb is also in Luke 7:4; 2 Tim 1:17; and Tit 3:13.

οὖν. This particle indicates that the sending of Epaphroditus is a result of the Philippians' concern for him (2:26–27).

ἔπεμψα. Aor act ind 1st sg πέμπω. Most interpreters refer to this as an "epistolary aorist," but see comments on ἡγησάμην in 2:25.

αὐτόν. Accusative direct object of ἔπεμψα. The antecedent is Epaphroditus.

ἵνα. Introduces a purpose clause.

ἰδόντες. Aor act ptc masc nom pl ὁράω (temporal).

αὐτόν. Accusative direct object of ἰδόντες. Antecedent remains Epaphroditus.

πάλιν. If this adverb is taken with the preceding participle, it means "see him again" (KJV and all modern translations). Hawthorne (119) and Silva (162), however, prefer it with χαρῆτε (see also Lightfoot, 124; O'Brien 1991, 339; Fee, 280 n39; Tyndale only), since Paul puts the adverb normally before the verb.

χαρῆτε. Aor act subj 2nd pl χαίρω. Subjunctive with ἵνα.

κἀγώ. Crasis for καὶ plus ἐγώ. Subject of ὦ.

ἀλυπότερος. Predicate adjective. Comparative of a *hapax legomenon* adjective with an *alpha* privative. The simple form of the adjective would mean "free from anxiety" (BDAG 48), so the comparative would be "less anxious (than now)" (NIV), or "relieved of anxiety" (Hawthorne, 114; Silva, 162). Fee (281 n40) prefers "may have less sorrow" (see KJV, JB).

ὦ. Pres act subj 1st sg εἰμί. Subjunctive with ἵνα. This combination appears only here in the NT and the LXX.

2:29 προσδέχεσθε οὖν αὐτὸν ἐν κυρίῳ μετὰ πάσης χαρᾶς καὶ τοὺς τοιούτους ἐντίμους ἔχετε,

προσδέχεσθε. Pres mid impv 2nd pl προσδέχομαι. The imperfective aspect, as in 2:18, raises the prominence given to Epaphroditus as the subject in this section (Reed 1997, 391). Rom 16:2 uses the same verb for the Romans to receive Phoebe.

οὖν. Indicates a transition from indicatives/subjunctives to an imperative, the first since 2:18.

αὐτόν. Accusative direct object of προσδέχεσθε.

ἐν κυρίῳ. The options for the meaning of this phrase range from sphere to manner if the phrase modifies the imperative προσδέχεσθε. If the phrase relates back to the previous word, αὐτόν, the sense could be "as a brother in the Lord" (O'Brien 1991, 340–41; GNB), and the following prepositional phrase would modify the imperative.

μετὰ πάσης χαρᾶς. Manner. "Receive him . . . with all joy."

καί. Connects the imperatives.

τοὺς τοιούτους. Direct object of ἔχετε in a double accusative construction.

ἐντίμους. Complement in a double accusative object-complement construction.

ἔχετε. Pres act impv 2nd pl ἔχω. The many nuances of this verb are often governed by its collocation with other forms. When ἔχω is followed by a direct object and predicate accusative, BDAG (421.6) defines it as "have an opinion about someth[ing], consider, look upon, view" (see also BDF §157.3). Since the second imperative in this verse is preceded by a direct object, it forms a chiasm with the first imperative that is followed by a direct object:

verb – προσδέχεσθε   direct object – αὐτόν
direct object – τοὺς τοιούτους   verb – ἔχετε

2:30 ὅτι διὰ τὸ ἔργον Χριστοῦ μέχρι θανάτου ἤγγισεν παραβολευσάμενος τῇ ψυχῇ, ἵνα ἀναπληρώσῃ τὸ ὑμῶν ὑστέρημα τῆς πρός με λειτουργίας.

ὅτι. Introduces a causal clause providing the reason for the imperatives in 2:29.

διὰ τὸ ἔργον. Cause. The translation "for the sake of" is preferred.

Χριστοῦ. Subjective genitive. This combination of Χριστοῦ in the genitive with the head noun ἔργον is unique in the NT, although the basic idea is often found. "The reading κυρίου (ℵ A P Ψ 33 81 syrh cop-bo arm eth) may have been substituted for Χριστοῦ by copyists who recollected the expression τὸ ἔργον τοῦ κυρίου in 1 Cor 15:58 and 16:10" (Metzger, 547). The unique expression, ἔργον Χριστοῦ, with early and wide support ($\mathfrak{P}^{46}$ B F G), is also the more difficult reading and more probable, also affirmed by THGNT.

μέχρι θανάτου. Temporal. Μέχρι is an unexpected preposition since Paul used the equivalent παραπλήσιον θανάτῳ in 2:27. This choice could be a deliberate play on 2:8, where Jesus became "obedient μέχρι θανάτου." Fee (282 n47) thinks that the Philippians would "have heard the echo."

ἤγγισεν. Aor act ind 3rd sg ἐγγίζω. While the verb contains the idea of "drawing near to" (Abbott-Smith, 127), it was often used transitively with prepositions like μέχρι to describe Jesus' drawing near to Jerusalem also to face death (Luke 19:41; 21:20, 28; 24:15).

παραβολευσάμενος. Aor mid ptc masc nom sg παραβολεύομαι (means). *Hapax legomenon*. Reumann (432) raises the question if Paul coined this word, but BDAG (759) states that the verb is the "passive use of παραβάλλω" and cites several Attic examples. See also LXX Ruth 2:16; Prov 2:2; 2 Macc 14:38. The reading in NA/UBS and THGNT, παραβολευσάμενος, has excellent manuscript support ($\mathfrak{P}^{46}$ ℵ A B D F G copsa). A variant reading, παραβουλευσαμενος, has later support (C Ψ 33 1739 𝔐 syr), with the only difference being the inclusion of an *upsilon*. The earlier word means that Epaphroditus "gambled with his life" (Lightfoot, 124). The later reading (TR/KJV) connotes only self-sacrifice.

τῇ ψυχῇ. Dative complement of παραβολευσάμενος. BDAG (759) documents the extra-biblical use of the dative with παραβολεύομαι. The article is used as a possessive pronoun. The noun does not describe the "soul" but "earthly life" (BDAG, 1098–99.1.b).

ἵνα. Introduces a purpose clause, but it is "close to result" (Reed 1997, 325).

ἀναπληρώσῃ. Aor act subj 3rd sg ἀναπληρόω. Subjunctive with ἵνα. BDAG (70) places this usage under "fill a gap, replace" with 1 Cor 16:17. "Epaphroditus made up for a lack or absence on the part of the Philippians" (Reumann, 433).

τὸ . . . ὑστέρημα. Accusative direct object of ἀναπληρώσῃ.

ὑμῶν. Subjective genitive.

τῆς . . . λειτουργίας. Objective genitive, related to ὑστέρημα. For the noun, see comments in 2:17 and its cognate in 2:25. BDF (§168.1) describes this "concatenation of genitives" as an example where the governing genitive (ὑμῶν) precedes the dependent genitive (τῆς . . . λειτουργίας).

Paul's readiness to credit his martyrdom to the account of the Philippians; Timothy's unselfish service for others; and Epaphroditus' devotion to mission at risk to his health all display the selfless care for others commended in 2:1–4 and reinforced by the example of Christ's self-emptying in 2:5–8 (see Bruce, 98).

3

Analysis of Philippians Three

Philippians 3:1

1 Finally, my brothers, rejoice in the Lord. To write the same things to you does not cause me hesitation and it is a protection for you.

Finally, my brothers, rejoice in the Lord. To write the same things *again* is no trouble to me, and it is a safeguard for you. (LSB)

Summary: Although it looks like Paul is heading toward a conclusion, this call to rejoice offers an opportunity for additional exhortations of a most serious nature.

3:1 Τὸ λοιπόν, ἀδελφοί μου, χαίρετε ἐν κυρίῳ. τὰ αὐτὰ γράφειν ὑμῖν ἐμοὶ μὲν οὐκ ὀκνηρόν, ὑμῖν δὲ ἀσφαλές.

Τὸ λοιπόν. Neuter accusative adjective functioning adverbially. When used this way, these adjectives are usually articular (Wallace, 293). Paul frequently initiates his conclusions with λοιπὸν or τὸ λοιπὸν (1 Thess 4:1, 2; 2 Thess 3:1; 2 Cor 13:11; Eph 6:10). In 3:2 the letter is interrupted, and Paul resumes his farewell at 4:8 with τὸ λοιπόν. The best translation is "furthermore," "finally," or "henceforth" (Moule, 161–62).

ἀδελφοί μου. While this nominative of direct address conveys affection, it is, as in its other uses (1:12; 3:13; 3:17; 4:1 with μου; 4:8), a transitional marker of focus (Reed 1997, 262 n397). The noun ἀδελφοί is used "in the collective sense of *brothers and sisters*" (CGELNT, 6).

χαίρετε. Pres act impv 2nd pl χαίρω. Some have taken this as a stereotyped greeting such as "hail" or "farewell" (Abbott-Smith, 478.2). This is doubtful because of the adjunct PP ἐν κυρίῳ and because the following words make more sense if this is a command to "rejoice." The idea of rejoicing is a theme throughout the book (1:18; 2:17, 18, 28; 4:4), and the possibility that the verb should suddenly acquire a new meaning here is unlikely (Bockmuehl, 178).

ἐν κυρίῳ. The language of indwelling is a way of highlighting the intimate nature of the relationship (see BDAG, 327.4.c).

τὰ αὐτά. The article functions as a nominalizer, changing the pronoun αὐτά into the direct object of γράφειν.

γράφειν. Pres act inf γράφω (substantival, subject of the implied verb; see Wallace, 601). "3:1a is part of a succession of imperatives begun in 2:29 and ending in 3:2. 3:1b (τὰ αὐτὰ γράφειν) punctuates these imperatives as an epistolary formula of disclosure" (Reed 1997, 392).

ὑμῖν. Dative indirect object of γράφειν.

ἐμοί. Dative of advantage (BDF §188).

μέν. Point-counterpoint with following δέ. The particle μέν is untranslated and "signals a forward-pointing correlation with an element introduced by δέ" (Runge, 55).

ὀκνηρόν. Predicate adjective. It is neuter in agreement with the entire infinitive subject clause. Most translations use "burdensome" or "troublesome." The other two NT occurrences mean "hesitant" (Matt 25:26, hesitant servant; Rom 12:11, not hesitant in zeal). BDAG (702.2) suggests "causing hesitation, reluctance." MM (444–45) lists papyrus examples where the cognate verb and adverb mean "without hesitation." Here ὀκνηρόν means "hesitating" rather than "troublesome" or "bothersome" (Reumann, 454).

ὑμῖν. Dative of advantage.

δέ. Signals shift in focus from ἐμοί to ὑμῖν. The particle is simply additive, not contrastive. See comment on μέν.

ἀσφαλές. Predicate adjective. Its use in Heb 6:19 as "firm" and in Acts 21:34; 22:30; 25:26 as "certain" reflects its meaning in Attic Greek (see BDAG, 147.1&2; GE, 326). Its meaning in 3:1 as "safe" reflects its usage in LXX 1 Sam 8:2 and Josephus, *Ant* 3.41 (BDAG, 147.3).

Philippians 3:2–6

2 Watch out for dogs, watch out for evil workers, watch out for those who mutilate the flesh. 3 For we are the circumcision, the ones who worship by the Spirit of God, who boast in Christ Jesus, and who do not put confidence in the flesh—4 although indeed I also had confidence in the flesh. If anyone else thinks he has grounds for confidence in the flesh, I have to a greater degree: 5 circumcised on the eighth day; of the race of Israel, of the tribe of Benjamin, a Hebrew born of Hebrews; regarding the law, a Pharisee; 6 regarding zeal, pursuing the church; regarding the righteousness that is in the law, blameless.

Beware of the dogs! Beware of the evil workers! Beware of the mutilation! For we are the circumcision, who worship by the Spirit of God and boast in Christ Jesus and put no confidence in the flesh, although I myself might have confidence even in the flesh. If anyone else has a mind to put confidence in the flesh, I far more: circumcised the eighth day, of the nation of Israel, of the tribe of Benjamin, a Hebrew of Hebrews; as to the Law, a Pharisee; as to zeal, a persecutor of the church; as to the righteousness which is in the Law, found blameless. (LSB)

Summary: After another call to rejoice, Paul's tone changes to one of warning. While he had proclaimed salvation by grace, some Jewish opponents taught that a person must earn credit by deeds of the law. Since salvation belonged to the Jews, people must be circumcised and, as it were, become Jews. Here, Paul excoriates these Jewish teachers and calls them three names, each of which is carefully chosen to throw their claims back upon themselves. While some have thought his language intemperate, the strong names reflect how deeply Paul felt about the gospel of grace. Then follows the most autobiographical passage in all the Pauline corpus.

3:2 Βλέπετε τοὺς κύνας, βλέπετε τοὺς κακοὺς ἐργάτας, βλέπετε τὴν κατατομήν.

Βλέπετε ... βλέπετε ... βλέπετε. "The threefold repetition of this verb, the use of alliteration (κυνάς, κακούς, κατατομήν), and the studied irony of the passage make this section a striking example of Paul's rhetorical power" (Silva, 152). This rhetorical figure of repetition is called *anaphora*. "The three imperative verbs precede the complement probably because the idea of 'caution' is the theme or is 'focal', not necessarily the objects of that caution (who are notably unidentified as are all of the implied opponents in the letter)" (Reed 1997, 392).

Βλέπετε. Pres act impv 2nd pl βλέπω. Kilpatrick (146–48) argues that when βλέπω is used with the accusative, it nowhere means "beware of" and that the simple meaning "consider, take note" is preferable. Kilpatrick, however, isolates the meaning of βλέπω and overlooks that the direct objects increase the urgency of the polemical warning which calls for "beware," not just "be aware of."

τοὺς κύνας. Accusative direct object of the first Βλέπετε. See both literal and metaphorical uses of κύων in GE, 1198. Dogs in antiquity were generally held in contempt as packs of scavengers (Ps 59:6, 14), not as house pets, and at best as guard dogs. A mosaic floor inside the door of a house in Pompeii has the graphic "beware the dog" (*cave canem*). Michel (TDNT 3:1101–4) suggests that Paul might have known the *logion* at Matt 7:6, "Do not give what is holy to dogs."

τοὺς κακοὺς ἐργάτας. Accusative direct object of the second βλέπετε. The noun ἐργάτης is used in some passages for those engaged in Christian ministry (Matt 9:37–38; 20:1, 2, 8; Luke 10:2; 2 Tim 2:15; see BDAG, 390.1.b). Bockmuehl (188) suggests "that there may be a deliberate pun on the opponents' claim to be doing the 'works of the Law'," a Qumran phrase (4QMMT C 27, *ma'asê ha-tôrah*).

τὴν κατατομήν. Accusative direct object of the third βλέπετε. *Hapax legomenon*. The noun does not appear in the LXX, but verb κατατέμνω is used for the forbidden practice of cutting the skin (Lev 19:28; 21:5; Deut 14:1). The noun is a *paranomasia* on περιτομή in 3:3, chosen to maintain the alliteration. Vincent (93) suggests that three classes are intended: κύνας, heathen; κακοὺς ἐργάτας, those in 1:15; and κατατομήν, Jews. LSB employs an exclamation: "Beware of the mutilation!" According to Bruce (104), Paul "denounces ... those who visited Gentile churches and insisted that circumcision was an indispensable condition of their being justified in God's sight."

3:3 ἡμεῖς γάρ ἐσμεν ἡ περιτομή, οἱ πνεύματι θεοῦ λατρεύοντες καὶ καυχώμενοι ἐν Χριστῷ Ἰησοῦ καὶ οὐκ ἐν σαρκὶ πεποιθότες,

ἡμεῖς. The presence of the personal pronoun with the monolectic verb is for emphasis. This is the only use of this pronoun in the book.

γάρ. Explains κατατομήν in 3:2.

ἐσμεν. Pres act ind 1st pl εἰμί. This is the only use of this verb form in the book. The unique collocation of ἡμεῖς and ἐσμεν calls attention to the truly circumcised.

ἡ περιτομή. Predicate nominative. The noun parallels τὴν κατατομήν in 3:2 and defines the groups over against each other, one being the false circumcision, only the "cutting," while "we" (ἡμεῖς) are the "true" (implied) circumcision. This is a use of "the abstract for the concrete" (BDAG, 807.2.b) referring to "the circumcised."

οἱ ... λατρεύοντες. Pres act ptc masc nom pl λατρεύω (substantival, in apposition to ἡμεῖς). The verb carries the general sense of "serve" in earlier Greek but with an instrumental dative it becomes the service of "worship" (GE, 1217). Interestingly, the CSB changed the HCSB translation of "serve" to "worship."

πνεύματι. Instrumental dative (Moule, 46). The NASB translation "who worship in the Spirit of God and glory in Christ Jesus" overlooks the distinction between the two datives, one without the preposition and the other with ἐν. Since the first dative is instrumental (Moule, 46), the ἐν plus dative is locative.

θεοῦ. Genitive of source. The formulation, οἱ λατρεύοντες πνεύματι θεοῦ, can be rendered either "the ones worshiping by God's Spirit" or "the ones worshiping God's Spirit." The verb λατρεύω is normally accompanied by the dative, hence the Spirit becomes the recipient of the worship (Hawthorne, 122). To avoid the idea of worshiping the Spirit, some scribes added another object in the dative case, θεω. Lightfoot (145) argues that λατρεύω had acquired a technical sense referring to divine worship, so one does not need to understand "God's Spirit" as the object of the worship. The verb does not have to include a direct object to convey that God is being worshiped by the Spirit. The reading of 𝔓[46] omitting θεοῦ is due to an accidental oversight.

καυχώμενοι. Pres mid ptc masc nom pl καυχάομαι (substantival, in apposition to ἡμεῖς). Wallace (281–83) considers the phrase οἱ ...

λατρεύοντες καὶ καυχώμενοι as a variant of the Granville-Sharp rule where both groups are identical.

ἐν Χριστῷ Ἰησοῦ. The language of indwelling is a way of highlighting the intimate nature of the relationship (see BDAG, 327.4.c). See ἐν κυρίῳ in 3:1.

ἐν σαρκί. Locative. In 1:22 and 24 the expression ἐν σαρκί was neutral, but here and in 3:4 it is pejorative (BDAG, 916.5, "earthly things or physical advantages"). The verb πέποιθα is usually followed by ἐπί plus dative (2 Cor 1:9), but its use with ἐν plus dative indicates that οὐκ negates ἐν σαρκί. While some grammarians suggest the use of οὐκ rather than μή with the participle reflects an earlier practice (BDF §430; MHT 1:231), this explanation is not necessary if οὐκ does not negate πεποιθότες.

πεποιθότες. Prf act ptc masc nom pl πείθω (substantival, in apposition to ἡμεῖς). Perfect with present meaning (BDF §341). The participle is substantival like λατρεύοντες καὶ καυχώμενοι because it is connected to them by a second καί and thus is governed by the same article οἱ. The stative aspect of the perfect tense form indicates a state of confidence. "The use of the perfect and pluperfect active involves what might be called grammatical metonymy, with a nominal aspect (cp. πειθώ) expressing in effect the product of persuasion which one receives; hence one can be said to get persuasion, i.e., have confidence" (CGELNT, 276.c).

3:4 καίπερ ἐγὼ ἔχων πεποίθησιν καὶ ἐν σαρκί. Εἴ τις δοκεῖ ἄλλος πεποιθέναι ἐν σαρκί, ἐγὼ μᾶλλον·

καίπερ ἐγὼ ἔχων πεποίθησιν καὶ ἐν σαρκί. As punctuated in the critical text, this is a concessive subordinate clause, not an independent sentence (as in KJV, RSV). It links and contrasts Paul's personal account in 3:4b–6 to how believers are described in 3:3. The linking words, πεποίθησιν and ἐν σαρκί, repeated from v. 3 (ἐν σαρκί πεποιθότες … πεποίθησιν καὶ ἐν σαρκί), form a chiasm.

καίπερ. Concessive conjunction (BDF §425.1; Robertson, 1129). Each of its five occurrences in the NT is used with a participle (see Heb 5:8; 7:5; 12:17; 2 Pet 1:12). The suffix -περ strengthens the meaning to "although indeed" (Ellicott, 80).

ἐγώ. Paul uses the first person singular pronoun 53 times in the letter, but only 4 times in the nominative case (see 3:4b, 13; 4:11). The use of the pronoun twice in this verse adds intensity to his autobiographical account.

ἔχων. Pres act ptc masc nom sg ἔχω (concessive).

πεποίθησιν. Accusative direct object of ἔχων. The word means actual present confidence, not merely grounds for confidence. A Pauline word (2 Cor 1:15; 3:4; 8:22; 10:2; Eph 3:12) that was "condemned by the Atticists" (Abbott-Smith, 353).

καί. Functions as "a marker of an additive relation which is not coordinate—'and, and also, also, in addition, even'" (LN 89.93). This word implies Paul's one-time confidence in the flesh was "also" like those he is criticizing.

ἐν σαρκί. Locative. "The expression ἐν σαρκί extends beyond περιτομή to all external privileges" (Lightfoot, 145).

Εἴ. Conditional particle introducing the protasis of a first class conditional clause.

τις ... ἄλλος. The indefinite pronoun τις functions as the subject of δοκεῖ and is modified by the adjective ἄλλος. Sumney (73) suggests that "ἄλλος may be construed as a substantive, to be understood as ἄνθρωπος is in the phrase τις ἄνθρωπος. The meaning is not changed either way."

δοκεῖ. Pres act ind 3rd sg δοκέω.

πεποιθέναι. Prf act inf πείθω (indirect discourse). The infinitive is "the object of a verb of saying or of thinking" (Burton §390). The subject of the infinitive is not expressed, because it is the same as the subject of δοκεῖ (BDF §396). "St Paul is using an *argumentum ad hominem;* in his own language, he is for the moment 'speaking foolishly,' is 'speaking not after the Lord,' 2 Cor. 11:17" (Lightfoot, 146).

ἐγὼ μᾶλλον. Apodosis of the conditional clause. It could be translated, "I rather," or "I to a greater degree."

3:5 περιτομῇ ὀκταήμερος, ἐκ γένους Ἰσραήλ, φυλῆς Βενιαμίν, Ἑβραῖος ἐξ Ἑβραίων, κατὰ νόμον Φαρισαῖος,

Seven items follow each other in 3:5–6 with no conjunctions. This asyndeton is similar to the practice in inscriptions. Hellerman (124,

162) describes this style as "syntactical economy."

περιτομῇ. Dative of reference (BDF §197; Robertson, 523).

ὀκταήμερος. *Hapax legomenon*. Predicate adjective, modifying ἐγώ at the end of 3:4. Literally "an eight-day-er" (Robertson, 657). There is no occurrence of this word in previous or contemporary Greek. Did Paul coin it? Later patristic writers evidently got it from Paul (PGL, 947).

ἐκ γένους. Source. BDAG (194.3) has "nation, people," but the English word "nation" carries political associations, and the term "people" suggests the Greek λαός, which could include proselytes. Racial descent is intended (O'Brien 1991, 370; Abbott-Smith, 91.3). LN (10.1) references Mark 7:26: "the woman was Greek in culture, of the Syrophoenician race" (τῷ γένει).

Ἰσραήλ. Epexegetical genitive. Ἰσραήλ is an indeclinable noun that refers to the descendants of the patriarch Jacob/Israel (TDNT 3:383–84).

φυλῆς. This genitive is governed by the same preposition ἐκ that appears in the previous phrase ἐκ γένους Ἰσραήλ.

Βενιαμίν. Epexegetical genitive (see Ἰσραήλ above). It is included in Paul's pedigree because Benjamin was one of the tribes that returned from captivity.

Ἑβραῖος. Predicate nominative. While Ἰουδαῖος is contrasted with Ἕλλην (Rom 1:16), Ἑβραῖος is contrasted with Ἑλληνιστής (Acts 6:1). The former terms convey a contrast of race and religion, whereas the latter two convey a difference of language and customs. When used of a Jewish person it is primarily a linguistic term, referring to one who knew the Hebrew language, even if it was not their only language. The term Ἑβραῖοι is used this way in the Greek Maccabean literature (see 2 Macc 7:31; 11:13; 15:37; 4 Macc 4:11; 5:2; 8:2; 9:6, 18). For further discussion, see NIDNTTE (2:73–75).

ἐξ Ἑβραίων. Source. The genitive Ἑβραίων is not the Hebrew superlative as in Ἁγία Ἁγίων (Heb 9:3), which many translations convey as "Hebrew of Hebrews" (NIV and most versions; e.g., NLT: "a real Hebrew if there ever was one!"). Nor is it a genitive "par excellence" (contra Wallace, 103 n84; and Sumney, 75). The preposition ἐξ denotes source, i.e., Paul's parents ("Hebrew born of Hebrews" [CSB], or "a

Hebrew born of Hebrew parents" [NJB]).

κατὰ νόμον. Reference. The preposition κατὰ with the accusative in this and the next three expressions "denotes a relationship to something, with respect to, in relation to" (BDAG, 513.B.6) and is also used with this sense in 1:12. This is the first of three parallel constructions with κατὰ and an anarthrous object followed by a predicate nominative or adjective.

Φαρισαῖος. Predicate nominative. The nominatives in this list are related to ἐγὼ in 3:4 by an implied equative verb like εἰμί. The noun appears 98 times in the NT, but this is the only example outside the Gospels and Acts (NIDNTTE, 4:593–94).

3:6 κατὰ ζῆλος διώκων τὴν ἐκκλησίαν, κατὰ δικαιοσύνην τὴν ἐν νόμῳ γενόμενος ἄμεμπτος.

κατὰ ζῆλος. Reference. The noun ζῆλος is usually masculine, but here and in 2 Cor 9:2 it is neuter (Abbott-Smith, 195, "late Greek"; see also GE, 891.2). The corrector of both Codex Sinaiticus and Codex Claromontanus changed it to the neuter ζῆλον. While Paul can use the word in its negative sense of "jealously, envy" (Rom 13:13), here it is used in its positive, although misguided, sense of "zeal, ardor" (BDAG, 427.1.2; see also Rom 10:2).

διώκων. Pres act ptc masc nom sg διώκω (substantival, functioning as a predicate nominative). It usually appears with an article, although the anarthrous form is not rare. Turner (151) sees an OT/LXX influence in these constructions. While not denying that the verb conveys the sense of "persecute" in a number of contexts, its clear meaning of "pursue" in 3:14 (κατὰ σκοπὸν διώκω) suggests that it is the nuance of "pursuing the church" to persecute it that is in Paul's mind in 3:6. This nuance then offers a powerful rhetorical contrast in these verses between what he had once wrongly pursued and what he now rightly pursues.

τὴν ἐκκλησίαν. Accusative direct object of διώκων. Western witnesses (F G Vulgate) expand the expression διώκων τὴν ἐκκλησίαν to διώκων τὴν ἐκκλησίαν θεοῦ, an apparent effort to harmonize Phil 3:6 with Gal 1:13. This is an example of the term ἐκκλησία being used to describe something wider than a local assembly (BDAG, 304.3.c, citing

Acts 9:31; 1 Cor 6:4; 12:28; etc.).

κατὰ δικαιοσύνην. Reference. This is the last of the seven autobiographical expressions and the third with κατά. BAGD (2.a) translates the noun δικαιοσύνη as "fulfilling the divine statutes ... the practice of piety originating from ... uprightness." While this substantive with its cognates has numerous shades of meaning in the NT, its meaning here is determined by the clause that follows.

τήν. The article functions as an adjectivizer, changing the PP ἐν νόμῳ into an attributive modifier of δικαιοσύνην. See also 3:9, δικαιοσύνην τὴν ἐκ νόμου.

ἐν νόμῳ. Locative, not instrumental. It is not within the scope of this volume to enter into the recent discussion about "covenantal nomism" in Second Temple Judaism. The language here limits νόμῳ to the Mosaic Law set within God's covenant with Moses and Israel and its sign of circumcision (Reumann, 487).

γενόμενος. Aor mid ptc masc nom sg γίνομαι (attributive). BDAG (199.7) translates the verb γίνομαι as "to come into a certain state or possess certain characteristics, to be, prove to be, turn out to be." The verb εἰμί stresses the state (see ἦν in the next verse); the verb γίνομαι stresses coming into that state.

ἄμεμπτος. Predicate adjective, "spotless." This is not a false boast, for it is what Yahweh asked of Abraham in LXX Gen 17:1: γίνου ἄμεμπτος. This is what Yahweh also requires in LXX Ps 14:2a: πορευόμενος ἄμωμος καὶ ἐργαζόμενος δικαιοσύνην. Of the seven asyndetic expressions in 3:5–6, the first four focus on Paul's birth and ancestry, while the last three describe his religious practices before his conversion (Sumney, 75). See further discussion of this word in 2:15.

Philippians 3:7–11

> [7] The things that were gain to me, these I consider to be a loss because of Christ. [8] Even more than that, I continue considering everything to be a loss because of the surpassing value of knowing Christ Jesus my Lord. Because of him I suffered the loss of all things and consider them garbage, in order that I may gain Christ [9] and be found in him, not having a righteousness of my own that is from the law, but one that is through faith in Christ—the

righteousness from God based on faith. ¹⁰ My goal is to know him and the power of his resurrection and the participation in his sufferings, being conformed to his death, ¹¹ assuming that I will somehow reach the resurrection from the dead.

¶ But whatever things were gain to me, those things I have counted as loss for the sake of Christ. More than that, I count all things to be loss because of the surpassing value of knowing Christ Jesus my Lord, for whom I have suffered the loss of all things, and count them but rubbish so that I may gain Christ and be found in Him, not having a righteousness of my own which is from *the* Law, but that which is through faith in Christ, the righteousness which *is* from God upon faith, that I may know Him and the power of His resurrection and the fellowship of His sufferings, being conformed to His death, in order that I may attain to the resurrection from the dead. (LSB)

Summary: Continuing his personal testimony Paul describes the total reorientation of his life because of his encounter with Jesus the Messiah. He employs accounting terminology (κέρδη, ζημίαν) and antithetic parallelism as he emphasizes the total re-alignment of his pre-Christian world view. He then states that his supreme goal is to know Christ fully and then expands this goal in terms of knowing the power of His resurrection as he participates in Christ's sufferings which every believer must experience. Employing the analogies of dying and rising, he indicates that this deeper relationship with Jesus is to be continually conformed to His death. Paul also yearned for the day when he would be raised from the dead, for only then will the redemption Christ has provided be complete and his knowledge of Christ become perfect. Although he looks forward to resurrection, the exact path by which he will reach it is not clear. As he was not clear in what he expected in chapter one, here he is not clear that he expects martyrdom or some other kind of death. Or will he be alive at the parousia?

The critical Greek texts, including THGNT, view 3:2–11 as one paragraph, but I have chosen to break the paragraph at 3:7 because of the change to a different stage of Paul's experience.

3:7 [Ἀλλ'] ἅτινα ἦν μοι κέρδη, ταῦτα ἥγημαι διὰ τὸν Χριστὸν ζημίαν.

The two clauses of 3:7 are finely balanced, each with a fronted pronoun, a predicate, an adjunct, and a direct object.
ἅτινα   ἦν   μοι   κέρδη,
ταῦτα   ἥγημαι   διὰ τὸν Χριστὸν   ζημίαν.

Ἀλλ'. The conjunction is bracketed in NA²⁸ and UBS⁵. 𝔓⁴⁶, 61 vid, ℵ* A G lack it, while B D ℵ² TR include it, as does THGNT with neither a bracket nor with the elided final α. The verse seems to demand a transitional particle, but this may have led scribes to add a conjunction, and asyndeton (BDF §462, §494) is not uncommon in Paul (see 3:17; 4:2). Fee (311 n1) argues against its inclusion although "the scribes have correctly read the context, which implies a contrast." "The insertion of αλλα ("but") at the beginning of this verse appears to be a scribal addition, intended to mark a contrast between Paul's behavior before becoming a Christian and his behavior afterwards" (Comfort).

ἅτινα. Nominative neuter plural subject of ἦν. This relative pronoun refers to the seven privileges of 3:5–6. The indefinite relative pronoun ὅστις is often equivalent to the simple relative pronoun ὅς (BDAG, 730.3). BDF (§293) states that the two are "no longer clearly distinguished in the NT" (also Wallace, 343–45).

ἦν. Impf act ind 3rd sg εἰμί. The neuter plural ἅτινα takes a singular verb, as it does in its four other occurrences in the NT (John 21:25; Gal 4:24; 5:19; Col 3:23).

μοι. Dative of advantage.

κέρδη. Predicate nominative in agreement with the plural subject. The anarthrous noun stresses the quality of "gain" rather than some indefinite idea like "a gain." According to BDAG (541), this noun refers to "something advantageous." It is used elsewhere only in 1:21 and Tit 1:11.

ταῦτα. Accusative direct object of ἥγημαι in an object-complement double accusative construction, fronted in the clause for emphasis. The demonstrative pronoun functions anaphorically by referring back to the seven privileges of 3:5–6 through the relative pronoun ἅτινα.

ἥγημαι. Prf mid ind 1st sg ἡγέομαι. The perfect tense here "grammaticalizes the speaker's conception of the verbal process as a state or condition" (Porter 1989, 257). That this perfect tense form cannot be temporal (i.e., past action with present results) is evident from the only other use of the perfect form of this verb in Acts 26:2, where Paul says to Agrippa: "I consider myself fortunate" (ἥγημαι ἐμαυτὸν μακάριον). One should note the shift to the present tense form (ἡγοῦμαι) twice in 3:8, where Paul regards his values as a process.

διὰ τὸν Χριστόν. Cause (BDAG (225.B.2.a; Fee, 315 n8; Robertson, 583–84). "Paul's threefold use of διά in verses 7–8 indicates the reason for which he has counted his former benefits as nothing" (Silva, 168).

ζημίαν. Complement in a double accusative object-complement construction. The singular noun conveys "one great loss" (O'Brien 1991, 385).

3:8 ἀλλὰ μενοῦνγε καὶ ἡγοῦμαι πάντα ζημίαν εἶναι διὰ τὸ ὑπερέχον τῆς γνώσεως Χριστοῦ Ἰησοῦ τοῦ κυρίου μου, δι' ὃν τὰ πάντα ἐζημιώθην, καὶ ἡγοῦμαι σκύβαλα, ἵνα Χριστὸν κερδήσω

ἀλλά. Conjunction that fulfills the contrastive function of the uncertain Ἀλλ' at the beginning of 3:7.

μενοῦνγε. Emphatic conjunction (Wallace, 673).

καί. Adverbial ("also"). The conjunction further strengthens the cumulative contrastive effect of three words at the beginning of 3:8.

ἡγοῦμαι. Pres mid ind 1st sg ἡγέομαι. The imperfective aspect with the adverbial καί and contrasted with the perfect tense form of this verb in 3:7 conveys a continuous *Aktionsart*. The aspect of the present tense is "continue to consider" (O'Brien 1991, 386). "The transition may be viewed as explanatory or even mildly corrective: 'Do not infer from what I have just said that my decision was limited or temporary—there is much more to it'" (Silva, 168).

πάντα. Functions both as the accusative direct object of ἡγοῦμαι and as the subject of the infinitive εἶναι.

ζημίαν. Predicate accusative. The noun ζημίαν stands in predicate relation to the adjective πάντα. Both terms are joined by the infinitive εἶναι.

εἶναι. Pres act inf εἰμί (indirect discourse).

διὰ τὸ ὑπερέχον. Cause. See comments on διὰ τὸν Χριστόν in 3:7.

ὑπερέχον is pres act ptc neut acc sg ὑπερέχω, "to exceed, be more prominent" (GE, 2201; substantival). Burton (§425) explains that "a neuter participle with the article is sometimes equivalent to an abstract noun," while BDF (§263.2) asserts that the use of the participle makes the idea more graphic than using the noun ὑπεροχή.

τῆς γνώσεως Χριστοῦ Ἰησοῦ τοῦ κυρίου μου. In this genitive chain, or "concatenated genitives," each successive genitive relates directly to the one that precedes it (BDF §168).

τῆς γνώσεως. Attributed genitive (Wallace, 90), in which the substantive ὑπερέχον functions as an adjective attributing its quality to the following genitive. There has been much debate about the Pauline meaning of γνῶσις, against the background of Hellenistic religion. The gloss in BDAG (203.2) about Paul's "personal acquaintance w[ith] Christ Jesus" is generally accepted, regardless of the precise nature of that acquaintance.

Χριστοῦ Ἰησοῦ. Objective genitive.

τοῦ κυρίου. Genitive in apposition to Χριστοῦ Ἰησοῦ. "Knowing Christ Jesus consists of knowing him as Lord (cf. 2:11), the one who occupies the position of supreme auhrity in one's life" (Moore, 190).

μου. Possessive genitive.

δι' ὅν. Cause. See comments on διὰ τὸν Χριστὸν in 3:7. The antecedent of the accusative relative pronoun is Χριστοῦ Ἰησοῦ.

τὰ πάντα. Accusative direct object of ἐζημιώθην (BDF §159.2). This accusative can be called "the accusative of retained object" that is used in constructions that involve "passive with an accusative object" (Wallace, 438–39). See also καρπὸν in 1:11.

ἐζημιώθην. Aor pass ind 1st sg ζημιόω. This verb appears only in the passive voice in each of its six NT occurrences. According to BDAG (428.1), the passive voice with the accusative means to "permit oneself … to sustain loss," so that the clause δι' ὅν τὰ πάντα ἐζημιώθην could be translated as "for whose sake I forfeited everything." This is an example of a verb with a θη- middle form where a passive translation makes no sense (Decker *Reading*, 17.25).

ἡγοῦμαι. Pres mid ind 1st sg ἡγέομαι. One should supply τὰ πάντα as direct object of ἡγοῦμαι, which in turn would be an expansion of the demonstrative pronoun ταῦτα that functions as direct object of ἥγημαι in 3:7.

σκύβαλα. Complement in a double accusative object-complement construction. The plural agrees with τὰ πάντα, which functions as direct object of ἡγοῦμαι in a double accusative object-complement construction. σκύβαλα is a *hapax legomenon*, appearing in the LXX only at Sirach 27:4. LSJ (1616) translates this noun as "dung, refuse, excrement," but GE (1933) mentions also the rendering "refuse, rubbish." Lightfoot (149), citing literary sources, suggests that the plural refers to "the refuse or leavings of a feast, the food thrown away from the table." He adds that "the Judaizers spoke of themselves as banqueters seated at the Father's table, of Gentile Christians as dogs greedily snatching up the refuse meat which fell therefrom. St Paul has reversed the image. The Judaizers are themselves the dogs (ver. 2); the meats served to the sons of God are spiritual meats; the ordinances, which the formalists value so highly, are the mere refuse of the feast." In either case, the σκύβαλα is food refuse, and Lightfoot's suggestion avoids the shocking figure of "crap" (Reumann, 491–92). The translation "garbage" or "rubbish" is adequate.

ἵνα. Introduces a purpose clause.

Χριστὸν. Accusative direct object of κερδήσω. This is the only direct object of κερδαίνω where Christ is the one to be gained, although 1:21 suggests that being with Christ is the benefit of death. "That Christ may be my wealth" catches the accounting overtones in the passage (Reumann, 492).

κερδήσω. Aor subj ind 1st sg κερδαίνω. Subjunctive with ἵνα. Paul has used the cognate noun to describe the "benefit" of his death (1:21) and of the lack of "benefits" from his achievements (3:7). While the verb can describe a monetary gain (Jas 4:13) and gaining the world (Matt 16:26 and parallels), it can also be used, as here, to "gain" or "win" a person (Matt 18:15; 1 Cor 9:19–22; 1 Pet 3:1).

3:9 καὶ εὑρεθῶ ἐν αὐτῷ, μὴ ἔχων ἐμὴν δικαιοσύνην τὴν ἐκ νόμου ἀλλὰ τὴν διὰ πίστεως Χριστοῦ, τὴν ἐκ θεοῦ δικαιοσύνην ἐπὶ τῇ πίστει,

καὶ εὑρεθῶ ἐν αὐτῷ. Completes the ἵνα clause introduced at the end of 3:8 and provides the last two elements of a chiasm:

ἵνα Χριστὸν (A)	κερδήσω (B)
καὶ εὑρεθῶ (B')	ἐν αὐτῷ (A')

The conjunction καί suggests a possible hendiadys so that 3:9a explains 3:8e (Fee, 320). BDF (§442.9) calls this clause "epexegetical." In other words, gaining Christ is to be found in union with him.

εὑρεθῶ. Aor pass subj 1st sg εὑρίσκω. Subjunctive with ἵνα. The passive voice "be found" (BDAG, 411.1.b) is used in Acts 8:40; 2 Cor 12:20; 1 Pet 2:22; and Rev 12:8. The subjunctive mood here "projects a possible realm" (Reed 1997, 411).

ἐν αὐτῷ. Locative. See 3:1, 3. The language of indwelling is a way of highlighting the intimate nature of the relationship.

ἔχων. Pres act ptc masc nom sg ἔχω (result). It is preceded by a negative particle μή. Since this participle follows the main verb, it describes the results of gaining Christ and of being found in Him ("so that I would not have my own righteousness," Wallace, 637–39). Another possibility is that it is modal, describing the manner in which Paul will be found perfectly in Christ (O'Brien 1991, 393).

ἐμήν. The possessive adjective is unusual without the definite article τήν. Of the 74 occurrences of the first person possessive adjective in the NT there are only 4 times that it appears without the article (see, e.g., 1:26: τῆς ἐμῆς παρουσίας). "This absence serves to focus attention strongly on the quality of this righteousness, that is, it is Paul's own. It is not simply the righteousness that he possesses but that which he has acquired (O'Brien 1991, 394; also Zerwick, 58).

δικαιοσύνην. Accusative direct object of ἔχων. See 3:6. For an excellent treatment of the various ways in which the δικαι- word group is used in its various contexts, see NIDNTTE (1:723–41).

τήν. The article functions as an adjectivizer, changing the PP ἐκ νόμου into an attributive modifier of δικαιοσύνην.

ἐκ νόμου. Source. This use of ἐκ with the genitive νόμου is contrasted with the following ἐκ θεοῦ that describes the correct source of righteousness.

ἀλλά. Conjunction that marks the stark contrast between the previous false righteousness and the following true righteousness.

τήν. The article functions as an adjectivizer, changing the PP διὰ πίστεως into an attributive modifier of δικαιοσύνην that is implied.

διὰ πίστεως. Means. According to LN (90.4), διά with genitive functions as "a marker of intermediate agent, with implicit or explicit causative agent—'through, by.'" The switch from ἐκ (νόμου) to διά is augmented by the ἐπὶ τῇ πίστει at the end of the verse.

Χριστοῦ. The genitive could be either objective or subjective based on theological/contextual arguments. A Greek argument for the objective genitive here is the anarthrous head noun πίστεως. Dunn (in Hays, 452–54) convincingly argues that when an anarthrous πίστις is the head noun it is followed by an objective genitive (Mark 11:22, ἔχετε πίστιν θεοῦ) and when it is arthrous the genitive is subjective (Rom 3:3, τὴν πίστιν τοῦ θεοῦ).

τὴν ... δικαιοσύνην. Accusative in apposition to the implied δικαιοσύνην in the previous clause. Whereas the earlier reference was to human righteousness, this occurrence is to a divine righteousness. "Within the teaching of Paul δικαιοσύνη can be a ref. to divine power (Rom 10:3; 2 Cor 3:9), a designation for Christ (1 Cor 1:30), a poss. synonym for God's glory (Rom 3:21–26), and a description of God's covenant faithfulness (3:5)" (NIDNTTE 1:740).

ἐκ θεοῦ. Source, in contrast to the previous PP ἐκ νόμου. The PP ἐκ θεοῦ is in the first attributive position, i.e., between the article and the noun, functioning as an attributive modifier of δικαιοσύνην ("the righteousness from God").

ἐπὶ τῇ πίστει. Cause ("on the ground of faith"). This is not a tautology but is added for emphasis. See "ἐπὶ τῇ πίστει" in Acts 3:16, which also contains the expression ἡ πίστις ἡ δι' αὐτου that is similar to διὰ πίστεως Χριστοῦ in 3:9. The article before πίστει is anaphoric, referring back to the anarthrous πίστεως.

3:10 τοῦ γνῶναι αὐτὸν καὶ τὴν δύναμιν τῆς ἀναστάσεως αὐτοῦ καὶ [τὴν] κοινωνίαν [τῶν] παθημάτων αὐτοῦ, συμμορφιζόμενος τῷ θανάτῳ αὐτοῦ,

τοῦ γνῶναι. Aor act inf γινώσκω (purpose). Some have regarded this infinitive as epexegetical, explaining what it means to "be found in him" and "to believe in him" (Collange, 131), because articular infinitives can occasionally be explanatory (Burk, 67). However, the infinitive with τοῦ is more often used to express purpose (Luke 24:29; 1 Cor 10:13; see BDF §400.5; Turner, 141; Burk, 64). This infinitive is then parallel to the purpose statements ἵνα Χριστὸν κερδήσω καὶ εὑρεθῶ ἐν αὐτῷ (3:8e–9a). Paul's expressed objectives in these purpose clauses are "to gain Christ," "to be found in Christ," and "to know Christ" (Hawthorne,

196; Moule, 128–29). Although this is a continuation of the previous sentence, many versions initiate a new sentence at this point for the sake of clarity.

αὐτόν. Accusative direct object of γνῶναι, the first of three.

τὴν δύναμιν. Accusative direct object of γνῶναι.

τῆς ἀναστάσεως. Genitive of source.

αὐτοῦ. Possessive genitive, the first of three.

[τὴν] κοινωνίαν. Accusative direct object of γνῶναι. The noun is best understood in its active sense of "participation" (see 1:5).

[τῶν] παθημάτων. Objective genitive. The semantic field of this word group (πάθημα and πάσχω) refers to "suffering" (LN 24.78), sometimes of Christ (7 times including here) and sometimes of Christians (7 times). The noun πάθημα also twice shares a semantic field with πάθος (LN 25.30) where it means "(sinful) passions" (Rom 7:5; Gal 5:24). NA[28] has the two articles bracketed, but the THGNT omits both articles. The manuscripts in favor of omission (𝔓[46] ℵ* A B) are older and better than those including them (ℵ[2] D F G Ψ 𝔐), which are Western or Byzantine. Scribes probably desired to conform the manuscript to the earlier direct object (τὴν δύναμιν), and the second corrector of Sinaiticus made the adjustments to conform to those later Byzantine readings.

αὐτοῦ. Possessive genitive.

συμμορφιζόμενος. Pres pass ptc masc nom sg συμμορφίζω (attributive), modifying the subject of τοῦ γνῶναι and the nominative subject of the verbs in 3:7–9. *Hapax legomenon,* although the cognate adjective σύμμορφος is in 3:21 and Rom 8:29. These help to define the verb as "to conform to" (Abbott-Smith, 423). It is not necessary to conclude that "Paul has simply let a long and complicated sentence get away from him" (Sumney, 82). "The participle indicates the process of development" (Vincent, 106).

τῷ θανάτῳ. Dative complement of συμμορφιζόμενος, governed by the συν- prefix of the participle.

αὐτοῦ. Possessive genitive.

3:11 εἴ πως καταντήσω εἰς τὴν ἐξανάστασιν τὴν ἐκ νεκρῶν.

εἴ πως. BDAG (εἴ, 279.6.n) translates εἴ plus the enclitic particle πως

Analysis of Philippians Three

as "if perhaps, somehow." It introduces a "simple particular" condition (BDF §371.1; §372.1.b). The collocation of these two particles elsewhere in the NT is only in Acts 27:12; Rom 1:10; 11:14. In the LXX εἴ πως is in 1 Kgs 20:31; 2 Kgs 19:4; Jer 28:8 (51:8). In all seven cases, both hope and doubt are involved. BDF (§375), however, calls it "an expression of expectation."

καταντήσω. Aor act subj 1st sg καταντάω. GE (1067) defines as "to arrive" or "to come to." "The Apostle states not a positive assurance but a modest hope" (Lightfoot, 151). The verb describes the desired path to maturity in Eph 4:13.

εἰς τὴν ἐξανάστασιν. Goal. This is the only attested occurrence of the compound ἐξανάστασις as "resurrection" (LXX Gen 7:4 means something different). Hellenistic Greek liked to add prefixes to strengthen words (Zerwick, 484; Silva, 169). CGELNT (132) defines as *"resurrection*, with focus on attendant vitality."

τήν. The article functions as an adjectivizer, changing the PP ἐκ νεκρῶν into an attributive modifier of ἐξανάστασιν (ME, 78).

ἐκ νεκρῶν. Source. This is a reference not to a general resurrection ("of the dead") but to a limited resurrection ("from the dead").

Philippians 3:12–16

> [12] Not that I have already reached this nor that I am already brought to this goal, but I am pursuing to take hold of that for which I also have been taken hold by Christ Jesus. [13] Brothers, I do not consider myself to have taken hold of it. But one thing I do: forgetting the things behind and reaching forward to the things ahead, [14] I pursue as my goal the prize of God's upward call in Christ Jesus. [15] Therefore, as many who think we are perfect, let us think this way. And if on anything you think amiss, this also God will reveal to you. [16] In any case, with respect to what we have attained, let us continue in the same way.

¶ Not that I have already obtained *it* or have already become perfect, but I press on so that I may lay hold of that for which also I was laid hold of by Christ Jesus. Brothers, I do not consider myself as having laid hold of *it* yet, but one thing *I do*: forgetting what *lies* behind and reaching forward to what *lies* ahead, I press on toward the goal for the prize of the upward call of God in Christ Jesus. Let us therefore, as many as are perfect, think this way; and if in anything you think differently, God will reveal that also to you. However, *let us* keep walking in step with the same *standard* to which we have attained. (LSB)

Summary: Having utilized some accounting analogies, Paul now turns to some athletic contests for his images. Although he has not reached perfection, he keeps pursuing a long-cherished ambition with the intention of *laying hold* on it, because the risen Jesus *laid hold* of him on the Damascus road, setting his life in a new direction. Further progress must be made, and only at the end of the race will he receive the prize. The apostle describes his earnest ambition by means of a series of clauses, the first group being negative (3:12–13a) with the second group (3:13b–14) stressing his determination to reach his ultimate goal. He then encourages his readers in their Christian growth by repeating his preceding assertions and by urging those who are mature to have the same Christ-centered ambition, while assuring them that God will lead them into his truth in these areas. Finally, he urges his readers to make progress in accord with the truth they had already received.

3:12 Οὐχ ὅτι ἤδη ἔλαβον ἢ ἤδη τετελείωμαι, διώκω δὲ εἰ καὶ καταλάβω, ἐφ' ᾧ καὶ κατελήμφθην ὑπὸ Χριστοῦ ['Ιησοῦ].

Οὐχ ὅτι. The negative particle plus conjunction function idiomatically and require an implied λέγω (BDF §480.5). In 4:11, 17 and other occurrences in the Pauline corpus (2 Cor 1:24; 3:5; 7:9; 2 Thess 3:9), this phrase qualifies a previous statement to avoid giving the wrong impression.

ἤδη. Temporal adverb repeated in the next clause.

ἔλαβον. Aor act ind 3rd sg λαμβάνω. Since the verb is usually transitive and followed by a direct object, the translation is difficult. The implied object is certainly what Paul is pursuing (διώκω), what he is not (τετελείωμαι), and what he has not taken hold of (καταλάβω). There is no need to express a direct object if that object has been mentioned.

In this case the object is τὴν ἐξανάστασιν in the preceding clause (3:11b; Silva, 174). Some Western manuscripts (D F G), as well as 𝔓⁴⁶ and a Latin text of Irenaeus, add the clause η ηδη δεδικαιωμαι following ἔλαβον. This addition has Paul declaring that he has not been justified, which is problematic in light of what he just wrote in 3:8–10 and elsewhere, e.g., in Romans. Although Comfort (612) defends the addition, no printed Greek texts from the Textus Receptus until today include it. The clause has sparse support, despite its inclusion in 𝔓⁴⁶, which is known for its singular readings. The NA²⁸ text exclusion, supported by the THGNT, has wide support among Alexandrian, Byzantine, and a few Western witnesses (𝔓⁶¹ ℵ A B Dc P Ψ 33 1739 itc vg syr cop). Silva (187) concludes that "if the clause is original, it would be an interesting example of a future-eschatological use of the verb (cf. Rom. 2:13), but the external evidence is so strongly in favor of the omission that the originality of the clause remains doubtful at best." Strangely, Metzger (547) states that the Textus Receptus contains the addition, but none of the TR texts (Stephanus, Elzevir, Scrivener) include it, nor is it in Erasmus' *Novum Instrumentum*.

ἤ. Particle used as a conjunction (ILNTG, 53).

τετελείωμαι. Perf pass ind 1st sg τελειόω. Among the variety of semantic nuances, BDAG (996.2) suggests, "bring to an end, bring to its goal/accomplishment." The verb τελειόω occurs nowhere else in Paul's letters, but its cognate ἐπιτελέω appears in 1:6: "bring to completion." Sumney (84) wisely warns against a "mirror hermeneutics" that sees a reference to mystery religions or perfectionist opponents, but "we do best to see this as Paul continuing to avoid misunderstanding" (contra BDAG, 996.3).

διώκω. Pres act ind 1st sg διώκω. Any direct object remains implied (see discussion of ἔλαβον). For the semantics of this verb, see 3:6 and 3:14.

δὲ. Signals development from a negative to a positive statement.

εἰ. While it is possible to regard εἰ as the introduction of the protasis of a conditional clause with διώκω as the apodosis, the particle simply introduces a statement of expectation (BDF §375). The idea is "that I am pursuing" or "making the effort to take hold."

καὶ. Adverbial ("also").

καταλάβω. Aor act subj 3rd sg καταλαμβάνω. Translators should resist viewing the augment κατα- as warrant for overtranslating the verb as "grab hold" (CEB) since its usage in the following clauses does not demand that.

There is a parallelism between the statements of 3:12 and 3:13–14:

A. I have not **reached** it (λαμβάνω) – 3:12a
    B. I **make an effort** (διώκω) that I may reach it (καταλαμβάνω) – 3:12b
A'. I do not think I have **reached** it (καταλαμβάνω) – 3:13a
    B'. I **make an effort** (διώκω) toward the goal – 3:14a

ἐφ' ᾧ. The Pauline meaning of this collocation is defined by BDAG (365.6.c) as "ἐφ' ᾧ = ἐπὶ τούτῳ ὅτι for this reason that, because." While some defend this causal meaning because of its use in Rom 5:12 and 2 Cor 5:4 (O'Brien 1991, 425; Wallace, 342), it is best to view the phrase as referring to the implied direct object of the preceding indicative verbs. Paul is pursuing that thing "for which" Christ has taken hold of him (Fee, 346 n1; Sumney, 85).

καί. Adverbial ("also"), although the sense of "already" may communicate best the attitude (Silva, 187).

κατελήμφθην. Aor pass ind 1st pl καταλαμβάνω. The change from the active voice (καταλάβω) to the passive voice here is a rhetorical switch of which Paul is fond. Note 1 Cor 8:2–3 (γνῶναι/ἔγνωσται); 1 Cor 13:12 (γινώσκω/ἐπιγνώσομαι); Gal 4:9 (γνόντες/γνωσθέντες).

ὑπὸ Χριστοῦ ['Ιησοῦ]. Agency (see BDAG, 1036.A.a.α). The omission of Ἰησοῦ in some significant witnesses (B D² Tertullian Clement of Alexandria) and its inclusion in others ($\mathfrak{P}^{46}$ $\mathfrak{P}^{61}$ ℵ A 𝔐) creates a decision that "is nearly impossible to call" (Fee, 338 n3), although with the scribal tendency to expand titles, it is probable that the short form is original. THGNT retains Ἰησοῦ without brackets.

3:13 ἀδελφοί, ἐγὼ ἐμαυτὸν οὐ λογίζομαι κατειληφέναι· ἓν δέ, τὰ μὲν ὀπίσω ἐπιλανθανόμενος τοῖς δὲ ἔμπροσθεν ἐπεκτεινόμενος,

The words ἀδελφοί, ἐγώ, and ἐμαυτόν are prominent "focal indicators" that lead up to κατειληφέναι (Reed 1997, 392). Because neither ἐγώ nor ἐμαυτόν are syntactically necessary, they provide further weight to Paul's strong self-evaluation: "I, for my part, do not consider myself ..."

ἀδελφοί. While addressing his readers 6 times with this nominative of address (1:12; 3:1, 13, 17; 4:1, 8), this is the only complete fronting of the word. The noun ἀδελφοί is used "in the collective sense of *brothers and sisters*" (CGELNT, 6).

ἐμαυτόν. Robertson (1037–39) called this an "accusative of general reference," but recent grammarians prefer a functional description like an "accusative subject of the infinitive" κατειληφέναι (Wallace, 192–97).

οὐ λογίζομαι. Pres mid ind 1st sg λογίζομαι. BDAG (598.3) translates this verb as "to hold a view about someth[ing], think, believe, be of the opinion." While the middle voice plus the reflexive pronoun ἐμαυτόν may seem redundant ("redundant middle," Robertson, 811), the force is intensified by the combination. "The reading οὐ, which is amply supported by 𝔓[46] B D G K Ψ 88 1739 most Old Latin vg syr[h] cop[sa] arm, appears to have been changed to οὔπω (ℵ A D[gr*] P 33 614 syr[h] cop[bo] goth eth Clement) by copyists who considered Paul to be too modest in his protestations" (Metzger, 548). THGNT retains the οὐ.

κατειληφέναι. Perf act inf (indirect discourse; see Robertson, 1038). This is the fourth use of (κάτα)λαμβάνω in vv. 12–13a.

ἕν. Either nominative or accusative singular. If the expression is used absolutely ("But one thing!"), it is nominative. Most suggest an implied ποιῶ or πράσσω ("But one thing I do"). Thus ἕν would be an accusative of direct object (BDF §481.1). This is an "example of ellipses common to Greek" (Robertson, 1202).

δέ. Signaling stronger than normal development, almost equivalent to ἀλλά. It functions as "a marker of contrast – 'but, on the other hand'" (LN 89.124).

τὰ ... ὀπίσω. The article functions as a nominalizer, changing the adverb ὀπίσω ("the things behind") into the accusative direct object of ἐπιλανθανόμενος.

μέν. The point-counterpoint with the following δέ is also balanced with the two articles τὰ/τοῖς and the two participles prefixed by ἐπι-.

ἐπιλανθανόμενος. Pres mid ptc masc nom sg ἐπιλανθάνομαι (manner or temporal). The adverbial participle modifies διώκω in 3:14 and conveys how the pursuit is done ("by forgetting") or, possibly, when the pursuit is done ("while forgetting"). Of its eight appearances, the verb is used in a good sense five times (here and Luke 12:6; Heb 6:10; 13:2, 16).

τοῖς ... ἔμπροσθεν. The article functions as a nominalizer, changing the adverb ἔμπροσθεν ("the things ahead") into the dative complement of ἐπεκτεινόμενος.

δὲ. See μὲν.

ἐπεκτεινόμενος. Pres mid ptc masc nom sg ἐπεκτείνομαι. BDAG (361) translates this verb as "stretch out, strain." *Hapax legomenon*. This lexeme combines a double prefix with the verb (επι + εκ + τεινω), something nowhere else seen in biblical Greek (Reumann, 539). Both of these participles (ἐπιλανθανόμενος and ἐπεκτεινόμενος) are used by Paul only here.

3:14 κατὰ σκοπὸν διώκω εἰς τὸ βραβεῖον τῆς ἄνω κλήσεως τοῦ θεοῦ ἐν Χριστῷ Ἰησοῦ.

The fronting of the prepositional phrase closely connects this verse to the last part of the sentence in 3:13b. The use of such words as σκοπὸν and βραβεῖον modifying the participle ἐπεκτεινόμενος raises the question if the passage is best understood against the background of athletic contests.

κατὰ σκοπὸν. Spatial (direction). BDAG (511.B.1.b) translates the preposition as "toward, to, up to." The noun σκοπὸν is a *hapax legomenon*, although the verb σκοπέω is used in 2:4 and 3:17. While athletic imagery is evident, the word had already been employed metaphorically as a "mark" or "goal" at which one aims in life (Polybius, *His.* 7.8.9; see TDNT 7:413–14).

διώκω. As in 3:12, this verb should be viewed as conveying a rhetorical contrast to Paul's history of "pursuing" or "persecuting" the church in 3:6. He once pursued the church; he now pursues Christ. The verb has a long Attic history as meaning "to pursue" and its usage as "persecute" ("pursue" with an evil intent) is a NT nuance (GE, 543). See its positive meaning here and in Rom 9:30; 1 Cor 14:1; 1 Thess 5:15; 1 Tim 6:11; 2 Tim 2:22.

εἰς τὸ βραβεῖον. Purpose. The noun βραβεῖον is used with the analogy of a runner in a race in 1 Cor 9:24. As was mentioned before about σκοπὸν, it may be possible that Paul was thinking about the games, but it is often simply used for "award" or "prize." Words such as ἆθλον and νικητήριον are more common in Greek literature for the athletic awards (BDAG, 183; GE, 1399).

τῆς ... κλήσεως. Epexegetical genitive. Compare Heb 3:1: κλήσεως ἐπουρανίου μέτοχοι. Because κλῆσις has such theological significance for Paul, one should be careful about pressing the analogy with the Greek games. There is no evidence that this word group (including καλέω) was used in that context.

ἄνω. An adverb in the first attributive position, functioning as a modifier of κλῆσις. Hence "upward(s)" (BDAG, 92.2).

τοῦ θεοῦ. Genitive of agency. The reading in NA^{28}/THGNT is supported by 𝔓^{61} ℵ A B D^2 I Ψ 33 1739 𝔐 it cop, followed by all the English versions. There are five textual variants, but each is so poorly attested that Metzger does not even discuss the issue (Metzger, 548), and there is no reason to doubt the critical texts.

ἐν Χριστῷ Ἰησοῦ. The prepositional phrase should be taken with κλήσεως (see 1 Cor 7:22, ὁ γὰρ ἐν κυρίῳ κληθεὶς). Its function is either locative, "in Christ Jesus" (Lightfoot, 153; O'Brien 1991, 433) or instrumental, "through Christ Jesus" (Collange, 134). If the first, the language of indwelling is a way of highlighting the intimate nature of the relationship.

3:15 Ὅσοι οὖν τέλειοι, τοῦτο φρονῶμεν· καὶ εἴ τι ἑτέρως φρονεῖτε, καὶ τοῦτο ὁ θεὸς ὑμῖν ἀποκαλύψει·

Ὅσοι ... τέλειοι. Nominative subject of φρονῶμεν. There is an implied verb like ἐσμέν or more likely εἰσίν.

Ὅσοι. Plural correlative pronoun (BDF §64.4), sometimes called an adjective (Friberg, Friberg, and Miller, 286).

τέλειοι. Predicate adjective within the subject clause. Paul's shift to the plural either indicates identity with his opponents for the sake of irony or an honest statement of his own status as "mature" (see O'Brien 1991, 433–37). Paul has, however, denied that he had reached the status of being τέλειος in 3:12 (Οὐχ ... τετελείωμαι). Most probably, with a touch of irony, he is describing the group whose error he is addressing as "perfect" or "initiated" (BDAG, 996.3; see also Lightfoot, 153). Then he exhorts the Philippians to share the humble perspective (φρονῶμεν) to which he has previously given expression (Silva, 177–78).

οὖν. In imperatival contexts (see the following hortatory φρονῶμεν), this inferential particle has an intensive force and is called an "οὖν-paräneticum" (BDAG, 736.1.b). Note its similar function in 2:1.

τοῦτο. Accusative direct object of φρονῶμεν. The antecedent of this demonstrative pronoun is not expressed but probably points back to the entire thrust of 3:12–14.

φρονῶμεν. Hortatory subjunctive. It marks a shift in subject from "I" (διώκω) to "we." The τοῦτο φρονῶμεν may correspond to the τοῦτο φρονεῖτε in 2:5.

καί. Connects two parallel clauses, both of which are anchored by different forms of the verb φρονέω. This polysyndeton style could easily be separated into a separate sentence with the conjunction καί being simply continuative.

εἴ. Conditional particle introducing the protasis of a first class conditional clause.

τι. Indefinite enclitic pronoun. Accusative direct object of φρονεῖτε.

ἑτέρως. Adverb. *Hapax legomenon*, but the genitive plural of the adjective ἕτερος is used in 2:4 ("other persons"). While BDAG (400) translates this adverb as "differently, otherwise," Silva's observation (187–88), following Lightfoot and LSJ, is that the adverb in Hellenistic Greek carries negative overtones and is best rendered "amiss" or "badly" (cf. Epictetus, *Discourses* 2.16.16; Josephus, *Ag. Ap.* 1.26; see also Bockmuehl, 226). GE (834) agrees: "in a different way (from how it ought to be), i.e., badly."

φρονεῖτε. Pres act ind 2nd pl φρονέω. Paul continues the creative use of this verb to convey his overall message. See 2:5.

καὶ τοῦτο ὁ θεὸς ὑμῖν ἀποκαλύψει. Apodosis of the conditional clause.

καί. Adverbial ("also").

τοῦτο. Accusative direct object of ἀποκαλύψει. See τοῦτο above.

ὁ θεός. Nominative subject of ἀποκαλύψει.

ὑμῖν. Dative indirect object of ἀποκαλύψει.

ἀποκαλύψει. Fut act ind 3rd sg ἀποκαλύπτω. This verb expresses a strong revelatory sense (contra NIV "make clear"). BDAG (112.b) places Phil 3:15 under the definition "revelation of transcendent secrets" along with Gal 1:16; 1 Cor 2:10; 14:30.

Analysis of Philippians Three

3:16 πλὴν εἰς ὃ ἐφθάσαμεν, τῷ αὐτῷ στοιχεῖν.

πλήν. Adverb used as a conjunction (ILNTG, 81–82), also in 1:18 and 4:14. Reumann (543) suggests "anyway." See 1 Cor 11:11 for a similar usage (GE, 1683).

εἰς ὅ. Reference. This is the only occurrence of this exact expression in the NT, although Rom 9:31 contains a rough parallel to the entire clause (εἰς νόμον οὐκ ἔφθασεν).

ἐφθάσαμεν. Aor act ind 1st pl φθάνω. BDAG (1053.3) translates this verb as "to come to or arrive at a particular state, attain." Although used extensively in Attic as "arrive first, reach" (GE, 2268–69), it is used only 5 times in Paul, twice in parallel Gospel passages, and always in the aorist indicative. With the preceding phrase it means "with respect to what we have attained."

τῷ αὐτῷ. Dative complement of στοιχεῖν.

στοιχεῖν. Pres act inf στοιχέω (imperatival). Along with Rom 12:15 (χαίρειν μετὰ χαιρόντων, κλαίειν μετὰ κλαιόντων) these "are apparently the only examples of this [usage] in the NT" (Wallace, 608; BDF §389). "Infinitive as substitute for imperative may be derived from the Hebrew infinitive absolute" (MHT 4:89). "Imperatival infinitives are to be found only in clauses with no main verb" (ME, 202). One might supply an impersonal verb like δεῖ (BDF §389). While originally a military term, "to take their place in line," στοιχέω developed a metaphorical meaning like "to be in line with" or simply "agree with" (NIDNTTE 4:378). All five NT instances are "fig[urative], to be in line with a pers[on] or thing, considered as standard for one's conduct, hold to, agree with, follow, conform" (BDAG, 946). See its indicative use in Acts 21:24; Rom 4:12; Gal 6:16; and its subjunctive use in Gal 5:25. The text of the end of the verse in NA²⁸ (τῷ αὐτῷ στοιχεῖν) has early manuscript and versional support ($\mathfrak{P}^{16}$ $\mathfrak{P}^{46}$ ℵ* A B 33 1739 cop). The reading reflected in KJV, τω αυτω στοιχειν κανονι, το αυτο φρονειν, has later support in a Byzantine corrector and manuscripts (ℵ² Ψ 𝔐) and conforms to Gal 6:16. The other variant, το αυτο φρονειν, τω αυτω στοιχειν with some small differences, is decidedly Western (D F G vg) and attempts to improve from the context what is the more difficult but better attested reading. The number of variant readings arose because of the rare use of the imperatival infinitive.

Philippians 3:17–21

> ¹⁷ Join in imitating me, brothers, and observe those who live in this way as you have us for an example. ¹⁸ For many live, about whom I have often spoken to you, and now I say again with tears, as the enemies of the cross of Christ. ¹⁹ Their end is destruction; their god is their stomach; their honor is in their disgrace; they are focused on earthly things. ²⁰ But our citizenship exists in heaven, from which we also eagerly wait for a Savior, the Lord Jesus Christ, ²¹ who will transform our humble body to be similar in form to his glorious body, because of the power that also enables him to subjugate everything to himself.

> ¶ Brothers, join in following my example, and look for those who walk according to the pattern you have in us. For many walk—of whom I often told you, and now tell you even crying—as enemies of the cross of Christ, whose end is destruction, whose god is *their* stomach and glory is in their shame, who set their thoughts on earthly things. For our citizenship is in heaven, from which also we eagerly wait for a Savior, the Lord Jesus Christ, who will transform the body of our humble state into conformity with the body of His glory, by His working through which He is able to even subject all things to Himself. (LSB)

Summary: Paul returns to his warning about false teachers (see 3:2–3), and the pattern again is one of comparison and contrast. He moves to plural rather than singular subjects so that the entire church is included. Some see a change of opponents while others see a reference to the Jewish false teachers previously condemned, and this is more probably the case. He describes them in very strong terms: enemies of the cross whose citizenship is only on earth rather than in heaven, and who do not have the same destiny as believers. An introductory statement sets the focus for these verses (3:17); he then describes the opponents (3:18–19); and he finally contrasts them with true believers (3:20–21).

3:17 Συμμιμηταί μου γίνεσθε, ἀδελφοί, καὶ σκοπεῖτε τοὺς οὕτως περιπατοῦντας καθὼς ἔχετε τύπον ἡμᾶς.

Συμμιμηταί. The fronting of the noun as a topical frame, collocated with the imperative γίνεσθε, marks a shift from Paul (3:12–15) to the Philippians. The noun is a true *hapax legomenon* because this is its only use in ancient Greek literature (GE, 2003), indicating that it may have been coined by Paul.

μου. Objective genitive. Wallace (130) mentions that it could be a genitive of association. The genitive object, however, is determined by the prefix συν- in the head noun.

γίνεσθε. Pres mid impv 2nd pl γίνομαι. This is the first imperative since 3:2.

ἀδελφοί. Nominative of direct address. The generic use of the word "brothers" is inclusive (BDAG, 18.2.a).

καί. Connects the two imperative clauses.

σκοπεῖτε. Pres act impv 2nd pl σκοπέω. Its meaning is not as it is used in Rom 16:17, "mark out and avoid," but "mark out and follow."

τοὺς ... περιπατοῦντας. Pres act ptc masc acc pl περιπατέω (substantival). It functions as a direct object of σκοπεῖτε (Wallace, 661). BDAG (803.2.a.γ) translates περιπατέω as "conduct one's life, comport oneself, behave, live as a habit of conduct."

οὕτως. An adverb in the first attributive position, functioning as a modifier of περιπατοῦντας ("those who live in this way").

καθώς. Comparative adverb. It is used here with a possible causal meaning, as in 1:7 ("since"; BDF §453).

ἔχετε. Pres act ind 2nd pl ἔχω.

τύπον. Complement in a double accusative object-complement construction. Only three NT references retain the concrete meaning of "a mark made as the result of a blow or pressure" (John 20:25, nail marks; Acts 7:43, an image; and Acts 23:25, a letter; BDAG, 1019.1). Other occurrences refer to a heavenly or OT archetype as a pattern or type (e.g., Acts 7:44; Rom 5:14; Heb 8:5) or to a human example or model, as here and in 1 Thess 1:7; 2 Thess 3:9; 1 Tim 4:12; Tit 2:7; and 1 Pet 5:3 (BDAG, 1020.6; see also NIDNTTE 4:505–8).

ἡμᾶς. Direct object of ἔχετε in a double accusative object-complement construction. This may be the only example of an "editorial we" in the epistle, but if taken literally, ἡμᾶς would include at least Timothy and Epaphroditus (2:19, 25). "Shrinking from the egotism of dwelling on his own personal example, St Paul passes at once from the singular μου to the plural ἡμᾶς" (Lightfoot, 154).

3:18 πολλοὶ γὰρ περιπατοῦσιν οὓς πολλάκις ἔλεγον ὑμῖν, νῦν δὲ καὶ κλαίων λέγω, τοὺς ἐχθροὺς τοῦ σταυροῦ τοῦ Χριστοῦ,

πολλοί. Nominative subject of περιπατοῦσιν.

γάρ. A "marker of clarification" (BDAG, 189.2) explaining why the Philippians should imitate Paul and consider those about him (cf. 3:3a, 20).

περιπατοῦσιν. Pres act ind 3rd pl περιπατέω. See περιπατοῦντας in 3:17.

οὓς πολλάκις ἔλεγον ὑμῖν. Relative clause.

οὕς. Accusative direct object of ἔλεγον in a double accusative object-complement construction.

πολλάκις. Adverb ("often").

ἔλεγον. Impf act ind 1st sg λέγω. The iterative action described comes from the pragmatics of πολλάκις and not from the imperfective aspect of the verb.

νῦν δέ. Signals development from past warnings to the present one.

καί. Connects ἔλεγον and λέγω.

κλαίων. Pres act ptc masc nom sg κλαίω (manner).

λέγω. Pres act ind 1st sg λέγω.

τοὺς ἐχθρούς. Complement in a double accusative object-complement construction, with the relative pronoun οὕς functioning as the direct object of ἔλεγον (see above). The article nominalizes the adjective ἐχθρός and makes the expression definite ("the enemies"). Many versions omit the article in translation (NASB, ESV, NIV), but a few include it (KJV, NET). As one of its many singular readings, 𝔓⁴⁶ inserts βλέπετε before τοὺς ἐχθρούς, thus tying 3:18 to the triple βλέπετε in 3:2 and to σκοπεῖτε in 3:17, another of its "unique" readings.

τοῦ σταυροῦ. Objective genitive. While 2:8 used this noun literally, here the word is a metonymy for the atoning death of Jesus (Abbott-Smith, 416). For how the language impacts a *theologia crucis*, see NIDNTTE (4:361–64).

τοῦ Χριστοῦ. Possessive genitive.

3:19 ὧν τὸ τέλος ἀπώλεια, ὧν ὁ θεὸς ἡ κοιλία καὶ ἡ δόξα ἐν τῇ αἰσχύνῃ αὐτῶν, οἱ τὰ ἐπίγεια φρονοῦντες.

Each of the first three relative clauses has an implied ἐστίν and each relates to τοὺς ἐχθροὺς of 3:18. The fourth clause has a nominative substantival participle that relates to the πολλοί of 3:18. The second and third clauses are connected by καί because they are more semantically parallel. Asyndeton again marks this colorful description of these "enemies of the cross."

> ὧν. Possessive genitive. Relative pronoun referring to τοὺς ἐχθροὺς.
> τὸ τέλος. Nominative subject of a verbless equative clause. Fee (370 n34) discerns a contrastive play on words with the positive cognates of τέλος in 3:12 (τελειόω) and 3:15 (τέλειοι).
> ἀπώλεια. Predicate nominative. Already used of spiritual "destruction" in 1:28, it was used of "perdition" even in Attic Greek (GE, 286).
> ὧν. Possessive genitive (see above).
> ὁ θεός. Nominative subject of a verbless equative clause.
> ἡ κοιλία. Predicate nominative. GE (1146) lists examples in Greek literature as "belly, stomach, intestines" as well as "excrement" — which certainly would add a nuance to Paul's point. Other negative examples of the noun are in Rom 16:18 and 1 Cor 6:13, but references to the word meaning simply the "womb" are also evident (e.g., Luke 1:41, 42; 2:21; 11:27).
> καί. Kennedy (462) suggests that the presence of the conjunction appearing only between the second and third clauses points to a possible proverbial saying. See below on αὐτῶν.
> ἡ δόξα. Nominative subject of a verbless equative clause. ὧν governs both ὁ θεός and ἡ δόξα. BDAG (257.3) translates δόξα as "fame, recognition, renown, honor, prestige." Reumann (573) sees here an effective rhetorical oxymoron: "whose prestige is in their disgrace." The translation "honor" communicates the same.
> ἐν τῇ αἰσχύνῃ. Locative. The noun appears only six times in the NT. Jude 13 compares libertine teachers to "wild waves of the sea, foaming up their **shame**." On the other hand, Paul and his co-workers have "renounced secret and **shameful** ways" (2 Cor 4:2, its only other occurrence in Paul).

αὐτῶν. Objective genitive. The single occurrence of this word as well as the connecting καὶ support the idea that this is a proverbial saying.

οἱ ... φρονοῦντες. Pres act ptc masc nom pl φρονέω (substantival). Sumney (94) regards this nominative as an apposition to πολλοὶ in 3:18. BDF (§468) describes the nominative as a grammatical anacoluthon, while Vincent (117–18) states that it simply stands in apposition to what precedes (see also BDF §136.1; §137.3).

τὰ ἐπίγεια. Accusative direct object of φρονοῦντες. The article nominalizes the adjective. The noun has a more material sense than κόσμος. GE (758) defines as: "on land, terrestrial."

3:20 ἡμῶν γὰρ τὸ πολίτευμα ἐν οὐρανοῖς ὑπάρχει, ἐξ οὗ καὶ σωτῆρα ἀπεκδεχόμεθα κύριον Ἰησοῦν Χριστόν,

ἡμῶν. Possessive genitive. The fronting of the personal pronoun is intended to focus on the great contrast between the characteristics of those "many" in 3:18–19 and "our" condition of spiritual riches. Note the fronting of ἡμεῖς in 3:3.

γὰρ. Postpositive conjunction. It is usually "causal and explanatory" (Reed 1997, 324, 356), functioning as a "marker of clarification" that can be translated "for, you see" (BDAG, 189.2). In this case, however, Zerwick (472) suggests opposition, "by contrast."

τὸ πολίτευμα. Neuter nominative subject of ὑπάρχει. *Hapax legomenon*. Lightfoot's classic explanation (156) with the appropriate Greco-Roman sources, is still worthy of consideration. "This may mean either (1) '[t]he state, the constitution, to which as citizens we belong' ... or (2) '[t]he functions which as citizens we perform'.... The singular points to the former meaning, which is also more frequent. In either case ἐξ οὗ 'whence' will refer not to πολίτευμα, but to οὐρανοῖς." See also GE, 1701. For the metaphor, see comments on 1:27 and the discussion of the city of Philippi as a Roman colony in the Introduction.

ἐν οὐρανοῖς. Locative. There seems to be no semantic difference between the singular and plural forms. Paul uses them about equally in its 21 occurrences.

ὑπάρχει. Pres act ind 3rd sg ὑπάρχω. This verb occurs 60 times in the NT. BDAG, while acknowledging that the verb sometimes simply means "be" (1029.2), distinguishes it from the stative as follows: "to really be there, exist, be present, be at one's disposal" (1029.1). On the basis of Attic usage, Montonari confirms this important nuance (GE, 2188–89). This verb occurs in Philippians only twice, each time with a heavenly context (see 2:6).

ἐξ οὗ. Source. The singular relative pronoun agrees grammatically with πολίτευμα, which supports the idea of the noun as a concrete place (e.g., "homeland"). Silva (189), however, adds: "There can be no strong objection to seeing the plural οὐρανοῖς as the real antecedent; such *ad sensum* constructions are very common." Furthermore, the plural οὐρανοῖς can be singular as well.

καὶ. Adverbial ("also").

σωτῆρα. Accusative direct object of ἀπεκδεχόμεθα. Fronting of this direct object also lends prominence to the "Savior." Surprisingly, Paul uses this title sparingly: in church letters elsewhere only in Eph 5:23 but ten times in the Pastoral Epistles.

ἀπεκδεχόμεθα. Pres mid ind 1st pl ἀπεκδέχομαι. There are no surviving examples of this word prior to the NT (GE, 233). Seven of its eight occurrences describe "eagerly waiting" for an eschatological hope (BDAG, 100), six of which are Pauline. Heb 9:28 uses it also of "eagerly waiting" for Christ, while it is used of God's own patient forbearance in 1 Pet 3:20.

κύριον Ἰησοῦν Χριστόν. Accusative in apposition to σωτῆρα.

3:21 ὃς μετασχηματίσει τὸ σῶμα τῆς ταπεινώσεως ἡμῶν σύμμορφον τῷ σώματι τῆς δόξης αὐτοῦ κατὰ τὴν ἐνέργειαν τοῦ δύνασθαι αὐτὸν καὶ ὑποτάξαι αὐτῷ τὰ πάντα.

ὅς. Nominative relative pronoun referring to σωτῆρα in 3:20 and functioning as the subject of μετασχηματίσει.

μετασχηματίσει. Fut act ind 3rd sg μετασχηματίζω. This is a Pauline verb appearing 5 times, three of which describe false apostles whose outward form is that of bearers of light (2 Cor 11: 13, 14, 15). The compound word means "to change the form (of something/someone, transform" (GE, 1329). Paul here "depicts the eschatological transformation that will take place in the physical existence of Christians" (NIDNTTE 4:416–17).

τὸ σῶμα. Accusative direct object of μετασχηματίσει.

τῆς ταπεινώσεως. Attributive genitive (Wallace, 86–88), our "humiliation-body."

ἡμῶν. Possessive genitive. LSB renders literally: "the body of our humble state."

σύμμορφον. Predicate adjective agreeing with σῶμα and with an implied verb such as "become." GE (2003) cites only one previous use of the adjective in secular Greek as "resembling." BDAG (958) translates it as "similar in form." This adjective is used elsewhere in the NT only in Rom 8:29 (with the genitive). The NA[28] and THGNT reading of σύμμορφον has the support of ℵ A B D* F G 1739 it cop. The TR reads εις το γενεσθαι αυτο συμμορφον, which is a scribal attempt to clarify Paul's terse syntax and is based on the later evidence of D¹ Ψ 33 𝔐 syr. 𝔓[46] is not cited as additional evidence for the shorter reading in NA[28], but the manuscript could not have contained the extra words found in the variant (see Comfort, 325).

τῷ σώματι. Dative complement of σύμμορφον. BDF (§194.2) calls it "associative dative" because of the συν- prefix in the compound σύμμορφον. Mathewson and Emig: "adjectives compounded with συν- (as here with σύμμορφον) are commonly accompanied by a dative" (27).

τῆς δόξης. Attributive genitive, his "glory-body."

αὐτοῦ. Possessive genitive.

κατὰ τὴν ἐνέργειαν. Causal. BDAG (512.B.5.a.δ) states that the meanings of the preposition as "in accordance with" and "because of" are merged. BDAG (335), defines the noun ἐνέργεια as "the state or quality of being active, working, operation, action." All eight occurrences of this noun are Pauline, and in each appearance the "power" is that of transcendent beings (Eph 1:19; 3:7; 4:16; Col 1:29; 2:12; 2 Thess 2:9, 11).

τοῦ δύνασθαι. Pres mid inf δύναμαι. Burk (67–68) lists this as an example of the "adnominal uses of the genitive articular infinitive." In such constructions the infinitive defines the noun to which it relates, and here that is ἐνέργειαν. Others call this an "epexegetical infinitive" (Wallace, 607).

αὐτὸν. Accusative subject of the infinitive τοῦ δύνασθαι.

καί. Adverbial ("also").

ὑποτάξαι. Aor act inf ὑποτάσσω (complementary). Originally a

Analysis of Philippians Three

military term (Polybius), ὑποτάσσω means "put under" or "subjugate" in the active voice (GE, 2234) and "obey" or "be subject" in the middle voice (Abbott-Smith, 463). While Paul uses it in 19 of its 32 appearances, this is its only occurrence in this book.

αὐτῷ. Dative indirect object of ὑποτάξαι. Wallace (324–25) sees this dative as an example of a personal pronoun used for a reflexive pronoun. He suggests that other examples of this usage can be found in Matt 6:19; John 2:24; and Eph 2:15.

τὰ πάντα. Accusative direct object of ὑποτάξαι. Everything under His control, an allusion to such texts as Ps 8:6 and 110:1 (see also 1 Cor 15:24–28 and Heb 2:5–9).

"Paul did not know, nor did he pretend to know, when the advent would take place. The so-called delay of the *parousia* involved no such agonizing reappraisal of his theology as has often been supposed. The certainty of the advent is accepted by faith; its timing is inaccessible to curious calculation. Each successive generation of the church has the privilege of living as though it were the generation that will greet the returning Christ" (Bruce, 135).

4

Analysis of Philippians Four

Philippians 4:1–3

> ¹ So then, my brothers, beloved ones and sadly missed—my joy and reward. In this way stand firm in the Lord, beloved. ² I urge Euodia and I urge Syntyche to be of the same mind in the Lord. ³ Yes, I also request, true comrade, that you help these women who have contended in the gospel ministry at my side, with Clement and the rest of my coworkers whose names are in the scroll of life.
>
> Therefore my brothers, loved and longed for, my joy and crown, in this way stand firm in the Lord, my beloved. ¶ I urge Euodia and I urge Syntyche to think the same way in the Lord. Indeed, I ask you also, genuine companion, help these women who have contended together alongside of me in the gospel, with also Clement and the rest of my fellow workers, whose names are in the book of life. (LSB)

Summary: Paul now returns to specific exhortations supported by both positive and negative models. The exhortation to "stand firm" is surrounded by affectionate expressions of his close relationship to the readers, echoing the letter's warm beginning (1:3–11). The second exhortation "to be of the same mind" is made to Euodia and Syntyche, two women who have leadership roles within the community. Since the same exhortation has also been given to the larger community

(2:2), it is likely that their differences have the potential of leading to a wider division. The third exhortation is given to his "true comrade," who is asked to assist the women in settling their differences (4:3). Is this person named Syzygos or is he one of Paul's co-workers, such as Timothy or Luke or Epaphroditus? Given Luke's association with Philippi in Acts and his desire for anonymity in the same book, one wonders if he is the best candidate. Paul's intended audience could undoubtedly recognize the allusion, even if we cannot.

4:1 Ὥστε, ἀδελφοί μου ἀγαπητοὶ καὶ ἐπιπόθητοι, χαρὰ καὶ στέφανός μου, οὕτως στήκετε ἐν κυρίῳ, ἀγαπητοί.

Ὥστε, ἀδελφοί ... ἀγαπητοὶ ... ἐπιπόθητοι, χαρὰ ... στέφανός ... στήκετε ... ἀγαπητοί. The consequential particle combined with six terms of address and the switch to the imperative mark a shift in the discourse (Reed 1997, 266). This should be noted because 4:1 is often viewed as the conclusion of 3:17–21. While the passages are certainly related, these distinct markers set off 4:1 as a fresh paraenetic emphasis in the Pauline writing strategy.

Ὥστε. This conjunction introduces an independent clause (BDAG 1107.1) and draws consequences from what precedes (3:17–21). The particle appears also in 1:13 and 2:12, each time beginning a new unit and initiating a statement of some consequence.

ἀδελφοί. Vocative, or more preferably, a nominative of direct address (Porter 1994, 86–87). The noun ἀδελφοί is used "in the collective sense of *brothers and sisters*" (CGELNT, 6).

μου. Possessive genitive.

ἀγαπητοί. Nominative adjective (substantival) in apposition to ἀδελφοί. Paul uses this adjective here and in 2:12 with the personal pronoun and following the particle Ὥστε.

ἐπιπόθητοι. Nominative adjective (substantival) in apposition to ἀδελφοί. *Hapax legomenon*, an adjective not found in any previous Greek literature. GE (784) defines it as "desired, sadly missed." It is utilized later in *1 Clem.* 65.1 and *Barn.* 1.3. Paul did use the verb ἐπιποθέω ("long for"), however, in Phil 1:8; 2:26, as well as in 2 Cor 5:2; 9:14; Rom 1:11; 1 Thess 3:6; and 2 Tim 1:4.

χαρά. Nominative in apposition to ἀδελφοί. The shift to the

collective singular indicates a more personal relationship to Paul and is further indicated by the repetition of the following μου. This joy is eschatologically focused.

καί. The use of the second καί at this point indicates that the two nouns χαρά – στέφανός function differently from the first two plural adjectives.

στέφανός. Nominative in apposition to ἀδελφοί. This noun means "wreath, crown" in its literal usage (BDAG, 943.1) and is often associated with the games. Trench's explanation of the contrast between στέφανός ("chaplet") and διάδημα ("kingly") crowns is helpful but needs nuancing (Trench, 74–77). GE (1961) removes the idea of "crown" by citing its already extensive metaphorical meaning of "prize, reward, reason for glory or honor." See NIDNTTE (4:371–72) for warnings about the appropriate semantic nuance. Paul addressed the Thessalonians with this term along with χαρά (1 Thess 2:19), so metaphorically στέφανος refers to eschatological "reward" (1 Cor 9:25; BDAG, 944.3).

μου. Possessive genitive.

οὕτως. This adverb refers back to the preceding passage, especially to the statement in 3:20 related to heavenly citizenship.

στήκετε. Pres act impv 2nd pl στήκω. The indicative στήκετε in 1:27, which expressed the apostle's hope for them, he now turns into a decisive imperative.

ἐν κυρίῳ. Locative, where the firm stand takes place.

ἀγαπητοί. The last of the five adjectives/nouns in apposition to ἀδελφοί is stressed by repeating the first one.

4:2 Εὐοδίαν παρακαλῶ καὶ Συντύχην παρακαλῶ τὸ αὐτὸ φρονεῖν ἐν κυρίῳ.

Εὐοδίαν. Accusative direct object of παρακαλῶ. A Greek name found in inscriptions (MM, 263). Some have occasionally suggested that the name could refer to a male (see KJV "Euodias"), but the feminine αὐταῖς in 3:3 makes it certain that both Εὐοδία and Συντύχη were women. The corresponding noun means "good journey" or "good success" (GE, 857).

παρακαλῶ. Pres act ind 1st sg παρακαλέω. Reed describes the use of the verbs παρακαλῶ and ἐρωτῶ (4:3) as "conventional epistolary language" in order to introduce a new topic in the discourse (1997, 265). He cites Mullins who documents the use of these verbs in ancient epistolary petitions (1997, 266 n406). This section has the highest concentration of imperatives in the book (4:1, 3, 4[2], 5, 6[2], 8, 9). In another section of concentrated imperatives (1:27–2:5), the theme is also unity.

Συντύχην. Accusative direct object of παρακαλῶ. The nearest cognate noun, συντυχία, means "good fortune, success" (GE, 2055). There is no semantic significance to the original meaning of these two names.

παρακαλῶ. Pres act ind 1st sg παρακαλέω. The repetition of the imperative is for added emphasis and to particularize the command for each person. "It is unusual to find it (i.e., παρακαλῶ) directed to single individuals rather than to the church as a whole, or at least to a segment of the community" (Sumney, 99).

τὸ αὐτὸ. Accusative direct object of φρονεῖν. Three examples of the direct object-verb (OV) word order in this verse indicate the prominence of both the subjects and the unity commanded. The collocation of αὐτός and φρονέω appeared earlier in 2:2.

φρονεῖν. Pres act inf φρονέω (indirect discourse). The dominance of φρονέω language (1:7; 2:2, 5; 3:15, 19; 4:10) continues to convey the main theme of the book: to think in unity.

ἐν κυρίῳ. Locative. Since this is where the firm stand must take place (see 4:1), it is also where similar thinking must take place.

4:3 ναὶ ἐρωτῶ καὶ σέ, γνήσιε σύζυγε, συλλαμβάνου αὐταῖς, αἵτινες ἐν τῷ εὐαγγελίῳ συνήθλησάν μοι μετὰ καὶ Κλήμεντος καὶ τῶν λοιπῶν συνεργῶν μου, ὧν τὰ ὀνόματα ἐν βίβλῳ ζωῆς.

ναὶ. The TR replaces this affirmative particle with the conjunction καὶ, reflected in the KJV, but this reading has been found in only two medieval manuscripts (131 1243). The affirmative particle ναὶ can also confirm a previous assertion (Robertson, 1150) or emphasize a point by repetition (BDAG, 665.c), "yes indeed."

ἐρωτῶ. Pres act ind 1st sg ἐρωτάω. The semantic field of the verb moves from "inquire" or "question" in Attic to "request" in LXX and NT (GE, 827).

καί. Adverbial ("also").

σέ. Accusative direct object of ἐρωτῶ.

γνήσιε. Vocative adjective.

σύζυγε. Vocative of σύζυγος, with γνήσιε: "true comrade" (BDAG, 954). *Hapax legomenon*. LSB renders as "genuine companion." Some translations (NJB NRSVmg NLTmg) have understood the noun to refer to a particular individual named Συζυγος ("Syzygus"), although no such name has survived from the Greco-Roman world (Fee, 392–93 n40; GE, 1993), nor was it adopted as a Christian name (Lampe, 1278). Because one "we" section in Acts ends and another recommences in Philippi, Hagner suggests that Luke was this "comrade" known to the church there (547 n1). This suggestion fits with Luke's apparent desire for anonymity and is worthy of thoughtful consideration.

συλλαμβάνου. Pres mid impv 2nd sg συλλαμβάνω. BDAG (955–56.4) translates this verb as "help by taking part w[ith] someone in an activity, support, aid, help."

αὐταῖς. Dative complement of συλλαμβάνου.

αἵτινες. Relative pronoun, nominative subject of συνήθλησάν.

ἐν τῷ εὐαγγελίῳ. Locative. As in 1:5, the noun refers not just to the message of "good news" but to the ministry of proclaiming that good news.

συνήθλησάν. Aor act ind 3rd plural συναθλέω. While Paul does not hesitate to imply athletic imagery, the compound verb evidently was not used that way in Attic (GE, 2018). In the NT it is used only here and in 1:27. BDAG (964) translates this verb as "contend, struggle along with." Combined with εὐαγγελίῳ and μοι, "they fought at my side in spreading the gospel."

μοι. Dative complement of συνήθλησάν.

μετὰ καί. This combination is pleonastic (BDF §442.13). In other words, καί does not need to be translated.

καὶ ... καί. If translated, the combination should not be "both ... and" but "also ... and."

μετὰ ... Κλήμεντος. Association.

τῶν λοιπῶν συνεργῶν. Association, governed by μετά. This is the fourth συν- word in the verse, which includes two verbs (συλλαμβάνου and συνήθλησάν), and two nouns (σύζυγε and συνεργῶν). Sinaiticus has καὶ τῶν συνεργῶν μου καὶ τῶν λοιπῶν ("and my coworkers and the others"), but this has been called "a scribal inadvertence" (Metzger, 549). The probable reading of 𝔓¹⁶, however, suggests that the women and Clement were not included under Paul's category of "coworkers."

μου. Genitive of association.

ὧν. Relative pronoun, possessive genitive. Efforts to join this word to other genitives (τῶν λοιπῶν συνεργῶν) are not needed because the relative pronoun does not take the case of its antecedent but the case appropriate to its function in the clause ("the names of whom").

τὰ ὀνόματα. Nominative plural subject of an implied verb such as ἐστίν, because of the neuter plural subject, or an implied participle construction like τῶν γεγραμμένων.

ἐν βίβλῳ. Locative. Although theological and thus metaphorical, at this time βίβλιον would have been a papyrus scroll, not a codex or "book"; see CEB: "scroll of life."

ζωῆς. Epexegetical genitive. No article accompanies either βίβλῳ or ζωῆς, which is either an example of Apollonius' canon (Moule, 114–15) or because the phrase follows a preposition (Turner, 180). OT antecedents of the expression βίβλῳ ζωῆς can be found in LXX Ps 68:29; 86:6; 138:16; Exod 32:32; Isa 4:3; Mal 3:16; Dan 12:1; Ezek 13:9, although no example contains the exact two words of Phil 4:3.

Philippians 4:4–7

> ⁴ Rejoice in the Lord always. Again I will say it: Rejoice! ⁵ Let your considerate spirit be known to all people. The Lord is near. ⁶ Do not worry about anything, but in everything, through prayer and petition with thanksgiving, let your requests be made known to God. ⁷ Then the peace of God, which surpasses every thought, will guard your hearts and your thoughts in Christ Jesus.

> ¶ Rejoice in the Lord always; again I will say, rejoice! Let your considerate *spirit* be known to all men. The Lord is near. Be anxious for nothing, but in everything by prayer and petition with thanksgiving let your requests be made known to God. And the peace of God, which surpasses all comprehension, will guard your hearts and your minds in Christ Jesus. (LSB)

Analysis of Philippians Four

Summary: There are two separate paragraphs of final exhortations (4:4–6, 8–9b), more general than 4:2–3 but still appropriate for the Philippians, and each is concluded with a promise of peace (4:7, 9c). The first set of exhortations differs both from those that immediately precede them (4:2–3) and those that follow (4:8–9), being less specific than the words spoken directly to Euodia, Syntyche, and a "true syzygos" and contain a miscellaneous collection of four independent exhortations ("rejoice," "let your gentleness be known," "do not worry," and "let your requests be made known to God") and one affirmation ("the Lord is near"). The exhortations are appropriate to the letter that has preceded. Rejoicing is a note heard repeatedly (1:3, 25; 2:2, 17–18, 28–29; 3:1; 4:1, 4, 10). "Gentleness" is needed by a congregation threatened with possible conflict. The statement made in the midst of the exhortations ("the Lord is near") keeps before the reader the eschatological thrust of the letter. Prayer as an antidote to worry is a fitting word for a community undergoing opposition and suffering. The militant guarding of hearts recalls the guarding of a city (2 Cor 11:32), to guard from the inside as well as the outside.

4:4 Χαίρετε ἐν κυρίῳ πάντοτε· πάλιν ἐρῶ, χαίρετε.

Χαίρετε. Pres act impv 2nd pl χαίρω. The strong emphasis on joy and rejoicing provides further evidence of an important theme in the book. The main theme of unity, which has been developed in the discourse analysis, is not displaced by this clear emphasis on joy. As is the case here and elsewhere in the book, joy is a byproduct of unity (4:2, 3; see also 2:1–2).

ἐν κυρίῳ. This phrase "may designate the object of their rejoicing or the sphere within which their rejoicing takes place. Perhaps these should not be separated" (Sumney, 101–2). This should remind us that many of these case usage decisions are determined by context and not by some clear indicator in the word itself.

πάντοτε. Adverb, modifying Χαίρετε.

πάλιν. Adverb, modifying ἐρῶ. The alliteration with πάντοτε is probably conscious since it also occurred in 1:4: πάντοτε ἐν πάσῃ δεήσει μου ὑπὲρ πάντων ὑμῶν.

ἐρῶ. Fut act ind 1st sg λέγω.

χαίρετε. Pres act impv 2nd pl χαίρω. See above. The intensity of the collocation with ἐρῶ is equivalent to a hortatory subjunctive (Zerwick, 117: "let me say it anew, rejoice!"). Mathewson and Emig (259) call attention to the rhetorical effect of the asyndeton here. The use of these short commands without intervening conjunctions is continued in the following exhortations (4:5–6).

4:5 τὸ ἐπιεικὲς ὑμῶν γνωσθήτω πᾶσιν ἀνθρώποις. ὁ κύριος ἐγγύς.

τὸ ἐπιεικὲς. The article nominalizes the neuter adjective which is the subject of γνωσθήτω. According to BDAG (371), τό ἐπιεικές is equivalent to ἡ ἐπιείκεια and suggests "forbearing spirit." Some versions (e.g., NIV) render the neuter substantive as "gentleness." Others prefer "gentle spirit" (NASB). I have opted, with the LSB, for "considerate *spirit*." GE (764) mentions that Plutarch personifies ἐπιείκεια as the character "Clemency." The fronting of the subject in the clause increases its markedness as a new subject (Porter 1994, 295–96).

ὑμῶν. Possessive genitive.

γνωσθήτω. Aor pass impv 3rd sg γινώσκω. This is one of only three aorist imperatives in the book (see 2:2 and 4:21). The shift to the third person does not lessen the urgency of the imperatival command (Wallace, 485–87; ME, 181 suggest "should be known"). The third person is used to accommodate the subject τὸ ἐπιεικὲς. Note also 4:6: τὰ αἰτήματα ὑμῶν γνωριζέσθω πρὸς τὸν θεόν. A passive imperative "is a different sort of command in which the recipient has a responsibility to see that the action gets done" (Boyer 1987, 49).

πᾶσιν ἀνθρώποις. Dative indirect object of γνωσθήτω. The noun is generic for "all people."

ὁ κύριος. Nominative subject of an implied verb like ἔστιν. Consistent with its other NT usages in an eschatological context, ὁ κύριος is undoubtedly a reference to Jesus (e.g., 1 Thess 4:15; Jas 5:7).

ἐγγύς. Predicate adjectival use of the adverb. The LXX passages with these words, such as Ps 118:151 and Ps 144:18, indicate the present nearness of the Lord. NT passages like Jas 5:8, Luke 21:31, and 1 Pet 4:7 use ἐγγύς or the cognate verb ἐγγίζω in an eschatological sense. 1 Cor 16:22 contains the Aramaic equivalent, μαράνα θά, so the expression was a familiar one in the early church. Compare *Barn.* 21.3, ἐγγὺς ὁ κύριος καὶ ὁ μισθὸς αὐτοῦ, which echoes these NT statements. The asyndeton leads some to think that ὁ κύριος ἐγγύς culminates 4:4–5a as the ground for the previous imperatives (Lightfoot, 160), while others see the clause as introducing the imperatives that follow in 4:6 (Chrysostom). The clause also may have both an anaphoric and a cataphoric function. Silva (198–99) observes that both what precedes (ἐπιεικὲς) and what follows (μηδὲν μεριμνᾶτε) are semantically connected. Fee (407 n35) also sees an "intentional double entendre."

4:6 μηδὲν μεριμνᾶτε, ἀλλ᾽ ἐν παντὶ τῇ προσευχῇ καὶ τῇ δεήσει μετὰ εὐχαριστίας τὰ αἰτήματα ὑμῶν γνωριζέσθω πρὸς τὸν θεόν.

μηδὲν. Accusative direct object of μεριμνᾶτε. Because this is the object of an intransitive verb, BDAG (647.2.b.β) calls this an "accusative of the inner object" that can be rendered "not ... at all." Moule (34) prefers an accusative of reference, or an implied cognate accusative; *μηδεμίαν μεριμνάν* μεριμνᾶτε literally means "be anxious about no anxiety" (Moule, 32).

μεριμνᾶτε. Pres act impv 2nd pl μεριμνάω: "to be anxious or distressed, worry, fret" (GE, 1313). The present imperative does not necessarily mean "stop being concerned" (contra Reumann, 614). Negated present imperatives convey general commands (Young, 142) unless the context indicates there is a behavior that must cease.

ἀλλ᾽. Conjunction that introduces the positive alternative to worry. "When ἀλλά links a negative characteristic or proposition with a following positive one, the negative proposition usually retains its relevance" (Levinsohn 2000, 115).

ἐν παντὶ. Locative.

τῇ προσευχῇ. Dative of means.

τῇ δεήσει. Dative of means. "While προσευχὴ is the general offering up of the wishes and desires to God, δέησις implies special petition for the supply of wants" (Lightfoot, 160).

μετὰ εὐχαριστίας. Manner. This word is used by Paul in 12 of its 15 occurrences.

τὰ αἰτήματα. Nominative subject of γνωριζέσθω. The three types of "prayer" are each distinguished by an accompanying article from the anarthrous εὐχαριστίας. The latter is not a type of "prayer" but describes the attitude in which the three types of prayer should be offered. Trench (176–80) has an excellent discussion of all these synonyms for prayer.

ὑμῶν. Genitive of source.

γνωριζέσθω. Pres pass impv 3rd sg γνωρίζω. Neuter plural subject can take a singular verb. Verbs ending in -ίζω are usually causative (Robertson, 140; compare γινώσκω, "know" with γνωρίζω, "make known"). See comments on the function of the passive imperative γνωσθήτω in 4:5.

πρὸς τὸν θεόν. Direction.

4:7 καὶ ἡ εἰρήνη τοῦ θεοῦ ἡ ὑπερέχουσα πάντα νοῦν φρουρήσει τὰς καρδίας ὑμῶν καὶ τὰ νοήματα ὑμῶν ἐν Χριστῷ Ἰησοῦ.

καὶ. A future tense (φρουρήσει) preceded by an imperative (γνωριζέσθω) and joined by καί functions like a result clause in a Semitic type of conditional clause: "make your request known, then the peace of God will guard your hearts" (BDF §227).

ἡ εἰρήνη. Nominative subject of φρουρήσει.

τοῦ θεοῦ. Genitive of source. Wallace (104–6) has suggested a new category which he calls the "genitive of producer" listing 4:7 as an example. He acknowledges, though, that "the discussion of this category is admittedly in seminal form" (105 n89).

ἡ ὑπερέχουσα. Pres act ptc nom fem sg ὑπερέχω. Attributive participle modifying εἰρήνη. BDAG (1033.3) translates ὑπερέχω as "to surpass in quality or value." This is the third appearance of this verb in the letter, each time in a participial form (see 2:3 and 3:8).

πάντα νοῦν. Accusative direct object of ὑπερέχουσα. BDAG (680.1.b) translates νοῦς as "understanding, mind as the faculty of thinking." It refers to "the reasoning power in each person, practical perception rather than an 'academic mind'" (Reumann, 615). This is the noun's only appearance in Philippians, which is surprising considering all that is said about thinking and thought, but see the following νοήματα.

φρουρήσει. Fut act ind 3rd sg φρουρέω. See the significance of the future tense in the comments about καί above. While some authors see this as a military term (Rogers and Rogers, 457), MM (677) and

BDAG (1066–67) offer many non-military and metaphorical examples, although the verbal paradox of εἰρήνη providing the guarding should not be overlooked. From 2 Cor 11:32 (ἐν Δαμασκῷ ὁ ἐθνάρχης Ἀρέτα τοῦ βασιλέως ἐφρούρει τὴν πόλιν Δαμασκηνῶν πιάσαι με), the idea may be to "guard from the inside," not the outside.

τὰς καρδίας. Accusative direct object of φρουρήσει. The noun καρδία refers to the center of each person, which is "the seat of courage and feeling" (GE, 1035A).

ὑμῶν. Genitive of possession.

τὰ νοήματα. Accusative direct object of φρουρήσει. The noun νόημα appears only 6 times in the NT, five of them in 2 Cor (2:11; 3:14; 4:4; 10:5; 11:3). Although frequent in extra-biblical Greek, the word is little used in the LXX. Its basic meaning, with the -μα suffix, is the result of the activity of the νους, or simply "thought(s)" (NIDNTTE 3:430; EDNT 2:470). Some Western witnesses (F G it[ar]) replace νοήματα with σώματα to expand the areas covered by καρδίας and νοήματα. There is no reason to question the wording in NA[28] and THGNT. A few Western witnesses (F G it) read τας καρδιας υμων και τα σωματα υμων. The third-century 𝔓[16] has the conflated τας καρδιας υμων και τα νοηματα και τα σωματα υμων, an evidence of protection of the psychological and physical life. The context favors protection over the thought-life.

ὑμῶν. Genitive of possession or source.

ἐν Χριστῷ Ἰησοῦ. See comments on ἐν κυρίῳ in 4:4.

Philippians 4:8–9

> [8] Finally brothers, whatever is true, whatever is honorable, whatever is right, whatever is pure, whatever is pleasing, whatever is commendable—if there is any virtue and if there is anything worthy of praise—let your mind dwell on these things. [9] Whatever you have also learned and accepted and heard and seen in me, do these things; thus the God of peace will be with you.

> ¶ Finally, brothers, whatever is true, whatever is dignified, whatever is right, whatever is pure, whatever is lovely, whatever is commendable, if there is any excellence and if anything worthy

of praise, consider these things. The things you have learned and received and heard and seen in me, practice these things, and the God of peace will be with you. (LSB)

Summary: Unlike the miscellaneous collection in the preceding paragraph, the second paragraph of exhortations is presented in a more eloquent and structured form. In 4:8 six virtues, introduced by a similar "whatever," are listed, followed by two conditional clauses and a present imperative ("think about these things"). The list of words is used for the things that should fill the Christian's thought-life. In 4:9 four verbs are listed and then followed by a present imperative ("keep on doing these things"). The paralleling of the two imperatives indicates that the two verses should be read together. Living by what we know and acknowledge will result in the life that Paul had sought to model. Not only will God's peace be found but also his abiding presence. The "peace of God" (4:7) is possible because of the "God of peace" (4:9).

4:8 Τὸ λοιπόν, ἀδελφοί, ὅσα ἐστὶν ἀληθῆ, ὅσα σεμνά, ὅσα δίκαια, ὅσα ἁγνά, ὅσα προσφιλῆ, ὅσα εὔφημα, εἴ τις ἀρετὴ καὶ εἴ τις ἔπαινος, ταῦτα λογίζεσθε·

Τὸ λοιπόν. Adjective functioning adverbially, repeated from 3:1. While many see this as a closure formula (GNB, "In conclusion"), because of its repetition and since the closing section actually begins with 4:10, Robertson (1146) and Thrall (25–26, 28) suggest that the word functions almost like οὖν, which has been used 5 times, the last of which was in 3:15. GE (1252) documents this adverbial usage in Plato and Polybius and also calls attention to its being used this way in Matt 26:45 and Mark 14:41. I propose that it functions not to introduce the "final" part of this letter but as a climactic οὖν which introduces the final summation of Paul's emphasis on "thought" and "thinking."

ἀδελφοί. Nominative of direct address. See 1:12 and 3:1 (with μου). The noun ἀδελφοί is used "in the collective sense of *brothers and sisters*" (CGELNT, 6).

ὅσα. Nominative neuter plural relative pronoun subject of ἐστὶν.

ἐστίν. Pres act ind 3rd sg εἰμί. Singular verb with ὅσα neuter plural subjects (BDF §133), which is implied in the remaining clauses.

ἀληθῆ. Neuter plural predicate adjective agreeing with ὅσα. Each of the following five clauses are structured in the same way: a relative pronoun that is the subject of an implied ἐστίν is followed by a predicate adjective. For each adjective the contextual gloss in BDAG will be listed as well as the reference to the further discussion of the adjective in NIDNTTE or in MM. Thus BDAG (43.2) defines ἀληθής as "true"; see also NIDNTTE (1:222–41).

σεμνά. BDAG (919.b) defines σεμνός as "honorable"; see also NIDNTTE (4:282–83).

δίκαια. BDAG (247.2) defines δίκαιος as "right"; see also NIDNTTE (1:723–41).

ἁγνά. BDAG (13.b) defines ἁγνός as "pure"; see also NIDNTTE (1:137–39).

προσφιλῆ. Hapax legomenon. BDAG (886–87) defines προσφιλής as "pleasing"; see also NIDNTTE (4:605–8).

εὔφημα. Hapax legomenon. BDAG (414) defines εὔφημος as "commendable"; see also MM (267).

εἴ. Conditional particle introducing the first protasis of a first class conditional clause. See 2:1 also where εἴ introduces the conditional clause assuming the reality of the protasis: "If ... as we assume."

τις ἀρετή. Nominative subject of the implied verb ἐστίν. BDAG (130.1) defines ἀρετή as "uncommon character worthy of praise, excellence of character, exceptional civic virtue"; see also NIDNTTE (1:388–91). Paul takes a term that was a commonplace in Greco-Roman ethical discussions (GE, 293) and refocuses it as a Christian virtue by surrounding it with accompanying virtues.

καί. Conjunction that connects coordinate elements in the dual protasis.

εἴ. Conditional particle introducing the second protasis of a first class conditional clause.

τις ἔπαινος. Nominative subject of the implied verb ἐστίν. BDAG (357.2) defines ἔπαινος as "a thing worthy of praise"; see also NIDNTTE (1:172–73). Silva agrees with Meyer's claim that each of the virtues "represents the Christian moral character generally, so that in reality the same thing is described, but according to the various aspects which commended it" (Meyer, 206–7), and adds that "all of these qualities could be subsumed under τὰ ἀγαθά" (Silva, 199).

ταῦτα λογίζεσθε. The apodosis of the conditional sentence.

ταῦτα. Accusative plural demonstrative pronoun, direct object of λογίζεσθε, fronted to function anaphorically by referring back to the previous neuter ὅσα.

λογίζεσθε. Pres mid impv 2nd pl λογίζομαι. Paul creatively varies his φρονέω-terminology (see 2:2) with this verb which BDAG (598.2) elaborates as "to give careful thought to a matter, think (about), consider, ponder, let one's mind dwell on"; see also NIDNTTE (3:123–27).

4:9 ἃ καὶ ἐμάθετε καὶ παρελάβετε καὶ ἠκούσατε καὶ εἴδετε ἐν ἐμοί, ταῦτα πράσσετε· καὶ ὁ θεὸς τῆς εἰρήνης ἔσται μεθ᾽ ὑμῶν.

Paul continues the same order that he used in 4:8 by fronting the relative clause followed by an anaphoric demonstrative pronoun and imperative command.

ἅ. Accusative relative pronoun functioning as the direct object of the following four verbs.

καὶ ... καὶ ... καὶ ... καὶ. Adverbial, "also ... and." All four verbs are preceded by καὶ; the polysyndeton style is intended to convey abundance in a staccato fashion (Robertson, 1182; BDF §460.3). An adjunctive sense for the first καὶ ("also") is preferable to an adversative sense.

ἐμάθετε. Aor act ind 2nd pl μανθάνω.

παρελάβετε. Aor act ind 2nd pl παραλαμβάνω. While μανθάνω ("learn") stresses learning by instruction, παραλαμβάνω ("accept") has a focus on agreement or approval (BDAG, 768.3.b; see 1 Cor 15:1).

ἠκούσατε. Aor act ind 2nd pl ἀκούω.

εἴδετε. Aor act ind 2nd pl ὁράω.

ἐν ἐμοί. Locative. Although following εἴδετε, some (e.g., O'Brien 1991, 511) consider this PP as also following the other three verbs. The Philippians saw (εἴδετε) what Paul's behavior was like when he was in Philippi and heard (ἠκούσατε) from others like Timothy and Epaphroditus what he was like elsewhere.

ταῦτα. Accusative direct object of πράσσετε. The demonstrative pronoun is fronted for emphasis and functions anaphorically by pointing back to the previous relative clause.

πράσσετε. Pres act impv 2nd pl πράσσω. The verb πράσσω is not to be interpreted as a contrast to λογίζομαι in 3:8. Unlike ποιέω it never refers to creative activity. Paul joins two elements found in Greek ethical writers: right thinking (4:8) and right doing (4:9). In this way he shows the connection between moral ideals and moral action (Moore, 235).

καί. Conjunction used as an adverb, "thus" (ILNTG, 57).

ὁ θεός. Nominative subject of ἔσται.

τῆς εἰρήνης. Genitive of product like in the expression ὁ θεὸς τῆς εἰρήνης in Rom 15:22 (Wallace, 106). It is possible that ὁ θεὸς τῆς εἰρήνης is intended to balance ἡ εἰρήνη τοῦ θεοῦ in 4:7, thus forming an *inclusio*, although a chiasm is more difficult to discern. While ὁ θεὸς τῆς εἰρήνης may function as a veiled critique of Roman propaganda about the *Pax Augusti* in this Roman colony (Reumann, 621–22), anti-Roman nuances should not be preferred over the simple contextual call for spiritual peace and unity in the letter. Note the balance in the inclusio regarding "the peace of God" (4:7) and "the God of peace" (4:13).

ἔσται. Fut act ind 3rd sg εἰμί. There is no need to take this clause as the apodosis of an implied condition ("if you do these things, then God will be with you"; NAB), since Paul has shown no hesitance in clearly conveying his conditional clauses (see 4:8b).

μεθ' ὑμῶν. Accompaniment. This unconditional indicative promise of the divine presence echoes covenant promises of the OT (Gen 21:22; Exod 3:12; Josh 1:5; Ps 23:4). See also Rom 15:33 and 2 Thess 3:16.

Philippians 4:10–14

> [10] Now I rejoiced through the Lord greatly because once again you have renewed your care for me. You were, in fact, concerned about me but lacked the opportunity to show it. [11] I do not say this out of need, for I have learned to be content in the circumstances where I am. [12] I know how to have a little, and I know how to have a lot. In any and all circumstances I am taught both to be satisfied and to be hungry, to be both in abundance and in need. [13] I am able to do all things through him who strengthens me. [14] Still, you did well by sharing with what distresses me.

¶ But I rejoiced in the Lord greatly, that now at last you have revived thinking about me; indeed, you were thinking about me *before*, but you lacked opportunity. Not that I speak from want, for I learned to be content in whatever circumstances I am. I know how to get along with humble means, and I also know how to live in abundance; in any and all things I have learned the secret of being filled and going hungry, both of having abundance and suffering need. I can do all things through Him who strengthens me. Nevertheless, you have done well to fellowship *with me* in my affliction. (LSB)

Summary: Paul turns finally to one of the main reasons for writing his letter: to express his gratitude to the Philippians for their generous gift sent through their apostle/messenger, Epaphroditus. In chapter two he has alluded to their kindness and expressed great affection for Epaphroditus, but he has not described the gift in detail until now. We might think that a note of thanks at the end of a letter may look like an afterthought. Because of the lapse of time between the arrival of Epaphroditus with that gift and the writing of this note, some scholars have suggested that 4:10–20 was a separate letter written by Paul soon after he received the gift from the Philippians. This purely hypothetical solution is to be rejected and has been by most recent scholars. There are better explanations for what some imagine as an irregularity.

4:10 Ἐχάρην δὲ ἐν κυρίῳ μεγάλως ὅτι ἤδη ποτὲ ἀνεθάλετε τὸ ὑπὲρ ἐμοῦ φρονεῖν, ἐφ᾽ ᾧ καὶ ἐφρονεῖτε, ἠκαιρεῖσθε δέ.

Ἐχάρην. Aor pass ind 1st sg χαίρω. Hawthorne (260) calls this an epistolary aorist, but it is a genuine past tense recalling Epaphroditus' arrival, not a present tense viewed from the perspective of the recipients. This verb is another indication of joy in the epistle.

δέ. Marks development from the paragraph (4:4–9) with the readers as the focus (one first person verb) to the paragraph (4:10–20) where Paul is again the focus (14 first person verbs). The translation "now" indicates that development more than conveying temporality.

ἐν κυρίῳ. Instrumental (see 2:19).

μεγάλως. Adverb, "greatly."

ὅτι. Most English versions since Tyndale have translated ὅτι as "that" (introducing the clausal complement of Ἐχάρην), but a causal clause ("because"; NET CEB) makes better sense and provides the ground for his rejoicing (BDAG 1075.1; Hawthorne, 196; Fee, 428 n21).

ἤδη ποτέ. Combination of a temporal adverb and a temporal enclitic particle. For this collocation BDAG (434, 856) suggests "now at last." This sounds like a rebuke in the KJV ("now at the last") or NEB ("after so long ... now"). There is nothing contextual, however, to suggest Paul is chiding the Philippians for delay; cf. Rom 1:10, εἴ πως ἤδη ποτέ εὐοδωθήσομαι ("if now at last the way may be opened").

ἀνεθάλετε. Aor act ind 2nd pl ἀναθάλλω. *Hapax legomenon,* also "very rare in Greek writings and only in the poets" (Thayer, 37; see also GE, 134). MM (33) mentions its use in LXX and in one papyrus. The question is whether this verb should be translated intransitively, "grow up again, bloom again" (BDAG, 63.1) or transitively, "cause to grow/bloom again" (BDAG, 63.2). Since it appears as transitive in the LXX both literally (Sir 50:10; Ezek 17:24) and figuratively (Sir 1:18; 11:22), it should be taken here as transitive with τὸ ὑπὲρ ἐμοῦ φρονεῖν as its object: "you have renewed your care for me."

τὸ ὑπὲρ ἐμοῦ φρονεῖν. Infinitival clause that functions as direct object of ἀνεθάλετε.

τὸ ... φρονεῖν. Pres act inf φρονέω (substantival). See comments on 1:7; 2:2, 5; 3:15, 19; 4:2.

ὑπὲρ ἐμοῦ. For this collocation with the verb φρονέω BDAG (1030.A.1.δ) has: "think of me = care for, be interested in me."

ἐφ᾽ ᾧ. Causal. BDAG (ἐπί, 363.6.c and ὅς, 725.1.k.δ) suggests that in the four passages with this combination (Phil 3:12; 4:10; 2 Cor 5:4; Rom 5:12) the meaning is causal, and the translation can vary between "for, indeed" and "for the reason that, because." The antecedent of the dative relative pronoun ᾧ is unclear. Moule (132) suggests that the antecedent is the previous ἐμοῦ, i.e., Paul, thus "for whom." His suggestion is grammatically sound and is consistent with the context. The CSB adopts this sense: "You renewed your care for me."

καί. Adverbial ("also").

ἐφρονεῖτε. Impf act ind 2nd pl φρονέω. Imperfective aspect portrays the process of their concern. This is the tenth occurrence of this verb in Philippians. Here it carries the idea of "think of someone in the sense to be concerned about him" (BDAG, 1065.1). "Paul, after assuring the Philippians that he had the right frame of mind toward them (1:7), and then rebuking them for not having the right frame of mind toward one another (2:2, 5; 3:15; 4:2), here at the end encourages them by recognizing a very positive trait in their attitude" (Silva, 208–9).

ἠκαιρεῖσθε. Impf mid ind 2nd pl ἀκαιρέομαι. *Hapax legomenon.* "A Hellenistic derivative from καιρός plus the *alpha* privative" (BDF §117.1). The adjective ἄκαιρος means "untimely, ill-timed" (Sir 20:19; 22:6) and contrasts with εὔκαιρος that means "favorable" (Mark 6:21). With the alpha privative, ἀκαιρέομαι would bear the sense of "you had no time or opportunity" (LN 67.7; GE, 62).

δέ. Marks the development from their intent to their capability.

4:11 οὐχ ὅτι καθ' ὑστέρησιν λέγω, ἐγὼ γὰρ ἔμαθον ἐν οἷς εἰμι αὐτάρκης εἶναι.

οὐχ ὅτι. BDAG (732.2.b) states that this combination is used "in ellipses" for οὐ λέγω ὅτι, as in 3:12 and 4:17. Fee (342 n17) adds that in idiomatic English it means something like "this is not to say that."

ὅτι. Introduces the clausal complement of the implied verb λέγω.

καθ' ὑστέρησιν. BDAG (512–13.5.a.δ) lists κατά in 4:11 among texts in which "the norm is at the same time the reason," so that "in accordance with" and "because of" have been merged. See Acts 3:17 (κατὰ ἄγνοιαν ἐπράξατε) and Rom 10:2 (ζῆλον θεοῦ ἔχουσιν ἀλλ' οὐ κατ' ἐπίγνωσιν). The noun ὑστέρησις is used elsewhere only to describe the widow in Mark 12:24 (ἐκ τῆς ὑστερήσεως αὐτῆς). CSB: "Out of need."

λέγω. Pres act ind 1st sg λέγω.

ἐγώ. The inclusion of the pronoun could be emphatic, but it is difficult to see why Paul would have needed to add such emphasis. It may simply have been added so γάρ could be in a postpositive position (Reumann, 651).

γάρ. A conjunction that can express cause, clarification, or inference. Here it is a "marker of clarification" that can be translated "for, you see" (BDAG, 189.2; ILNTG, 43).

ἔμαθον. Aor act ind 1st sg μανθάνω. The tense functions as a consummative aorist (Wallace, 559–561), stressing the accomplishment of his learning. "If he has learned how to be content in every circumstance, then he is not speaking out of needing more from them" (Moore, 243).

ἐν οἷς. Temporal. The careful choice of the relative pronoun ὅς rather than the indefinite relative ὅστις has semantic implications that most versions do not indicate. Paul is not expressing a theoretical idea, "in whatever circumstances I am in" (KJV, NASB, NIV, ESV) but an actual idea, "in what circumstances I am." These words describe the actual experiences that Paul is having (ILNTG, 72, 74). Lightfoot (174) proposes the following translation: "in the position in which I am placed."

εἰμί. Pres act ind 1st sg εἰμί. BDAG (284.3.c) translates the formulation ἐν οἷς εἰμι as "in the situation in which I find myself."

αὐτάρκης. Nominative predicate adjective. *Hapax legomenon*, but the noun αὐτάρκεια occurs in 2 Cor 9:8 and 1 Tim 6:6: "godliness ... with contentment." In the LXX αὐτάρκης occurs only 5 times, but the word describes "a central concept in Greek ethical discussion from the time of Socrates" (TDNT 1:466–67; see also GE, 340). See also NIDNTTE (1:395–97). While recognizing that αὐτάρκης had an important place among virtues which the Stoic philosopher desires, Collange (150) observes that "Paul gives the concept a very un-Stoical meaning: a man does not find true freedom within himself but in God who gives it to him (v. 13)."

εἶναι. Pres act inf (complementary or direct object of ἔμαθον).

4:12 οἶδα καὶ ταπεινοῦσθαι, οἶδα καὶ περισσεύειν· ἐν παντὶ καὶ ἐν πᾶσιν μεμύημαι, καὶ χορτάζεσθαι καὶ πεινᾶν καὶ περισσεύειν καὶ ὑστερεῖσθαι·

οἶδα. Prf act ind 1st sg οἶδα. BDAG (693) explains that this is "really the perf[ect] of the stem εἰδ- (Lat. video), but used as a pres[ent]." Its specific focus in this occurrence is not simply "to know" but "to know/ understand how, can, be able." (694.3).

καί. Correlative conjunction (Wallace, 672) that pairs with the following καί in another of Paul's "both ... and" series (see on 1:7 and 2:13).

ταπεινοῦσθαι. Pres pass inf ταπεινόω (direct object of οἶδα). The sense is better conveyed if "how" is understood before the two infinitives. "I know how to be humbled." This verb also recalls Christ's action in 2:8 (ἐταπείνωσεν ἑαυτὸν).

οἶδα. Repetition to stress the counterbalance of the two verbs.

καί. See καί above.

περισσεύειν. Pres act inf περισσεύω (direct object of οἶδα).

ἐν παντί. Temporal, as ἐν οἷς in 4:11.

ἐν πᾶσιν. Temporal. The expression ἐν παντὶ καὶ ἐν πᾶσιν would be best translated "in any and all circumstances."

μεμύημαι. Prf pass ind 1st sg μυέω. *Hapax legomenon.* BDAG (660) and GE (1367) provide evidence where this verb functions as a technical term of the mystery religions that means "initiate (into the mysteries)." Some translations attempt to convey this influence with the rendering "I have learned the secret" (NIV; LSB), but readers unfamiliar with the mystery religions may understand this translation quite differently from what was intended by Paul. On the other hand, see the KJV, "I am instructed." Indeed, there may be serious question whether Paul intended such a connection at all. The verb appears in Jewish sources only once in this technical meaning (3 Macc 2:30), but there is much evidence for a non-technical meaning since μυέω is common in the Greek Fathers for Christian initiation and instruction (PGL, 887). Patristic interpreters favored the translation "be tested, practiced, taught in," and the Vulgate uses *institutus sum* ("I am instructed"). Silva (204) concludes that Paul uses it as "a colorful stylistic variant for ἔμαθον and οἶδα" and that it is unlikely that he is alluding to cultic initiations; see also NIDNTTE (3:350–57).

καί. This καί is also correlative and is paired with the following ones (BDF §444.5.3).

χορτάζεσθαι. Pres pass inf of χορτάζω (complementary). This verb should be translated intransitively ("to be satisfied"; see Abbott-Smith, 482) rather than transitively ("to fill w[ith] food, feed, fill," BDAG, 1087.1.b). Its meaning is the opposite of the following infinitive πεινᾶν. These verbs also appear as opposites in Matt 5:6.

πεινᾶν. Pres act inf πεινάω (complementary). BDAG (792.1) translates πεινάω as "hunger, be hungry."

περισσεύειν. Pres act inf περισσεύω (complementary). BDAG (805.1) translates περισσεύω as "to be in abundance, abound." Its meaning is the opposite of the following infinitive ὑστερεῖσθαι.

ὑστερεῖσθαι. Pres mid inf ὑστερέω (complementary). BDAG (1043.3) translates ὑστερέω as "to be in need, be needy, lack." This meaning in the middle voice developed from the active "to be behind or late" (GE, 2241–42). Compare its parallel meaning in 1 Cor 1:7. The verb appears also as paired with περισσεύω in 1 Cor 8:8. Heb 11:37 uses this verb to describe the deprivation of some who suffered for their faith.

4:13 πάντα ἰσχύω ἐν τῷ ἐνδυναμοῦντί με.

πάντα. Adverbial accusative of reference (Wallace, 203–4). Strangely, Robertson (478) calls πάντα a "cognate accusative." If the following verb contains the idea of "I am able to do," then the πάντα would be its direct object. The substantive should be measured by the context of contentment in the face of suffering (4:11–12), and not absolutized to cover every endeavor from winning at sports to losing weight.

ἰσχύω. Pres act ind 1st sg ἰσχύω. The term πάντα above could be parallel to πολὺ in the expression in Jas 5:16: πολὺ ἰσχύει δέησις δικαίου, "the prayer of a righteous person is able to do much" (see BDAG, 484.2.a).

ἐν τῷ ἐνδυναμοῦντί. Instrumental.

τῷ ἐνδυναμοῦντί. Pres act ptc masc dat sg ἐνδυναμόω (substantival). BDAG (333.1) translates it as "strengthen." In 3:10 this "strength" or "power" (δύναμις) was clearly indicated as being found in "his resurrection."

με. Accusative direct object of ἐνδυναμοῦντί. Some Western manuscripts (F G Jerome) and the Byzantine text, reflected in the KJV, add Χριστῷ at the end of this clause. The omission, however, has wider and stronger attestation. The variant is clearly a scribal addition (correctors of ℵ and D) intended to clarify that it was Christ who strengthened Paul. "If the word had been present in the original text, there would have been no reason to omit it" (Metzger, 550). NA/UBS and THGNT do not include Χριστῷ. Note the scribal addition, in a "cruder" hand, of the word as a *nomen sacrum* in Codex Sinaiticus:

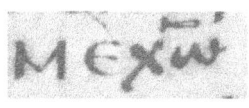

Courtesy of BibleWorks

4:14 Πλὴν καλῶς ἐποιήσατε συγκοινωνήσαντές μου τῇ θλίψει.

Πλὴν. Adverb used as a conjunction. Because πλὴν is a "marker of someth[ing] that is contrastingly added for consideration" (BDAG, 826), it functions to further develop an already expressed thought.

καλῶς ἐποιήσατε συγκοινωνήσαντές. There is a parallel construction in Acts 10:33, σύ τε καλῶς ἐποίησας παραγενόμενος ("You have done well in coming").

καλῶς. The adverb modifies the verb ἐποιήσατε (ME, 68: "you did well"). Although this adverb is often used with an ironic tone (Matt 15:7; Mark 7:9; Luke 20:39; John 4:17; Rom 11:20; 1 Cor 14:17; 2 Cor 11:4; Gal 4:17; Jas 2:8, 19), here its use is quite sincere.

ἐποιήσατε. Aor act ind 2nd plural ποιέω.

συγκοινωνήσαντές. Aor act ptc masc nom pl συγκοινωνέω (complementary, "you did well to share" as in NET and LSB, or means, "you did well by partnering" as in CSB). GE (1988) "to participate, take part." On whether this verb reflects financial support, see comments on κοινωνία in 1:5. In its two other NT appearances the verb συγκοινωνέω with a dative describes sharing in sinful deeds (Eph 5:11) and sharing in the sins of Babylon (Rev 18:4). The CSB[17] altered the HCSB translation "sharing with me" to "partnering with me."

μου. Objective genitive. Of the 18 occurrences of this form in the book, only here and in 2:2 (μου τὴν χαρὰν) does it appear before its head noun. Vincent (146) and Lightfoot (164) suggest that the bringing forward of μου emphasizes the Philippians' special relationship to Paul. The pronoun μου has been understood in an associative sense, with the following dative being locative – "shared with me in (my) distress" (Reed 1997, 209 n210). With κοινωνέω and its cognate verb, however, the following object is in the dative case; cf. BDAG, 952.1 on συγκοινωνέω: "to be associated w[ith] someone in some activity, be connected τινί with someth[ing]." The parallel idea in 4:15 illustrates this same use of the dative following another κοινωνέω verb (μοι … ἐκοινώνησεν).

τῇ θλίψει. Dative complement of συγκοινωνέω. BDAG (457.1), defines θλῖψις as "trouble that inflicts distress, oppression, affliction, tribulation" and suggests the translation, "you showed an interest in my distress." See also GE (946): "oppression, affliction."

Philippians 4:15–20

¹⁵ And you Philippians know that in the early days of the gospel, when I left Macedonia, no church shared with me in the matter of giving and receiving except you alone. ¹⁶ For even in Thessalonica more than once you sent gifts for my need. ¹⁷ Not that I wish for the gift, but I wish for the profit that increases to your account. ¹⁸ But I have received everything in full, and I have an abundance. I am fully supplied, because I have received from Epaphroditus what you provided—a fragrant offering, an acceptable sacrifice, pleasing to God. ¹⁹ And my God will supply all your needs according to his wealth in glory in Christ Jesus. ²⁰ Now to our God and Father be honor forever and ever. Amen.

¶ And you yourselves also know, Philippians, that at the first preaching of the gospel, after I left Macedonia, no church fellowshipped with me in the matter of giving and receiving but you alone. For even in Thessalonica you sent *a gift* more than once for my needs. Not that I seek the gift itself, but I seek the fruit which increases to your account. But I have received everything in full and have an abundance; I have been filled, having received from Epaphroditus what you have sent, a fragrant aroma, an acceptable sacrifice, pleasing to God. And my God will fulfill all your needs according to His riches in glory in Christ Jesus.

Now to our God and Father *be* the glory forever and ever. Amen. (LSB)

Summary: Though Paul was content whatever be his circumstances, he was still grateful for the help the Philippians sent with Epaphroditus. They gave of their means when they shared with the apostle in his troubles. In the very beginning of their Christian experience (Acts 16), they alone shared with him in material things. And when Paul was in Thessalonica on his second missionary journey (Acts 17:1) they sent him aid twice. He was not looking for a gift simply to satisfy his own needs but desired that credit should accrue to their account (accounting language again!). Paul did not want them to think that he was still looking for more. What they had sent with Epaphroditus

(2:25–30) had an effect both on him and God, for the gifts were the fragrant offering of a sacrifice well-pleasing to God. God would "repay" the Philippians, because they had met Paul's needs, so He would now meet theirs. He would not only bless them *from* His bounty but also *in accordance with* His glorious riches in Christ Jesus.

4:15 οἴδατε δὲ καὶ ὑμεῖς, Φιλιππήσιοι, ὅτι ἐν ἀρχῇ τοῦ εὐαγγελίου, ὅτε ἐξῆλθον ἀπὸ Μακεδονίας, οὐδεμία μοι ἐκκλησία ἐκοινώνησεν εἰς λόγον δόσεως καὶ λήμψεως εἰ μὴ ὑμεῖς μόνοι,

Although the NA[28] and THGNT texts view 4:10–20 as one paragraph, the post-positive δὲ that opens 4:15 (as in 4:10) combined with the direct address Φιλιππήσιοι justifies dividing this paragraph into two sections (4:10–14/4:15–20).

οἴδατε. Prf act ind 2nd pl οἶδα. See 4:12.
δὲ. Marks development from the Philippians to other churches.
καὶ. Adverbial ("also").
ὑμεῖς. Emphatic subject of οἴδατε. The use of this pronoun combined with two conjunctions again provides the emphasis to initiate a new paragraph.
Φιλιππήσιοι. Nominative plural of direct address. First and only time the readers are addressed in this manner. The other two times that Paul addresses his readers by their city name are in the context of intense and personal appeals (2 Cor 6:11; Gal 3:1).
ὅτι. Introduces the clausal complement of οἴδατε. "As it often does, ὅτι designates the content of what is known with verbs of thinking and knowing" (Sumney, 115).
ἐν ἀρχῇ. Temporal. BDAG (138.1.a) translates the phrase ἐν ἀρχῇ τοῦ εὐαγγελίου as "when the gospel was first preached."
τοῦ εὐαγγελίου. Objective genitive. See comments on τὸ εὐαγγέλιον in 1:5. This is a *nomen actionis* (Reumann, 660), the action aspect of his gospel missionary activity (NIDNTTE 1:415).
ὅτε. Introduces a temporal clause.
ἐξῆλθον. Aor act ind 1st sg ἐξέρχομαι. Common verb used many times for departing from some place.
ἀπὸ Μακεδονίας. Spatial (separation). The preposition often appears with verbs of motion such as ἐξέρχομαι.

οὐδεμία. Modifies the feminine ἐκκλησία.

μοι. Dative complement of ἐκοινώνησεν.

ἐκκλησία. Nominative subject of ἐκοινώνησεν. In 3:6 the word referred to its universal sense of "the church," while here the focus is on a local congregation but certainly not yet as a "church building."

ἐκοινώνησεν. Aor act ind 3rd sg κοινωνέω. See comments on συγκοινωνέω in 4:14. GE (1149) cites its usage in Attic as "to take part in, participate" and defines the verb here as "to enter into fellowship with" and classifies it as a "Christian" usage. The verb speaks of sharing in financial matters in Rom 12:13 and Gal 6:6, as it does here. Careful attention should always be given to the context of this verb, because in Rom 15:27 the sharing is in spiritual gifts and in 1 Tim 5:22 the verb speaks of sharing in sin. See also the compound συγκοινωνέω in 4:14.

εἰς λόγον. According to BDAG (290.4.g), εἰς plus the accusative "is used for the dat[ive]." BDAG (601.2.b) translates λόγος as "settlement of a mutual account (lit., 'of giving and receiving,' 'of debit and credit')." See also 4:17: εἰς λόγον ὑμῶν.

δόσεως. Objective genitive. The noun δόσις occurs elsewhere only in Jas 1:17. BDAG (259.2) translates it as "debit" when paired with λήμψις (see also GE, 551).

λήμψεως. Objective genitive of λήμψις. *Hapax legomenon*, although used in extra-biblical Greek in commercial contexts (BDAG, 593, "receiving" or "credit"). See also GE (1236) as "receiving" or "acquiring, acquisition." The spelling λήψις was widespread and explains the slight variants in some texts. In light of the "financial" context and because of their extensive use with this meaning in extra-biblical Greek, it is difficult to understand why Sumney (115) states that the two words δόσεως καὶ λήμψεως are used as friendship terms and that this meaning is their primary referent here.

εἰ μὴ. A common combination appearing 86 times in the NT. It literally means "if not," but it is rendered "except" by most translations.

ὑμεῖς μόνοι. This is the only use of the plural of the adjective μόνος in Philippians and the only combination of these two words in the NT. The adjective μόνοι is certainly emphatic.

4:16 ὅτι καὶ ἐν Θεσσαλονίκῃ καὶ ἅπαξ καὶ δὶς εἰς τὴν χρείαν μοι ἐπέμψατε.

ὅτι. Since the ὅτι clause that is introduced with this conjunction follows in the same sentence a substantival ὅτι clause in 4:15, it could also be substantival and translated "that" (Reumann, 659). If it is a parallel substantival clause, however, ὅτι would be preceded by a continuative καί. Since it is followed by an adverbial καί the clause must be causal (O'Brien 1991, 535).

καί. Adverbial ("also"), or, more probably, ascensive ("even").

ἐν Θεσσαλονίκῃ. Locative.

καί ... καί. Paul's fondness for the "both ... and" use of the conjunction καί is evident throughout this section (see 4:9, 12).

ἅπαξ καὶ δίς. An idiom (lit. "once and twice") for "repeatedly" (Reed 1997, 315) or at least "more than once" (BDAG, 97.1).

εἰς τὴν χρείαν. Purpose. See 2:25 where Paul called Epaphroditus λειτουργὸν τῆς χρείας μου, whom Paul was undoubtedly referencing by ἅπαξ.

μοι. Dative of possession. That this was read as possession by the scribes is evident from the variant reading μου (Dc F P and a few uncials) reflecting a scribal clarification for the less often used μοι. Also, εἰς was omitted early ($\mathfrak{P}^{46}$) in an apparent effort to provide a direct object (τὴν χρείαν) and an indirect object μοι. The reading in NA[28] and THGNT has extensive early Alexandrian (ℵ B), Western (D F G lat) and Byzantine ($\mathfrak{M}$) support, as well as being the more difficult reading.

ἐπέμψατε. Aor act ind 2nd pl πέμπω. BDAG (795.2) translates this usage here as "you have sent me (what was necessary) to satisfy my needs."

4:17 οὐχ ὅτι ἐπιζητῶ τὸ δόμα, ἀλλ' ἐπιζητῶ τὸν καρπὸν τὸν πλεονάζοντα εἰς λόγον ὑμῶν.

οὐχ ὅτι. Same usage as in 4:11. Here it also has an implied λέγω: "I do not say that ..."

ἐπιζητῶ. Pres act ind 1st sg ἐπιζητέω. BDAG (371.2) translates is as "wish for."

τὸ δόμα. Accusative direct object of ἐπιζητῶ. Although rarely used in Attic Greek (GE, 547), the noun appears over 60 times in the LXX, often for sacred gifts. It appears only 5 times in the NT giving way to the favored δῶρον which appears 19 times. The noun δόσις (see 4:15)

Analysis of Philippians Four

refers to the "act of giving" or "gifting" (GE, 551) whereas δόμα is the "result of giving" or the "gift."

ἀλλ'. Conjunction that marks a correction of the idea in the preceding clause. BDAG (45.1) translates it as "on the contrary, but, yet, rather." THGNT includes the word without eliding the final α.

ἐπιζητῶ. Same as above.

τὸν καρπὸν. Accusative direct object of ἐπιζητῶ. While the noun may refer to eschatological reward, it does not have this meaning in its seven other appearances in Paul (Rom 1:13; 6:21, 22; 15:28; 1 Cor 9:7; Gal 5:9; Phil 1:11). In Rom 15:28 it refers to the collection for Jerusalem, so it refers here to present "fruit," although in a metaphorical sense.

τὸν πλεονάζοντα. Pres act ptc masc acc sg πλεονάζω (attributive, modifying καρπὸν). The imperfective aspect supports the idea that the fruit is in the process of "increasing." BDAG (824.1) translates πλεονάζω as "grow, increase" but cites no evidence for its use in a financial sense. GE lists some Attic examples (1678).

εἰς λόγον. See 4:15. See its use with this meaning ("account") also in 4:15. Some interpreters see the monetary context extending the noun καρπὸν to "interest in your account" (Sumney, 117).

ὑμῶν. Possessive genitive.

4:18 ἀπέχω δὲ πάντα καὶ περισσεύω· πεπλήρωμαι δεξάμενος παρὰ Ἐπαφροδίτου τὰ παρ' ὑμῶν, ὀσμὴν εὐωδίας, θυσίαν δεκτήν, εὐάρεστον τῷ θεῷ.

ἀπέχω. Pres act ind 1st sg ἀπέχω. BDAG (102.1) translates this verb as "to be paid in full, receive in full" and indicates that ἀπέχω was a "commercial t[echnical] t[erm]" in contemporary Greek documents, especially the papyri. LXX Gen 43:23 also uses the verb to indicate receiving money. While the examples in MM (57) often point to a commercial use, the numerous examples in GE (237) do not indicate anything other than a general sense of "to receive" with a number of different complements. Paul's use of the verb to counsel Philemon to "receive back" Onesimus (Philm 15) is closer to its general usage in several different contexts. The papyri *do* illustrate how the ἀπο- prefix gives the present tense a "perfectivizing" sense, "I have received" (MM, 57).

πάντα. Accusative direct object of ἀπέχω.

καὶ περισσεύω. Pres act ind 1st sg περισσεύω. See notes on the word in 4:12, where it contrasts with ὑστερέω.

πεπλήρωμαι. Prf pass ind 1st sg πληρόω. See notes on πληρόω in 1:11 (about the Philippians), in 2:2 (about Paul), and in 4:19 (about the Philippians).

The words of Paul's prayer in 1:9–11 also appear in 4:10–20, the two passages forming an *inclusio* to the letter.

1:11 πεπληρωμένοι →	4:18 πεπλήρωμαι 4:19 πληρώσει
καρπὸν →	4:17 καρπὸν
1:9 περισσεύῃ →	4:12 περισσεύειν (2) 4:18 περισσεύω
1:11 εἰς δόξαν →	4:20 δόξα

This *inclusio* provides further evidence for the unity of the book.

δεξάμενος. Aor mid ptc masc nom sg δέχομαι (causal).

παρὰ Ἐπαφροδίτου. Source. Moule (51–52) states that παρὰ with the genitive indicates "emanation from" as in Mark 5:26 (τὰ παρ' αὐτῆς πάντα) and Luke 10:7 (τὰ παρ' αὐτῶν). Epaphroditus was commended earlier in 2:25.

τὰ. The article functions as a nominalizer, changing the PP παρ' ὑμῶν into the accusative direct object of δεξάμενος.

παρ' ὑμῶν. Source.

ὀσμήν. Accusative in apposition to τὰ παρ' ὑμῶν. With these three phrases (ὀσμὴν εὐωδίας, θυσίαν δεκτήν, εὐάρεστον τῷ θεῷ) Paul shifts any metaphor of financial language to sacrificial language. Appears over 80 times in the LXX.

εὐωδίας. Attributive genitive. Paul may have chosen this noun as a word play on the name of the woman in 4:2, Εὐοδίας, who needed to live up to the fragrance of her name. The word was also used in many LXX cultic contexts (Muraoka, 308).

θυσίαν. Accusative in apposition to τὰ παρ' ὑμῶν.

δεκτήν. Attributive adjective, modifying θυσίαν. The adjective is used 9 times in LXX Leviticus to describe an "acceptable" sacrifice and 10 times in Proverbs to describe "acceptable" behavior (Muraoka, 142).

εὐάρεστον. Attributive adjective, modifying θυσίαν. Unlike the previous adjectives, εὐάρεστος does not have a cultic association in the LXX. It describes secular Greek citizens who do "pleasing" things (BDAG, 403) and is used in the NT of believers who are "pleasing" to the Lord (Rom 14:18; 2 Cor 5:9; Eph 5:10).

τῷ θεῷ. Dative of advantage that complements both εὐάρεστον and θυσίαν, and probably also ὀσμήν.

4:19 ὁ δὲ θεός μου πληρώσει πᾶσαν χρείαν ὑμῶν κατὰ τὸ πλοῦτος αὐτοῦ ἐν δόξῃ ἐν Χριστῷ Ἰησοῦ.

ὁ ... θεός. Nominative subject of πληρώσει.
δὲ. Signals a change of focus from Paul to the Philippians.
μου. Possessive genitive.
πληρώσει. Fut act ind 3rd sg πληρόω. Paul's need is "filled" (πεπλήρωμαι – 4:18) and now he assures his readers that God will "fill" their need. Instead of the indicative some Western manuscripts (D* F G Ψ 33 1739 1881) have the optative πληρωσαι. While this could be a simple scribal mistake of one letter, the change was probably motivated by someone taking issue with the confident statement. But the reading supported by both Alexandrian and Byzantine witnesses (𝔓⁴⁶ ℵ A B D² 𝔐 cop) is consistent with the context where Paul promises that God will provide spiritual needs (κατὰ τὸ πλοῦτος αὐτοῦ ἐν δόξῃ) in response to their caring for his physical needs.

πᾶσαν χρείαν. Accusative direct object of πληρώσει. See χρεία in 2:25 and 4:16.
ὑμῶν. Possessive genitive.
κατὰ τὸ πλοῦτος. Standard (Wallace, 743); see note on κατὰ in 1:20, "in accord with." GE defines as "wealth" and mentions that Ploutos was the "god of wealth" (1687). The noun appears 22 times in the NT, always in the singular. It is usually masculine, but it is neuter here and in 2 Cor 8:2 (BDF §51.2).
αὐτοῦ. Possessive genitive that refers to θεός.
ἐν δόξῃ. Locative, modifying πλοῦτος and indicating the sphere where God's wealth is found. This follows the use of the word in the LXX where it is often a synonym for God himself, rendering the Hebrew כָּבוֹד (NIDNTTE 1:762–63).
ἐν Χριστῷ Ἰησοῦ. Locative. God's glory is located in Christ Jesus.

4:20 τῷ δὲ θεῷ καὶ πατρὶ ἡμῶν ἡ δόξα εἰς τοὺς αἰῶνας τῶν αἰώνων, ἀμήν.

τῷ ... θεῷ καὶ πατρὶ ἡμῶν. Dative of advantage. The single article with two substantives connected by καί is a clear example of the Granville Sharp Rule (Wallace, 274).

δέ. Signals development from a focus on the readers to a focus on God.

ἡ δόξα. Subject of an implied verb, probably the optative εἴη. The noun probably has the sense of "honor" (BDAG, 257.3) as in the doxology of Eph 3:21 and Rev 5:13. If the noun retains the sense of a divine attribute (see 4:19), the "glory" is ascribed as in 1 Pet 4:11.

εἰς τοὺς αἰῶνας. Temporal. The noun αἰών appears around 60 times linked with εἰς in references to the future. The most common construction is εἰς τὸν αἰῶνα, but there are many examples of both εἰς τοὺς αἰῶνας and εἰς τοὺς αἰῶνας τῶν αἰώνων (12 times in Revelation). This construction reflects 30 LXX references in the Psalms to the singular εἰς τὸν αἰῶνα, while the plural εἰς τοὺς αἰῶνας is limited to the Apocrypha and to Daniel (Theodotian).

τῶν αἰώνων. Suggestions about the use of the genitive with a cognate head noun (such as Wallace, 103 n84) are not necessary because the construction reflects an OT influence and is not a usual Greek construction. The singular head noun plus singular genitive appears 25 times in the LXX, but the double plural construction here in Phil 4:20 appears in the LXX only in Tobit 14:15 and 4 Macc 18:24.

ἀμήν. An indeclinable particle that is a transliteration of the Hebrew particle אָמֵן, originally an adjective meaning "trustworthy." The LXX transliterated this word only a few times (1 Chr 16:36; Neh 5:13; 8:6); it is usually translated with the optative verb γένοιτο, "may it be" (e.g., Deut 27:15–17). The Greek word occurs 128 times in the NT, most of which are the double appearances in the dominical sayings. Paul uses the word 15 times, usually ending a doxology (GE, 108), but once to indicate that all divine promises are guaranteed in Christ (2 Cor 1:20).

Philippians 4:21–23

> [21] Greet every saint in Christ Jesus. The brothers who are with me greet you. [22] All the saints greet you, but especially those from the emperor's household. [23] May the grace of the Lord Jesus Christ be with your spirit.

Greet every saint in Christ Jesus. The brothers who are with me greet you. All the saints greet you, especially those of Caesar's household. The grace of the Lord Jesus Christ be with your spirit. (LSB)

Summary: Paul began his letter according to contemporary epistolary practice but enhanced it with the recognition of what both writers and readers were because of their Christian calling. He now ends it in the same way. He again describes the readers as *saints* (see 1:1). Because they are *in Christ Jesus* they are truly *brothers* (and sisters!). Greetings are conveyed, and included among those who sent them are *those who belong to Caesar's household*. Whether that was in Rome or not, they were at least employed in either the domestic or administrative establishment of the Emperor, and it is significant that there were loyal believers in that imperial service. The letter closes as it began with a prayer for *the grace of the Lord Jesus Christ*, who energizes our human *spirit*.

4:21 Ἀσπάσασθε πάντα ἅγιον ἐν Χριστῷ Ἰησοῦ. ἀσπάζονται ὑμᾶς οἱ σὺν ἐμοὶ ἀδελφοί.

Ἀσπάσασθε. Aor mid impv 2nd pl ἀσπάζομαι. The verb has a general meaning "to welcome affectionately or gladly" (GE, 318), but is used 23 times as "greet" the readers in NT letter closings and 21 times by Paul (16 times in Rom 16:3–16).

πάντα ἅγιον. Accusative direct object of Ἀσπάσασθε.

ἐν Χριστῷ Ἰησοῦ. This is the twentieth time that this preposition has been used with either Χριστός or κύριος as the object (1:1, 13, 14, 26; 2:1, 5, 19, 24, 29; 3:1; 3, 9, 14; 4:1, 2, 4, 7, 10, 19, 21). Grammatical labels like locative and sphere do not adequately portray the Christ-centered focus that motivates all the indicatives and imperatives in the book.

ἀσπάζονται. Pres mid ind 3rd pl ἀσπάζομαι.

ὑμᾶς. Accusative direct object of ἀσπάζονται.

οἱ ... ἀδελφοί σὺν ἐμοί. Nominative subject of ἀσπάζονται. These are Paul's companions or co-workers. The noun ἀδελφοί is used "in the collective sense of *brothers and sisters*" (CGELNT, 6).

In his subscriptions at the end of 1 Corinthians, Galatians, Philemon, Colossians and 2 Thessalonians, Paul writes a farewell greeting that he says is in his own hand, not the hand of an amanuensis/secretary. Therefore, "it is reasonable to infer that he followed this practice in his other letters as well" (Reece, *Paul's Large Letters*, 45). Perhaps even in prison a secretary was available. For a thorough treatment of this subject, see the volume by Reece just cited.

4:22 ἀσπάζονται ὑμᾶς πάντες οἱ ἅγιοι, μάλιστα δὲ οἱ ἐκ τῆς Καίσαρος οἰκίας.

ἀσπάζονται. Pres mid ind 3rd pl ἀσπάζομαι.
ὑμᾶς. Accusative direct object of ἀσπάζονται.
πάντες οἱ ἅγιοι. Nominative subject of ἀσπάζονται.
μάλιστα. The superlative form of the Attic μάλα (BDAG, 613; GE, 1277). The comparative form is μᾶλλον (GE, 1277; see 1:9, 23; 2:12; 3:4).
δὲ. Signals development from all the believers to the ones in Caesar's household.
οἱ. The article functions as a nominalizer, changing the PP ἐκ τῆς Καίσαρος οἰκίας into the nominative subject of the elided verb ἀσπάζονται.
ἐκ τῆς ... οἰκίας. Source. The expression appears only here in the NT and corresponds to the Latin *domus*. The household could include the lowest menial slaves to soldiers and the highest functionaries.
Καίσαρος. Possessive genitive. This would be the emperor Nero, but the entire expression would not necessarily include his immediate family members. This is the strongest evidence for a Roman provenance. "It does not, however, limit the possibilities to one city. Caesar's household included soldiers, free people, and slaves. There were other places, in particular Caesarea and Ephesus, that also had a contingent of members of Caesar's household" (Sumney, 123). See the comments on "Provenance" in the Introduction for the "Roman" view.

4:23 Ἡ χάρις τοῦ κυρίου Ἰησοῦ Χριστοῦ μετὰ τοῦ πνεύματος ὑμῶν.

Ἡ χάρις. Nominative subject of an unexpressed verb, as with

δόξα in 4:21. "The use of χάρις at the beginning (see 1:2) and end of the apostle's letters should not be viewed as a polite wish; rather, it refers pointedly to 'the grace of the Lord Jesus Christ' " (NIDNTTE 4:658).

τοῦ κυρίου Ἰησοῦ Χριστοῦ. Genitive of source. This is only the second occurrence of this full title (see 1:2), so that the title serves as another *inclusio*, bookending the discourse. Grace is not only unmerited favor; it includes all the spiritual blessings which are communicated to a believer from the Lord Jesus Christ.

μετὰ τοῦ πνεύματος ὑμῶν. Accompaniment. The grammatical anomaly between singular πνεύματος and plural ὑμῶν is explained again by Paul's emphasis on unity, stressed through the singular πνεύματος with individuality stressed through the plural ὑμῶν. By "spirit" a believer's whole life is intended as governed and dependent on his Lord for guidance, strength, and sanctification.

The reading τοῦ πνεύματος has superior support ($\mathfrak{P}^{46}$ ℵ* A B D F G P 6 88 itg vg copsa arm eth) while the variant reading πάντων (ℵ^c K L Ψ 𝔐 syrh and TR) appears to be the substitution of a more familiar word for a benediction (see 1 Cor 16:24). Furthermore, an ἀμήν was added by scribes in accord with liturgical practice. Although there are significant manuscripts and versions that contain it ($\mathfrak{P}^{46}$ ℵ A D K L P 𝔐 vg syr, h cop^{bo} arm eth), if it was original, it is difficult to understand why it was omitted in B F G 6 1739* 1836 1908 it syr cop. The THGNT, in one of the few places where it differs from the NA/UBS texts, includes it, agreeing with its presence in the TR. See the following image.

This grace benediction is one of the most regular features in the Pauline letter subscriptions. The wording is identical with Philm 23 and is similar to Gal 6:18 (see also 2 Tim 4:22 for the final μετὰ τοῦ πνεύματος ὑμῶν). For such grace benedictions outside the Pauline letters, see Heb 13:25 and Rev 22:21.

The "benediction" included by the apostle should be distinguished from the "subscription" which was added by later scribes. These subscriptions vary from Προς Φιλιππησιους in ℵ A B* (D F G) Ψ 33 to Προς Φιλιππησιους εγραφη απο Ρωμης δια Επαφροδιτου in 1739 1881 Maj (TR). It is quite certain that no book had an original title ("inscription") or a subscription.

Image of Philippians 4:22–23 in Codex Sinaiticus.

Note the nomina sacra for κυρίου Ἰησοῦ Χριστοῦ and πνεύματος in 4:23, the addition of πάντων by a corrector in the right margin, and the inclusion of the final Ἀμήν.

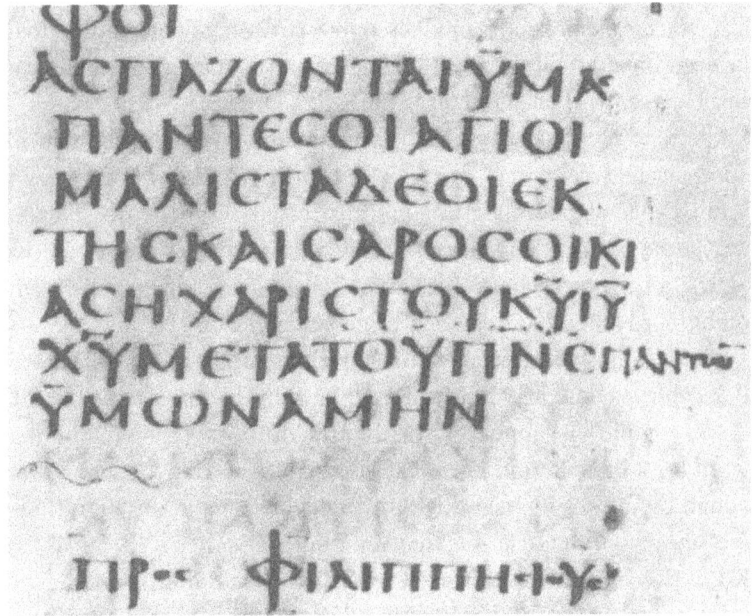

Courtesy of Bible Works

Conclusion: "It is not easy for us in the Western world today to imagine what it must have felt like to belong to a small community of 'citizens of heaven' in one of the eastern provinces of the Roman empire in the first century A.D. The society in the midst of which the Philippian Christians lived might be described as 'crooked and depraved', but they were commended for shining 'like stars in the universe' and offering it the 'word of life.' Every church was to be a missionary church … and among those was the church of Philippi, and like the other Macedonian churches, it holds an honored place" (Bruce, 161–62).

Glossary

Adjectivizer – In Greek syntax, this term refers to an article that is used to change a non-adjective into an adjectival modifier. Thus, in the phrase, ἀπὸ παντὸς ἔθνους τῶν ὑπὸ τὸν οὐρανόν, the article τῶν changes the prepositional phrase, ὑπὸ τὸν οὐρανόν, into an attributive modifier of παντὸς ἔθνους.

Adnominal – Attached to or modifying a noun.

Aktionsart – A term used in relation to verb tense that refers to the supposed objective quality of the action of the verb, e.g., whether it is punctiliar, durative, iterative, inceptive, etc.

Anacoluthon – A construction involving some sort of break in grammatical sequence.

Anaphoric – Referring back to, i.e., coreferential with, a preceding word or group of words. Thus, pronouns are anaphoric references to participants that have already been introduced into the discourse.

Anarthrous – Lacking an article.

Antecedent – An element that is referred to by another expression that follows it. Thus, the antecedent of a relative pronoun is that element in the preceding context to which the relative clause provides additional information.

Apodosis – The second part ("then" clause) in a conditional construction.

Arthrous/Articular – Including an article.

Ascensive – In Greek, this term is most often used in relation to conjunctions, especially καί. It refers to a usage that is intensive or expresses a final addition or point of focus. In such instances, the conjunction is typically translated, "even."

Aspect – This term is used in relation to verb tense and refers to the writer's/speaker's subjective choice of how to portray the verbal action, e.g., perfective or imperfective.

Asyndeton – A literary technique of linking clauses without the use of a conjunction.

Attraction – Relative pronouns at times take on or "attract" to the case of their antecedent. For example, in the text, Πάντων δὲ θαυμαζόντων ἐπὶ πᾶσιν οἷς ἐποίει εἶπεν πρὸς τοὺς μαθητὰς αὐτοῦ ("While everyone was marveling at all that he was doing, he said to his disciples"), the expected case for the relative pronoun would be accusative (οὓς) since it functions as the direct object of ἐποίει. Instead, it has been attracted to the case of its antecedent (πᾶσιν).

Background – This term is used to refer to information that is off the event line, or storyline, i.e., those events or material that do not move the narrative forward. Instead, background information comments on, amplifies, or otherwise supports the narration.

Cataphoric – Referring forward to, i.e., coreferential with, a following word or group of words. The demonstrative οὗτος is frequently used in this manner.

Causative – Causative verbs or constructions denote that a new state of affairs is brought about or "caused" by the action of the verb or construction. Both δίδωμι and ποιέω are examples of verbs that can

Glossary

be used to form a causative construction. For example, in the text, δὸς τοῖς δούλοις σου μετὰ παρρησίας πάσης λαλεῖν τὸν λόγον σου (lit. "Give to your servants to speak your word with all boldness") the imperative and infinitive verbs (δὸς and λαλεῖν) form a causative verb phrase ("cause to speak").

Clausal complement – This type of complement is structurally a direct object, but since it is a clause rather than a noun phrase scholars often use the language of "complement" rather than "direct object." For example, ὅτι is often used to introduce complement clauses with verbs of speech that represent what was said: λέγω γὰρ ὑμῖν ὅτι δύναται ὁ θεὸς ἐκ τῶν λίθων τούτων ἐγεῖραι τέκνα τῷ Ἀβραάμ ("For I tell you that God is able to raise up children for Abraham from these stones.")

Clitic – A word that is written as a separate word in the syntax but is pronounced and accented as if it were part of another word. There are two types. Enclitics give their accent to the preceding word; proclitics shift the accent to the following word.

Cohesion – A means of linking clauses and sentences into larger syntactical units of a discourse Lexical cohesion is accomplished by the use of the same word or by words from the same semantic domain. Relational and referential cohesion are other types which help to hold a discourse together.

Collocation – The conventional association of two or more words that produces a particular nuance is termed a collocation. In Mark 5:41–42, the collocation of ἐγείρω, which can mean either "wake up" or "arise," with ἀνέστη ... καὶ περιεπάτει clarifies that the meaning in this context is "arise."

Complement – In this volume this term is used in two ways in addition to its use in the phrase, "clausal complement": (1) A constituent, other than an accusative direct object, that is required to complete a verb phrase. Verbs that include a prepositional prefix often take a complement whose case is determined by the prefix. For example, verbs with the prefix συν- characteristically take a dative complement. (2) The second element in a double accusative construction, which completes the verbal idea. In the sentence, "I call my son Superman," Superman would be the complement.

Copula/Copular Clause – A copula is a linking verb that joins a subject and predicate into an equative or copular clause. In the copular clause, Ἡ γενεὰ αὕτη γενεὰ πονηρά ἐστιν ("This generation is a wicked generation"), the copula is ἐστιν.

Crasis – The merging of two words through the use of contraction, e.g., κἀμοί for καὶ ἐμοί.

Elative – An adjectival form that denotes intensity or superiority.

Ellipsis – The omission of a word or phrase that is able to be understood from the context.

Enclitic – A clitic is a word that appears as a discreet word in the syntax but is pronounced as if it were part of another word. *En*clitics "give" their accent to the *preceding* word.

Equative verb/clause – An equative verb, like εἰμί, γίνομαι, or ὑπάρχω, is a verb that joins a subject and predicate to form an equative clause ("something is something"), e.g., Ἡ γενεὰ αὕτη γενεὰ πονηρά ἐστιν ("This generation is a wicked generation").

External evidence – In textual criticism the evidence available from manuscripts and versions is described as external evidence. See also *internal evidence*.

Final (clause) – An older term for a purpose clause; it may also be applied to the function of individual elements such as the infinitive or participle.

Focal/focus – A focal constituent (i.e., a constituent in focus) is a constituent that is the most important new information in a clause.

Glossary

Foreground – This term is used to refer to information that is on the event line, or storyline, i.e., those events that move the narrative forward.

Fronting – Placing a constituent earlier in the sentence than its default order, most commonly in a pre-verbal position.

Genitive of relationship – Wallace (83) prefers to limit this label to *familial* relationships, but we have followed Young (25–26) in applying it to a variety of *social* relationships as well, including slaves, friends, and enemies.

Haplography – The accidental omission of text.

Hendiadys – When two words, connected by the same article, combine to form one idea.

Imperfective (aspect) – The semantic value of the present and imperfect tenses that indicates that the writer/speaker is portraying the situation as a process.

Inclusio – An "envelope" or "bookend" structure in which the same or similar language is used to begin and end a unit of discourse.

Intransitive – A type of verb that does not require a direct object. Some verbs may be either transitive or intransitive depending on the statement in which they are used.

Litotes – A figure of speech in which a statement is made by negating the opposite idea. For example, "she is *not* a *bad* tennis player" means "she is a *good* tennis player."

Marked – Departing from the normal or neutral pattern, or having additive features. At various levels of grammar, speakers/writers have a choice between various options. One option will typically be viewed as the "default" or "unmarked" member of the set. The other members are "marked." Something that is "marked" may be more prominent, in focus, emphatic, etc.

Metonymy/Metonym – Metonymy is a figure of speech in which one term is used in place of another with which it is associated. In the expression, "he was reading the prophet Isaiah," the writer ("the prophet Isaiah") is used as a metonym for his writings ("the book that the prophet Isaiah wrote").

Nominal (clause) – A nominal is a noun or something that functions like a noun. In a nominal clause, a nominative noun stands alone in the clause without a verb, and sometimes without any other elements.

Nominalizer – In Greek syntax, this term refers to an article that is used to change a word, phrase, or clause into a substantive. Most commonly, nominalizers are used to make an adjective or participle substantival.

Perfective (aspect) – The semantic value of the aorist tense that indicates that the writer/speaker is portraying the situation in summary as a whole with no reference to any process that might be involved. See also *imperfective aspect* and *stative aspect*.

Peak – A climactic development within a discourse.

Polysyndeton – A literary technique in which conjunctions are used in quick succession even when they could be removed.

Prominence – The "semantic and grammatical elements of discourse that serve to set aside certain subjects, ideas or motifs of the author as more or less semantically or pragmatically significant than others" (Reed 1997, 75–76).

Protasis – The first part ("if" clause) in a conditional construction.

Stative (aspect) – The semantic value of the perfect and pluperfect tenses that indicates that the writer/speaker is portraying a situation as a state or condition with no reference to any process or expenditure of energy. See also *imperfective aspect* and *perfective aspect*.

Storyline (discourse structure) – This term is used to refer to information that moves the narrative forward. In the narrative genre of the NT, this is most commonly expressed with aorist tense forms or sometimes narrative presents.

Synecdoche – A figure of speech in which one term is used in place of another with which it is associated, specifically involving a part-whole relationship. In the sentence, "Do you have your own *wheels*?" the word "wheels" stands for the entire "vehicle" of which it is a part.

Unmarked – The unmarked or default choice between two or more options refers to a writer choosing not to signal the presence of some feature (Runge §9.2).

Bibliography

Abbott-Smith, George. *A Manual Greek Lexicon of the New Testament*. 3rd ed. New York: Charles Scribner's Sons, 1937.

Barth, Karl. *Epistle to the Philippians: 40th Anniversary Edition*. Louisville: Westminster John Knox Press, 2002.

Bengel, Johann Albrecht. *Gnomon of the New Testament*. Edited by M. Ernest Bengel and J. C. F. Steudel. Translated by James Bryce. 4 vols. Edinburgh: T&T Clark, 1860.

Black, David Alan. "The Discourse Structure of Philippians: A Study in Textlinguistics." *Novum Testamentum* 37 (1995a): 16–49.

_____. *It's Still Greek to Me: An Easy to Understand Guide to Intermediate Greek*. Grand Rapids: Baker Books, 1998.

_____. *Linguistics for Students of New Testament Greek*. Grand Rapids: Baker Books, 1995b.

_____. "Paul and Christian Unity: A Formal Analysis of Philippians 2:1–4." *JETS* 28 (1985) 299–308.

Bockmuehl, Markus. *The Epistle to the Philippians*. Black's NTC. Peabody, Mass: Hendrickson, 1998.

Boyer, James L. "A Classification of Imperatives: A Statistical Study." *Grace Theological Journal* 8 (1987): 35–54.

_____. "First Class Conditions: What Do They Mean?" *Grace Theological Journal* 2 (1981): 75–114.

Brewer, Raymond R. "The Meaning of *Politeuesthe* in Philippians 1:27." *Journal of Biblical Literature* 73 (1954): 76–83.

Bruce, Frederick F. *Philippians*. New International Biblical

Commentary 11. Peabody, Mass: Hendrickson Publishers, 1989.
Burk, Denny. *Articular Infinitives in the Greek of the New Testament: On the Exegetical Benefit of Grammatical Precision*. New Testament Monographs 14. Sheffield: Sheffield Phoenix Press, 2006.
Burton, Ernest de Witt. *Syntax of the Moods and Tenses in New Testament Greek*. Grand Rapids: Kregel Publications, 1976.
Campbell, Constantine R. *Advances in the Study of Greek: New Insights for Reading the New Testament*. Grand Rapids: Zondervan, 2015.
_____. *Basics of Verbal Aspect in Biblical Greek*. Grand Rapids: Zondervan, 2008.
_____. *Colossians and Philemon: A Handbook on the Greek Text*. Baylor Handbook on the Greek NT. Waco, Tex.: Baylor University Press, 2013.
Carson, D.A. *Basics for Believers*. Grand Rapids: Baker Books, 2018.
Collange, Jean-François. *The Epistle of St. Paul to the Philippians*. Translated by A. W. Heathcote. London: Epworth, 1979.
Comfort, Philip W. *New Testament Text and Translation Commentary*. Carol Steam, Ill.: Tyndale House Publishers, 2008.
Cullman, Oscar. *Christology of the New Testament*. Louisville, KY: Westminster John Knox, 1964.
Decker, Rodney J. *Mark: A Handbook on the Greek Text*. Volume One. Waco: Baylor University Press, 2014.
_____. *Reading Koine Greek: An Introduction and Integrated Workbook*. Grand Rapids: Baker Academic, 2014.
Ellicott, Charles J. *A Critical and Grammatical Commentary on St. Paul's Epistles to the Philippians, Colossians, and to Philemon*. Ellicott's Commentaries, Critical and Grammatical, on the Epistles of Saint Paul. London: Parker, 1857.
Fanning, Buist M. *Verbal Aspect in New Testament Greek*. Oxford Theology and Religion Monographs. Oxford: Clarendon, 1990.
Fee, Gordon D. *Paul's Letter to the Philippians*. The New International Commentary on the New Testament. Grand Rapids: Eerdmans, 1995.
Friberg, Timothy, Barbara Friberg, and Neva F. Miller. *Analytical Lexicon of the Greek New Testament*. Grand Rapids: Baker Books, 2000.
Funk, Robert W. *A Beginning-Intermediate Grammar of Hellenistic*

Greek. 3rd ed. Salem, OR: Polebridge Press, 2013.

Garland, David E. "The Composition and Unity of Philippians: Some Neglected Factors." *Novum Testamentum* 27 (1985): 141–73.

Guthrie, George H. "Cohesion Shifts and Stitches in Philippians." Pages 36–59 in *Discourse Analysis and Other Topics in Biblical Greek*. Edited by Stanley E. Porter and D. A. Carson. Journal for the Study of the New Testament Supplement Series 113. Sheffield: Sheffield Academic Press, 1995.

Hagner, Donald A. *The New Testament: A Historical and Theological Introduction*. Grand Rapids: Baker Academic, 2012.

Hawthorne, Gerald F. *Philippians*. Word Biblical Commentary 43. Waco, Tex.: Word, 1983.

Hays, Richard B. *The Faith of Jesus Christ: The Narrative Substructure of Galatians 3:1–4:11*. 2nd ed. Grand Rapids: Eerdmans, 2001.

Hellerman, Joseph H. *Exegetical Guide to the Greek New Testament: Philippians*. Edited by Andreas J. Kostenberger and Robert Yarborough. Nashville: B&H Academic, 2015.

Holmstrand, Jonas. *Markers and Meaning in Paul: An Analysis of 1 Thessalonians, Philippians, and Galatians*. Translated by Martin Naylor. Coniectanea Biblica: New Testament Series 28. Stockholm: Almqvist & Wiksell International, 1997.

Johnson, L. T. *The Letter of James*. AB 37A. New York: Doubleday, 1995.

Kennedy, Harry A. A. "The Epistle to the Philippians." Pages 397–473 in *The Expositor's Greek Testament*. Volume 3. Edited by W. R. Nicoll. Grand Rapids: Eerdmans, 1976.

Kilpatrick, George D. "ΒΛΕΠΕΤΕ, Philippians 3:2." Pages 146–48 in *In Memoriam Paul Kahle*. Edited by Matthew Black and Georg Fohrer. Berlin: A. Töpelmann, 1968.

Köstenberger, Andreas, and Raymond Bouchoc. *The Book Study Concordance of the Greek New Testament*. Nashville: Broadman & Holman Publishers, 2003.

Lenski, Richard C. H. *The Interpretation of Paul's Epistles to the Galatians, to the Ephesians, and to the Philippians*. Columbus, Ohio: Lutheran Book Concern, 1937.

Levinsohn, Stephen H. "A Discourse Study of Constituent Order and the Article in Philippians." Pages 60–74 in *Discourse Analysis and Other Topics in Biblical Greek*. Edited by Stanley E.

Porter and D. A. Carson. Journal for the Study of the New Testament: Supplement Series 113. Sheffield: Sheffield Academic Press, 1995.
_____. *Discourse Features of New Testament Greek*. Dallas: SIL International, 2000.
Lightfoot, Joseph B. *Saint Paul's Epistle to the Philippians*. Classic Commentaries on the Greek New Testament. London: Macmillan, 1913.
Longacre, Robert. *The Grammar of Discourse*. Topics in Language and Linguistics. 2nd ed. New York: Plenum, 1996.
Louw, Johannes P., and Eugene A. Nida, eds. *Greek-English Lexicon of the New Testament Based on Semantic Domains*. 2 vols. New York: United Bible Societies, 1988.
Martin, Ralph P. *Philippians*. New Century Bible 57. London: Marshall, Morgan & Scott, 1976.
McKay, Kenneth L. "Aspect in Imperatival Constructions in New Testament Greek." *Novum Testamentum* 27 (1985): 201–26.
Mathewson, David and Elodie Emig. *Intermediate Greek Grammar*. Grand Rapids: Baker, 2016.
Metzger, Bruce M. *A Textual Commentary on the Greek New Testament*. 2nd ed. Stuttgart: Deutsche Bibelgesellschaft, 1994.
Meyer, Heinrich A. W. *Critical and Exegetical Handbook to the Epistles to the Philippians and Colossians and to Philemon*. New York: Funk & Wagnalls, 1889.
Montonari, Franco, ed. *The Brill Dictionary of Ancient Greek*. Leiden: Brill, 2015.
Moore, Thomas. *Philippians: An Exegetical Guide for Preaching and Teaching*. Grand Rapids: Kegel Academic, 2019.
Moule, Charles F. D. *An Idiom Book of New Testament Greek*. 2nd ed. Cambridge: Cambridge University Press, 1959.
Mullins, Terence Y. "Disclosure: A Literary Form in the New Testament." *Novum Testamentum* 7 (1964): 44–50.
Muraoka, T. *A Greek-English Lexicon of the Septuagint*. Leuven, Belgium: Peeters, 2009.
Novenson, Matthew V. *Christ among the Messiahs: Christ Language in Paul and Messiah Language in Ancient Judaism*. New York: Oxford University Press, 2012.

Oakes, Peter. *Philippians: From People to Letter*. Society for New Testament Studies Monograph Series 110. Cambridge: Cambridge University Press, 2001.

O'Brien, Peter T. *The Epistle to the Philippians: A Commentary on the Greek Text*. New International Greek Testament Commentary. Grand Rapids: Eerdmans, 1991.

———. "The Fellowship Theme in Philippians." *Reformed Theological Review* 37 (1978): 9–18.

Porter, Stanley E. "Discourse Analysis and New Testament Studies: An Introductory Survey." Pages 14–35 in *Discourse Analysis and Other Topics in Biblical Greek*. Edited by Stanley E. Porter and D. A. Carson. Journal for the Study of the New Testament: Supplement Series 113. Sheffield: Sheffield Academic Press, 1995a.

———. "How Can Biblical Discourse Be Analyzed? A Response to Several Attempts." Pages 107–16 in in *Discourse Analysis and Other Topics in Biblical Greek*. Edited by Stanley E. Porter and D. A. Carson. Journal for the Study of the New Testament: Supplement Series 113. Sheffield: Sheffield Academic Press, 1995b.

———. *Idioms of the Greek New Testament*. 2nd ed. Biblical Languages: Greek 2. Sheffield: Sheffield Academic Press, 1994.

———. *Linguistic Analysis of the Greek New Testament*. Grand Rapids: Baker Academic, 2015.

———. *Verbal Aspect in the Greek of the New Testament with Reference to Tense and Mood*. Studies in Biblical Greek 1. New York: Peter Lang, 1989.

Reece, Steve. *Paul's Large Letters: Paul's Autographic Subscriptions in the Light of Ancient Epistolary Conventions*. London, et.al.: Bloomsbury, 2016.

Reed, Jeffrey T. *A Discourse Analysis of Philippians: Method and Rhetoric in Debate over Literary Integrity*. Journal for Study of the NT: 136. Sheffield: Sheffield Press, 1997.

———. "Identifying Theme in the New Testament: Insights from Discourse Analysis." Pages 75–101 in *Discourse Analysis and Other Topics in Biblical Greek*. Edited by Stanley E. Porter and D. A. Carson. Journal for the Study of the New Testament: Supplement Series 113. Sheffield: Sheffield Academic Press, 1995.

Reumann, John. *Philippians: A New Translation with Introduction and*

Commentary. Anchor Yale Bible 33B. New Haven, Conn.: Yale University Press, 2008.

Richards, E. Randolph. *Paul and First Century Letter Writing*. Downers Grove, IL: IVP Academic, 2004.

Roberts, Richard. "Old Texts in Modern Translation, Philippians 1:27." *Expository Times* 49 (1937–1938): 325–28.

Robertson, Archibald T. *A Grammar of the Greek of the New Testament in the Light of Historical Research*. 4th ed. Nashville: Broadman, 1934.

Roetzel, Calvin J. *The Letters of Paul: Conversations in Context*. 6th Edition. Louisville: Westminster John Knox Press, 2015.

Rogers, Cleon, Jr., and Cleon Rogers III. *New Linguistic and Exegetical Key to the Greek New Testament*. Grand Rapids: Zondervan, 1998.

Runge, Steven E. "Contrastive Substitution and the Greek Verb: Reassessing Porter's Argument." *Novum Testamentum* 56 (2014): 154–73.

———. *A Discourse Grammar of the Greek New Testament*. Peabody, Mass.: Hendrickson Publishers, 2010.

Runge, Steven E. and Christopher Fresch, eds. *The Greek Verb Revisited*. Lexham Press, 2016.

Sellew, Philip. "Laodiceans and the Philippians Fragments Hypothesis." *Harvard Theological Review* 87 (1994): 17–28.

Silva, Moisés. *Philippians*. 2nd ed. Baker Exegetical Commentary on the New Testament. Grand Rapids: Baker Academic, 2005.

Silva, Moisés, ed. *New International Dictionary of New Testament Theology and Exegesis*. 2nd ed. 5 vols. Grand Rapids: Zondervan, 2014.

Snyman, A. H. "A Rhetorical Analysis of Philippians 1:12–26." *Acta Theologica* 25 (2005): 89–111.

Sumney, Jerry L. *Philippians: A Greek Student's Intermediate Reader*. Peabody, Mass.: Hendrickson Publishers, 2007.

Thayer, Joseph Henry. *A Greek-English Lexicon of the New Testament*. Translation and revision of Grimm's Wilke's *Clavis Novi Testamenti*. New York, 1897.

Thrall, Margaret E. *Greek Particles in the New Testament. Linguistic and Exegetical Studies*. Leiden, 1962.

Trench, Richard Chevenix. *Synonyms of the New Testament*. 9th ed. London: James Clarke, 1880.

Turner, Nigel. *A Grammar of New Testament Greek. III: Syntax*. Edinburgh: T&T Clark, 1963.

Varner, William. *The Book of James, A New Perspective: A Linguistic Commentary Applying Discourse Analysis*. 2nd Edition, 2017.

Vincent, Marvin R. *Critical and Exegetical Commentary on the Epistles to the Philippians and to Philemon*. ICC. New York: Scribner's, 1922.

Wallace, Daniel B. *Greek Grammar Beyond the Basics: An Exegetical Syntax of the New Testament*. Grand Rapids: Zondervan, 1996.

Watson, Duane F. "A Rhetorical Analysis of Philippians and Its Implications for the Unity Question." *Novum Testamentum* 30 (1988): 57–88.

Weima, Jeffrey A. *Paul the Ancient Letter Writer*. Grand Rapids: Baker Academic, 2016.

Witherington, Ben III. *Paul's Letter to the Philippians: A Socio-Rhetorical Commentary*. Grand Rapids: Eerdmans, 2011.

———. "The Case of the Imprisonment That Did Not Happen: Paul at Ephesus," *JETS* 60, no. 3 (2017): 525–32.

Young, Richard A. *Intermediate New Testament Greek: A Linguistic and Exegetical Approach*. Nashville: Broadman & Holman, 1994.

Zerwick, Maximilian. *Biblical Greek: Illustrated by Examples*. Translated by Joseph Smith. SPIB 114. Rome: Pontifical Biblical Institute, 1985.

www.ingramcontent.com/pod-product-compliance
Lightning Source LLC
Chambersburg PA
CBHW050316120526
44592CB00014B/1938